Taunton's

BUILD LIKE A PRO®
Expert Advice from Start to Finish

Remodeling a
Basement

REVISED EDITION

Remodeling a Basement

REVISED EDITION

ROGER GERMAN

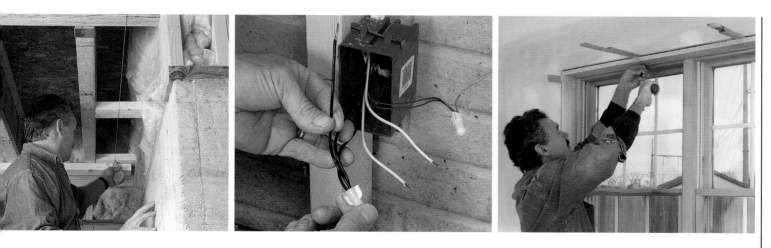

The Taunton Press

 **The Taunton Press**
Inspiration for hands-on living®

The Taunton Press, Inc., 63 South Main Street, Newtown, CT 06470-2344

e-mail: tp@taunton.com

PRODUCED BY WORDWORKS   A 3ROGERS PROJECT

EDITORS: Roger Holmes and Sarah Disbrow

INDEXER: Brigid A. O. Wilson

ART DIRECTION: Deborah Fillion/Image & Word

COVER DESIGN: Kimberly Adis

INTERIOR DESIGN: Lori Wendin

ILLUSTRATOR: Mario Ferro

Photographer: Roger Bruhn, except for Front cover (right): © Sylvain Côte and AbsoluteGreenHomes.com

Taunton's Build Like a Pro® is a trademark of The Taunton Press, Inc.,

registered in the U.S. Patent and Trademark Office.

Library of Congress Cataloging-in-Publication Data

German, Roger.
  Remodeling a basement / author, Roger German. -- Rev. ed.
      p. cm. -- (Taunton's build like a pro)
  Includes index.
  ISBN 978-1-60085-292-3
  1. Basements--Remodeling. I. Title.
  TH4816.3.B35G47 2010
  643'.5--dc22

                                    2009033545

Printed in the United States of America

15 14 13 12 11 10 9 8

The following manufacturers/names appearing in *Remodeling a Basement* are trademarks: ACQ Preserve®, Band-Aid®, Benseal®, Bilco®, Bonsal SUREWALL®, Congoleum®, Corian®, Crown Sprã-tool®, Dritite®, Durabond®, E-Z Ancor®, Formica®, Goof-Off®, Icynene®, LePage® PL Premium PL 200 and PL 300, Lufkin®, Natural Select®, Natural Wood®, ProTecta®, ProZIP®, Purdy®, Quik-Gel®, Romex®, Scratch Protection®, Sheetrock®, Sonneborn NP-1®, Stanley®, Surform®, Teflon®

Construction is inherently dangerous. Using hand or power tools improperly or ignoring safety practices can lead to permanent injury or even death. Don't try to perform operations you learn about here (or elsewhere), unless you're certain they are safe for you. If something about an operation doesn't feel right, don't do it. Look for another way. We want you to enjoy the remodeling process, so please keep safety foremost in your mind whenever you're working on your project.

To those who will use this book, and stain it with coffee and glue and sweat, and scribble in it and cuss its mistakes and appreciate its help.

It has been a gift to me to write it for you.

Acknowledgments

First, I need to thank Roland Casburn. When I was a freshman in college, Roland took me on his crew and kept me on, though I broke his hammer, cut his saw cord, and generally tested his patience. What I know of carpentry is built on the skillfulness of his framing.

Ron Olson deciphered the framing square for me and, more importantly, taught me how much fun it is to work hard with a good friend. Randy Ware taught me how to trim, and I have yet to meet anyone who can approach his quality and speed in finish work.

Josie Weber and Jim Patten taught me to write concisely. This sentence is for them. My editor, Roger Holmes, I thank for his friendship, his questions, and his belief in the book. And I thank Tim Snyder and Helen Albert at The Taunton Press for the chance to write it. Roger Bruhn is responsible for the remarkable photography. I thank him for his professionalism and his patience with a truly untutored "model."

I'm indebted to many professionals in Lincoln, Nebraska, in particular to Mike Kroese of Green's Plumbing, Heating, Cooling, and Electrical; to Scott Huenink of Electrical Enterprises; to Bob Codr of ABC Electric; to Gary Stratton of Roberts Plumbing; and to Dave Drohman of Drohman Drywall.

Joan Yien of Floor Works, Bob Barber at Lincoln Paint, and Doug and Chuck Krogman of Krogman Tile gave me time, advice, and professional tips, when I know they had other things to do. And Mel Goddard, Chief Building Inspector for the City of Lincoln, was kind enough to review the work for code compliance.

What accuracy inheres in this book I owe to them; any errors or omissions are mine alone.

I thank Barb Rowlan for the coffee, Terry Loos and Dick Noble for their friendship.

My thanks to Southeast Community College for giving me the chance to teach the class that led to this book. To former students Steve and Tami Sufficool, Kathy Lehnert, Mike and Denise Szatko, and Jeff Gilmore, thanks for allowing us to photograph their basements.

Lastly, and with great respect, I thank my class of 2002–2003 for working within the constraints of producing this book; Matt and Amanda Dowse for allowing us to photograph their basement as the class worked on it; and Curt and KayCee Sherrill for the use of their basement as well.

Contents

Introduction

THIS BOOK IS designed to help you remodel your basement. I strongly urge you to read (or at least skim) all of it before you pound a nail. Doing so will help you make informed decisions about the nature and scope of your project. You'll be able to determine how much you want to tackle yourself, when it makes sense to hire a professional, and how much the project will cost, both financially and emotionally.

In the chapters that follow, I'll take you step-by-step through the entire process of remodeling a basement, from evaluating the basement you've got now to polishing off the last detail of the one you've created. You'll learn about designing and planning; how to frame walls and run electrical wire and water pipe; how to hang, tape, and finish drywall, install doors, cabinets, and trim; how to lay carpet and ceramic tile; and much more.

As you design, remember that it's your home, your space. Be creative. As you tackle the actual building, have fun. Of course, there will be times when the work won't be fun. That's when you have to keep the long view in mind. Persevere. Or, if you're truly stumped, do what the professionals do: Hire a professional to help.

I am convinced that you can do the job (most of it, anyway) yourself. These are not just hopeful words of encouragement. I know from experience. For 15 years I have taught a basement-remodeling adult-education class at Southeast Community College in Lincoln, Nebraska, where I'm a remodeling contractor. The class meets for 18 weeks, one night a week for three hours. I like the hands-on approach, so I pick one of the student basements and we remodel it as a class. We don't complete the project in our 54 hours of class time, but we get a lot of it done.

When we start, some students hardly know which is the business end of a hammer. Nevertheless, the results are remarkable. Whether it's the class basement or students' individual projects, I'm always impressed by the level of craftsmanship and attention to detail that I've seen in the finished basements.

Almost all of the photos of the remodeling processes shown in this book were taken during the course of a class remodeling project. The charts, plans, and materials lists included in the book are also taken from this project. I hope this continuity will give you a sense of what a real project is like as you work your way through the chapters.

The two most common questions I hear in class are "Can I save money doing the work myself?" and "How long will it take?"

Yes, you can save money doing it yourself. How much? About half of what a pro would charge. For basement remodels I've done, the overall costs are about half for material and half for labor. Of course, if you throw in a $6,000 whirlpool tub, the percentages change. But, in general, doing the work yourself will save about half the cost.

When I'm asked, "How long it will take?" my answer is always, "Longer than you think it will." I'm not being coy. As a professional, I've worked for months on a single basement project. That's 8 to 10 hours a day, 5 to 6 days a week, and with professional subcontractors who have the tools, time, and experience to do the work as efficiently as possible. Just making a basement rec room and a half-bath will take a professional a month if everything goes right, which is rare in any kind of remodeling project.

I bring this up not to discourage, but to encourage you. So it takes you six months or a year. The thing is to start. And, if you keep chipping away at it, you'll eventually have the basement of your dreams, and the satisfaction of having done it (or most of it) yourself.

Getting

CHAPTER ONE
Started

T hat new basement rec room, bedroom, and office you've dreamed of is about to take shape. If you're like me, once you decide to tackle a project, you can't wait to get going. But before you start to clear out the old stuff, or pound a single nail, you need to spend some time looking closely at the basement as it is now.

It makes no sense to spend time, effort, and not a little cash installing beautiful new rooms in an unsound structure. Do your walls lean? Is the floor cracked? Are your electrical service and furnace capable of handling new demands? And, most important of all, does your basement leak? Are there mold or mildew problems?

Identifying and fixing, or mitigating, these basic problems is essential to a successful remodel. In this chapter, we'll take a look at this detective work. The information you uncover will help you determine the scope and cost of your project—its limits, perhaps, as well as its potential.

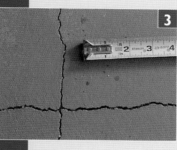

IN DETAIL

If you are remodeling the basement of an older home, it's a good idea to evaluate your mechanical systems. Once you enclose old pipes, wiring, and ductwork in new walls and ceilings, it's painful and expensive to uncover them for replacement. If you're uncertain about the condition of existing systems, ask a professional to evaluate them.

Old and New

For prospective remodelers, there are really only two types of basements—those built with no thought that the space might one day be finished, and those built with an eye toward habitable rooms. Older homes more often have the first type, and newer homes the second. In the Midwest, where I live, contractors working as early as the 1930s gave thought to basements as possible living space. In general, though, the idea of building homes with basements to live in didn't start taking hold until the 1950s and 1960s. By the 1970s, it had become the norm.

If you have a newer home, you're going to have an easier time remodeling the basement. Plumbing is usually in place for a bathroom; pipes, wires, and ducts are tucked in tight to the ceiling or consolidated in a few areas; and the stairs are more accessible and built with better headroom.

In older homes, basements were built as places to put the furnace and to store things that the next owner of the home would throw away. Many older basements have dirt floors or floors of thin concrete. Some have a furnace pit with a crawl space around the exterior and a room for coal and a coal chute. Old convection furnaces were inverted octopuses of huge ducts; with the advent of the forced-air furnace, most of those leviathans were replaced with much smaller units.

New furnaces free up space in older homes. But to make the space practical and in compliance with codes, you often need either to lower the floor or to raise the house, jobs requiring skid loaders, dumptrucks, house jacks, jackhammers, and considerable contractor liability insurance. If your basement requires either measure, have a professional builder do the work. Then you can embark on finishing the basement yourself. Fortunately, many older basements, like most newer ones, pose less daunting, more owner-friendly remodeling problems.

Adequate headroom makes a basement easier to remodel as well as more comfortable to use.

If your home is older, you may want to redo an existing live-in basement.

The mechanical systems in newer homes are often installed with an eye to future basement remodeling.

Water: The Bane of Basements

There is simply no point in finishing your basement if it leaks water. Covering up a water problem will only defer the damage from mold, mildew, and rot. The time to fix water-incursion problems is before they're covered up with insulation and drywall.

Almost all the basement-water problems I've encountered in 30 years of remodeling and house construction are the result of surface water (rainfall and runoff) and bad drainage. These problems can almost always be fixed by making sure water drains away from the house foundation. You can often do this work yourself. (See Water Problems on p. 44–45.)

If the surface-water drainage is fine, but you still have leaks, ground water may be the reason.

Anatomy of a Basement

Old or new, most basements have outside walls made of concrete or cement block, a center bearing wall, and stairs for access. A common variation of the hole-in-the-ground basement is the walkout basement, where at least one wall has grade-level access to the outdoors. That outside wall is often a frame wall rather than concrete, or a combination of the two.

The center wall is called "bearing" because the floor joists for the first level of the house rest, or bear, on the wall for support. To carry the load, a bearing wall is supported by a footing underneath the concrete floor. If you want to remove or insert a doorway in a bearing wall, you have to provide something to carry its load. Your basement may already have a steel beam that replaces part of a bearing wall and makes a wide opening between the two halves of the basement. A "curtain" wall carries no load and has no footing. Removing it causes no structural problems.

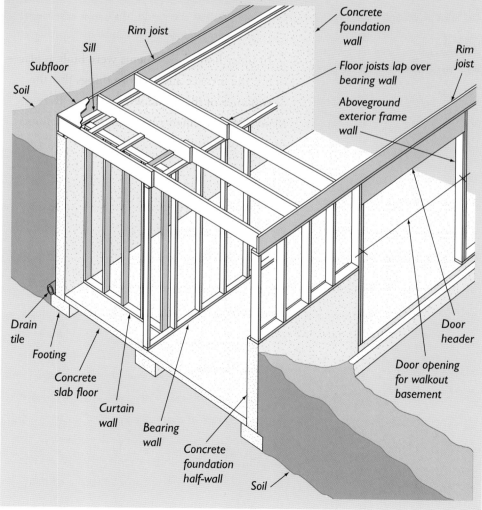

Rim joist

Sill

Subfloor

Soil

Concrete foundation wall

Floor joists lap over bearing wall

Rim joist

Aboveground exterior frame wall

Drain tile

Footing

Concrete slab floor

Curtain wall

Bearing wall

Concrete foundation half-wall

Soil

Door header

Door opening for walkout basement

PRO TIP

If your basement leaks when it rains (or when it doesn't rain), or is seasonally or constantly damp, find out why and fix it before remodeling.

IN DETAIL

You can determine if a crack in a wall is stable by measuring the width at a certain spot. Mark the spot and write the width on the wall with a marker. Measure it again every couple of months. If the crack gets larger or smaller, you may have a problem. Call an expert to help you evaluate further.

Mold and mildew, the result of a damp basement, can ruin drywall. They make a basement musty and unpleasant, particularly for allergy sufferers.

A sump pump removes ground water that would otherwise seep into a basement. The pump is designed to turn on automatically.

Ground water is subterranean, moving through the soil from areas of high to low water pressure. Leaks caused by ground water require removing or redirecting the water from around the foundation with drain tile and a sump pit and pump. In my area, these are often installed in new houses at the time they're built because it's easy to do then.

New and old houses can be retrofitted with drain tile and sump, too. Drain tile (which today is usually perforated plastic pipe rather than clay tile) can be laid inside or outside. The sump pit and pump are usually installed inside. An inside installation involves cutting out the floor around the perimeter of the basement about 1 ft. to 1½ ft. in from the wall, excavating enough dirt to drop in some gravel, the drain tile, and a sump pit, and then pouring a new floor over the gravel. Water seeping around or under the foundation and floor flows to the lowest point (the gravel and drain tile), drains to the sump pit, and is pumped away.

Installing drain tile and sump systems is an arduous task and requires some special skills and tools, so I recommend you hire it done. If you suspect ground-water problems, start by consulting a specialist or a knowledgeable builder.

Evaluating Walls and Floors

There are three things to know about concrete; it gets hard, it cracks and it is not impervious to water. All but the newest basement walls and floors will show some cracks.

Cracked walls

In block walls, cracks tend to follow the mortar joints. In poured walls, they can be anywhere. Cracks are usually of little concern if they've stopped moving. The National Association of

Home Builders (NAHB) has established criteria for acceptable cracking in order to lessen the friction that can arise between homeowners and builders. In block walls, cracks up to ¼-in. wide are acceptable; larger cracks must be addressed by the builder. Cracks in concrete walls must not allow water to leak into the basement.

Observe cracks over time to see if they're active or stable (see In Detail on the facing page.) If a crack is still moving, look for the cause. Perhaps a tree growing too close to the foundation is putting pressure on the wall. Or, more commonly, there is water pressure against the wall, and either the water pressure alone, or a cycle of freezing and thawing, or both, is moving the wall. Fix the problem before doing anything else. Simply clean and caulk stable cracks (see p. 46). This will eliminate some seepage and keep out bugs.

Bowed walls

Basement walls usually bow for the same reason that they crack—water pressure. As a rule of thumb, if the wall is bowed in less than an inch and is no longer moving, it won't be a problem. You could straighten it out, but this is costly and time consuming, and really not necessary. Just hide it behind the framed walls of your remodel. Of course, if the bow is still moving, the first thing to do is find out why and fix the cause. Professional advice is worth seeking out here.

If a wall is bowed in more than an inch, you probably need to straighten it. I say probably, because I've been in basements with the walls bowed in more than a foot. (I didn't stay long, but I've been in them.) They've been that way for dozens of years, inching their way in, and at some point, they'll cave. When you're investing time and money in a basement remodel, I don't think it makes sense to gamble that a questionable wall will hold up for years to come.

Cracked walls often indicate current or past drainage problems. Fix the problem before remodeling.

A 2×4 frame wall hides minor cracks and bows in exterior walls.

PRO TIP

Cracks are inevitable in concrete floors. Worry about them only if they're moving. Fix them only if they'll telegraph through your flooring.

IN DETAIL

Natural forces are not the cause of all wall problems. I've been in new basements where the walls were poured more than an inch out of plumb. These walls aren't structurally deficient, just sloppily built. If there are no signs of outside forces moving a wall, you can live with it. See Chapter 5 for how to frame basement walls to mitigate the sins of the folks who poured a poor foundation.

Cracked floors

Because of the expansion and contraction of large concrete slabs, cracks in basement floors are inevitable. Concrete floors and similar surfaces are constructed to direct the cracks along predetermined lines called control joints. These are visible as troweled joints on driveways, sidewalks, and some floors. Basement floors often have hidden control joints instead of troweled joints. Before

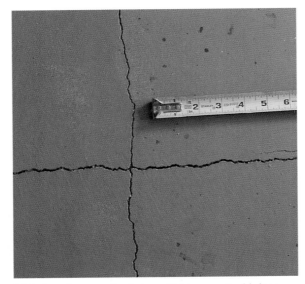

This floor has cracked along hidden control joints. The cracks are narrow and the floor remains flat.

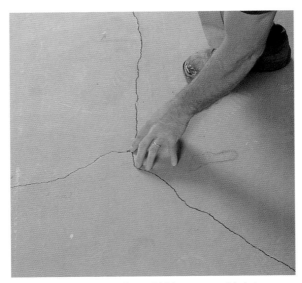

Cracks here diverge from hidden control joints. They're about 1/4 in. wide and offset about 1/8 in. and will require repair if the floor is to be tiled.

the concrete cures, the finishers slice through the thickness of the concrete along a grid pattern and trowel lightly over the top of these joints to make a smooth surface. When the cured slab moves, it cracks along these fault lines.

The NAHB guidelines allow a 3/16-in. separation and/or vertical displacement for cracks in basement floors. There are a number of ways to deal with floor cracks that fall within acceptable guidelines. One is to do nothing. If you're stretching a carpet and pad over the floor, most of the differences and separations will disappear. If you're laying a thinner covering, such as low-pile carpet or linoleum, cracks and heaves will telegraph through. You'll need to smooth out the differences with a grinder or a floor leveling compound (see Patching Concrete Floors on p. 150).

Serious cracks or large vertical displacements in floors are harder to ascribe to a cause and more work to fix. Fortunately, they're also less common, especially in newer homes. Here in the Midwest, bad floor problems are most often caused by a substrate of clay. The clay expands as it absorbs water and can exert enough pressure to bust up a concrete floor. The only solutions to this problem involve eliminating the source of water or removing the clay. Both are difficult tasks. If you have badly cracked, separated, or heaved floors, consult a professional to see what's going on and what can be done.

Checking the Mechanical Systems

The heating, ventilation, and air-conditioning system (HVAC) and the electrical system play a part in every basement remodel, and plumbing (for a bathroom or laundry room) almost always does. So, before you go any further with a remodel, check out each of these systems.

HVAC

In most newer homes, the furnace and air conditioner are sized to include a finished basement. Those in older homes are generally up to the task, too, although you may need some supplemental heat. Codes require that certain amounts of air be provided for each room and for the safe operation of the furnace. You can figure out for yourself what is needed (see Chapter 6). But if you're the least bit unsure of requirements and safety, hire an HVAC contractor to do an evaluation.

While the contractor is there, ask for suggestions on the best way to lay out the supply ducts and return air required by code. You may also want to ask the contractor for a bid to do the work, which isn't always the most enjoyable task in a project.

Electrical system

The electrical-service panel in newer homes is usually adequate for a basement remodel. An older home may need a new higher-amperage panel to service the additional demands of a remodel. In general, if your panel has fuses, you'll need to upgrade your service and replace the panel with a circuit-breaker panel.

If yours is already a circuit-breaker panel, see if there are enough blank knockouts below the installed circuit breakers to accommodate the new circuits you plan. Call in an electrician if you are unsure of what your panel will accommodate.

Plumbing

Newer homes are often plumbed to allow easy installation of a basement bathroom. These bathroom "rough-ins" usually include drains for a toilet, a tub or shower, and a sink. A 4-in.-round PVC sewer line, capped at floor level or a bit above, accommodates a toilet. A drain and vent stack (usually 2 in.) running from the floor to the ceiling serves the sink. Nearby should be a roughly 12-in. square plastic cover set in the floor.

Furnaces in newer homes are usually sized to accommodate a finished basement.

Check your electrical service box for unused circuit-breaker knockouts.

This basement has been preplumbed for a bathroom, with a toilet drain (center), a vent stack for a sink (right), and a black plastic knockout (left) covering the tub-shower drain.

IN DETAIL

There's a lot of wiring even a novice can do in a basement. But installing a panel isn't on that list. It's a good idea to consult with a pro even if you don't need a new panel. If you want to do some, but not all, of the project's wiring, be sure to arrange it with your electrician beforehand. Some pros are flexible enough to accommodate homeowner help. Others aren't. Be specific and realistic about what you can do and when you'll do it.

It protects a drain line set below the concrete for a bathtub or shower. Some tub rough-ins are thinly covered with concrete. You can find these by tapping on the surface of the concrete with a hammer. Solid concrete has a flat, dull sound. As you tap, you'll hear the recess where the rough-in hides as a change in pitch. Older rough-ins may simply be boxed by 2×4s, exposing a small square area of sand covering the capped drain line.

If you lack these rough-ins, or want them in a different spot than at present, call in a professional plumber. Jackhammering concrete to install or move drains is hard work, and you'll want to make sure it is done right. Once the basics are in place, there's plenty of installation you can do.

The Critical Path

Most successful projects, like successful journeys, follow a road map. I use a "critical path" map for basement remodels. It is one of the most important tools of any remodeling project. It will help you see where you are, where you want to go, and how you will get there. It will help keep you sane. It has worked so well for me that I've organized this book to follow the critical path for a typical basement remodel.

The critical path breaks a project into a series of logical bite-sized steps. It identifies each step that is critical to another step. For example, you don't need to paint before you lay carpet (although it's a good idea), but you do have to drywall before you can paint. Otherwise, there's nothing to paint. And before you can drywall, you have to frame the walls.

The critical path seems self-evident, and most of it is. But if you're not familiar with general construction, it is the best way to understand and organize the process.

The critical path also helps you spread your decisions over a reasonable length of time. You have hundreds of decisions to make, from paint colors, to the location of doorways, to where,

Unwanted Critters

As you're examining your basement, be sure to look for evidence of home-wreckers like termites and carpenter ants. Termites leave telltale tunnels when they travel over nonwood surfaces. Carpenter ants leave little piles of sawdust under their exit and entry holes. Both pests will hollow out boards right up to the surface, so that what looks like a solid board is actually just a shell. I've done demolition work in which I've grabbed a 2x4 to give it a whack, and it crumbled in my hand. Nothing inside but a bit of dust and maybe a critter or two.

If you have the faintest suspicion that your basement might harbor either of these villains, call a professional pest expert.

Red Flags

Given enough money and time, any basement can be remodeled in accordance with local building codes. But there are several requirements that can be project stoppers unless you've got very deep pockets. Most codes require a height of 7 ft. or more from the basement floor to the bottom of the joists of the floor above. (Ductwork and resultant soffits can project below 7 ft.) Less clearance than that and you won't get a building permit. That's a project stopper unless you can afford to lower the basement floor or raise the house above it.

Codes also require that basement bedrooms contain an egress window (see the facing page). Though not as expensive as lowering and pouring a new floor, installing an egress window can be a budget buster.

EGRESS WINDOWS

For years, building codes have required all basement bedrooms to contain an egress window (a window large enough to serve as an avenue of escape). And for years people have remodeled basements with a nod and a wink to that requirement. To avoid the expense of installing an egress window, bedrooms were called all sorts of things on the permit plans. Our chief building inspector once told the homebuilders association that it was a wonder any retail clothing outlets could survive, what with all the sewing rooms built in basements.

But as a volunteer firefighter for 10 years, I understand how important it is to have a functional secondary exit. When the stairs are on fire and the smoke is thick, few adults and fewer children can escape through those small, metal hatches that serve as windows in most basements.

If you plan to have someone sleeping in the basement on a regular basis, call the room a bedroom and install an egress window. (Technically, any room with a closet or direct access to a bathroom is considered a bedroom by the codes department.) A professional installation will cost $2,000 to $3,000. You can save up to half that cost by doing the installation yourself. But unless you're an experienced builder, consider hiring a professional. All kinds of bad things can happen if you don't know what you're doing when you punch a hole in your foundation, let alone try to set a window correctly and reseal everything.

Ample window wells allow an egress window to shed considerable light into a room. Required in basement bedrooms, egress windows are large enough to crawl out of and can save lives.

TRADE SECRET

Computer spread-sheet and project-tracking software can be a great help organizing a large complicated project. A basement remodel seldom reaches that level of complexity. Still, I've erased and rewritten on enough paper critical-path charts to appreciate the ease with which a computer program allows you to fine-tune or alter a schedule. I wouldn't buy such software just for a basement project, but if you already know your way around a tracking program, by all means, use it.

Critical Path Timeline	August	September	October	November
Repair work	████			
Draw plan	██			
Get permit	◆			
Buy material	··· Framing material ···		Tub-shower ···	···
Frame		████████		
Inspections (call ahead)			Framing ◆ ◆ Plumbing	Electrical ◆
HVAC rough-in			██	
Plumbing rough-in			███	
Electrical rough-in				████
Insulation/vapor barrier				██
Drywall (hang and finish)				
Finish carpentry				
Paint, stain, clear finish				
Door handles (not a critical path element, but good timing)				
Flooring: linoleum and tile				
Plumbing finish				
Electrical finish				
HVAC finish				
Flooring: carpet				
Bathroom accessories				
Door bumpers, touchup paint				
Final Inspection				

About Ordering Material
The time line shown here is for buying items that are in stock locally. If you're ordering material, allow 3 to 5 weeks minimum delivery time. Ask suppliers about specific delivery times and call periodically for an update.

exactly, you want this jog in this wall. You can't think about all of these decisions at once, and you don't need to. The critical path provides a schedule to ensure that all necessary choices are made and the materials and tools are on hand at the right time. I lay out critical path charts on gridded note paper. I usually have to tape a couple of sheets end to end.

Critical elements on the path

Here's a summary of the journey represented in the chart above and followed in this book.

The plan. Although your project may be crystal clear inside your head, construction can't begin until you have a building permit. The permit requires a plan. Chapter 3 covers how to go about making and drawing a plan.

Demolition and repair. Before you can build anything new, you've got to get rid of the old and unwanted, and repair, if necessary, what's left. Chapter 4 covers this stage.

Framing. Here you assemble the skeleton: building walls, framing doors and windows, and boxing in soffits, as described in Chapter 5.

Mechanicals. Installing the heating and air-conditioning ducts, roughing in the plumbing and electrical service, and stringing phone, cable, and speaker lines are covered in Chapter 6.

Drywall. With everything inside the walls finished, you can add insulation and then drywall, as outlined in Chapter 7.

Finish carpentry. I like to install doors, hang cabinets, and install wood trim after drywall-ing, as covered in Chapter 8. If you like to paint

December	January	February	March	April	May

Carpet, cabinets · Vanity countertop · Doors, trim · Linoleum and tile · Sink faucet, shower valve · Door handsets · Light fixtures · Bath accessories

Final ◆

Christmas time off

Staying on Schedule, or Not
Inevitably, there will be some tasks on the schedule that will "slip" and others that may move faster than planned. Remember, this is your schedule. If it begins to look unrealistic, refigure and redraw it, and move on.

The critical-path chart shown here maps the remodel that will serve as an example throughout the book.

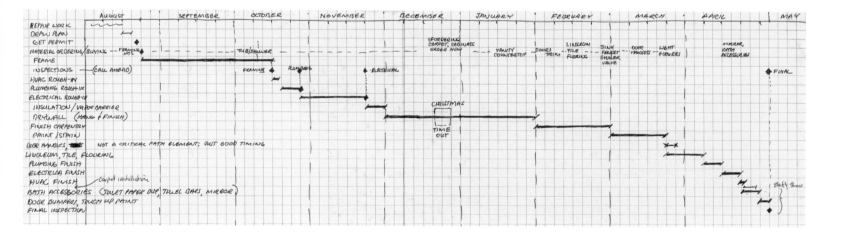

walls first, or stain or paint the trim before installing it, just reverse the order on your critical path.

Paint, stain, and floors. Another of my preferences is to paint and stain before installing floor coverings. As explained in Chapter 9,

I think it makes better use of time and material, but you can reverse the order if you wish.

Finishing up. Installing sinks, toilet, towel holders, mirrors, outlets, and light fixtures makes the basement ready for use. These final touches are covered in Chapter 10.

Inspiration and

CHAPTER TWO

Ideas

1 Rec Rooms, p. 18

Before you embark on your remodeling adventure, I'd like to show you what is possible. All the work shown in this chapter was done by students in my basement remodeling classes.

2 Bedrooms, p. 21

There are lots of good ideas in these photos. More important, I think, is the knowledge that these handsome rooms were designed and made by people just like you. They include a single mom with a full-time job, an insurance underwriter, a nurse, an accountant, and a business supervisor. Some of them were handy with a hammer before we started. Others had never driven a nail.

3 Bathrooms, p. 21

As you look through this chapter, see if you can distinguish the basements done by someone with experience from those done by someone without. That should give you the confidence to forge ahead.

4 Laundry and Utility Rooms, p. 22

IN DETAIL

If you're tight for space, consider installing a pocket door rather than a swinging door. As shown in the photo below, a pocket door slides neatly into a space in a wall that has been specially framed to accommodate it.

Opening up the stairway to the basement with a half-wall makes an attractive entrance.

Rec Rooms

Almost every finished basement has a recreation ("rec") room. Very few of the ones my students have done are the same. One student's recreation is throwing darts, so his rec room has an electronic dartboard and a wet bar to keep the dart throwers happy. Another student's children practice the piano as well as play video games in her rec room.

Most common in rec rooms are entertainment centers and, recently, big-screen TVs. These centers are ideal for children, who appreciate a place to hang out with their friends, and for parents, who appreciate not having to retreat to the bedroom when the kids have friends over. Fireplaces are popular with all age groups, as much for their cozy feel as for the actual heat they produce. In fact, sitting by the fireplace is the most popular activity in several of the rec rooms I've been in.

Television and entertainment centers are popular rec-room features. This one shares a room with the wet bar at top left on the facing page. Note the recessed lights—set into the ceiling they don't take up any precious headroom.

An otherwise awkward corner with a low soffit is a fine spot for a wet bar (above left). Adding a sink to the service and storage area (above right) makes it easy to entertain in the room shown in the photo at bottom left. A bearing wall originally separated the spaces shown in the two photos. Replacing it with a load-bearing beam made this large, comfortable room possible.

PRO TIP

Whether your passion is chess or pool, make sure you size the rec room to allow adequate space to play the game.

IN DETAIL

Recessed lights are ideal for basements. Set into the ceiling, they don't take up any precious headroom.

This rec room provides a sunny spot for exercising. The floor is an easy-to-install composite-wood system.

A curved wall transitions nicely from a rec room to a hallway that leads to a bathroom and a bedroom.

Basement rooms are excellent places for exercise equipment. Enthusiasts may install a small gym in a separate room. Many of my students have devoted an area of a larger multi-purpose room to a stationary bike or weight machine.

Regardless of a rec room's use, you can add interest to it (and other rooms) in a variety of ways. An angled or curved wall is fairly easy to build and makes a big impact. You can remove part of the wall along the stairs, adding a newel post, balusters, and a rail to enhance the room's character—and make it easier to move bulky items into the basement. Attractive flooring, subtle or dramatic lighting, a striking painting scheme—all can add flair to your remodel.

Bedrooms

Basement bedrooms are often "spare" bedrooms, so they tend to be a bit austere. But there's no reason they should be spare in either sense of the word. I haven't built a master bedroom suite in a basement, but it can be done. Natural light may be plentiful in a walkout basement, or in an enclosed basement with the installation of one or more egress windows. If you're cramped upstairs, the basement provides room not only for a master bedroom, but for that large walk-in closet or ensuite bathroom you've dreamed of.

A spare bedroom can also become a sewing room, an office space, or a library, complete with built-in bookshelves. With so many comfortable sofabeds on the market, you can have the spare bedroom, office, and sewing room all in one.

I regularly run computer cable into basements these days, often into a spare bedroom or office. It is easy to provide cable for high-speed internet connections when you remodel (much easier than trying to run cable into existing walls).

The bedrooms shown above and at left double as an office and a library. The bookshelves took advantage of a jog in the wall of the bathroom shown below.

Bathrooms

If bedrooms tend to get short shrift in basements, bathrooms make up for it. Here's where my students and clients often lavish attention (and a good chunk of the budget).

Sinks range from simple wall-hung units, to elegant pedestal lavatories, to marble-topped vanities. One-piece tub-shower combinations are the most versatile, and the most popular, choice. If you can't get a one-piece unit down the stairs (check before you buy), good fiberglass tub-showers are available in two- and three-piece kits. Of course, you can also install a whirlpool tub, a spacious tiled shower, or a traditional cast-iron tub with claw feet, if that's what you fancy.

Flooring choices in basements tend toward the durable and relatively inexpensive: carpet,

The students who built this bathroom used a striking paint job and handsome ceramic tile to make the most of an unavoidably awkward space.

PRO TIP

To save wear and tear on your legs and your heavy-laundry-basket-carrying arms, situate your laundry room close to the stairway.

IN DETAIL

Most of the "guts" of a basement—furnace, water heater, ducts, and wiring—can be hidden behind walls and ceilings when you remodel. The electrical-service panel, however, must be accessible. A common solution is to frame a wall around the panel, and then cover the panel with a door that matches the trim in the room.

By making this bathroom (above and right) wider than usual, the owners were able to place the tub-shower and a built-in linen closet and drawers against the longer wall.

linoleum, and vinyl tile. Again, bathrooms are often an exception, with ceramic tile a favorite material. An easy-to-install underfloor heating system can add comfort to the good looks of a tile floor. It's cozier to step out of the tub onto a warm floor.

In the standard layout of a bathroom, the tub stretches along the back wall, across the width of the room. Given more space, some of my students have placed tub-showers to accommodate built-in storage. Sometimes you can also box-in between studs to pick up a little extra shelving.

Laundry and Utility Rooms

Just because a room is utilitarian doesn't mean it has to be ugly. A well-lit room with nicely painted ceiling and walls and an easy-to-clean linoleum floor may not make washing and drying clothes a pleasure, but it will make laundry less of a chore.

A large laundry room can also include a backup refrigerator or freezer. If you've always wanted a pantry, here's your chance. You can build shelves into a utility-room closet, or line the walls of an entire room with shelves.

A generous vanity and mirror is featured in this bathroom (left), as well as a whirlpool bath and a shower with a ceramic-tile surround (above).

This spacious laundry has a washer, dryer, and ironing board, as well as a deep sink and refrigerator-freezer.

A utility-room closet can serve as a pantry or provide extra storage.

Design and

CHAPTER THREE
Planning

I f you, like many other people, get nervous when design is mentioned, relax. It's not the esoteric activity you fear. Design, at least in our context, is figuring out what you want in your basement, what will work, what won't, and what you can afford.

Planning, the next step, organizes the work your design requires. Breaking things into a sequence of bite-sized pieces keeps a big project from becoming overwhelming.

Design is where the fun starts. What do you want in your basement? A guest bedroom? A clean, well-lighted space for doing the laundry? What do you see yourself doing in your basement? Are you in a recliner watching a football game? Luxuriating in a whirlpool bath? Or do you see the kids enjoying a game of pool or having a sleepover?

Now it's time to put your dreams on paper, and this chapter will help you do so.

IN DETAIL

A good tape measure makes all the measuring you need to do much easier. It will serve you well through the rest of the project, too. If you don't already have a tape, buy a 25-footer, with a good recoil spring and at least a 6-ft. stand-out. That is, the tape will extend horizontally 6 ft. without falling. This is very useful when measuring behind furnaces or across wide openings. I've had good luck with Stanley® and Lufkin® tapes.

TRADE SECRET

Many students in my class have used inexpensive computer software to make scale drawings that are just as useful as plans made with design programs that cost thousands of dollars. Computer-aided drawings are easy to alter, so they're particularly helpful for trying out different design ideas.

Design

It's possible to march down to your basement and start slamming walls together. It's not smart, but it's possible. It's better to have a blueprint. And the blueprint starts with knowing what you have, so you can make informed decisions on what's possible, what's reasonable, and what's simply out of reach.

Draw what you've got

So, the first thing to do before you lift a hammer to drive a nail is to map out your basement. Make a rough sketch (don't worry about scale now) and write down measurements. Be sure to include:

- The length and width of the basement and all the jogs in and out
- Rooms or other defined spaces
- Bathroom rough-in
- Bearing walls or support posts and beams (see Identifying a Bearing Wall on p. 32)
- Stairway
- Windows and doors
- Furnace
- Main sewer drain (where it drops down from above)
- Electrical service panel
- Water heater, water softener
- Everything permanently attached to water, power, or sewer services
- Heating-duct runs
- Lights, switches, and outlets

Scale drawings. Now, use your sketch and measurements to make a scale drawing of your existing basement. This drawing (or versions of it) will guide you through the entire project. You'll use it to work out your ideas, then to make your working drawings ("blueprints"), and to submit for building permits.

I make scale drawings the simple old-fashioned way, on sheets of paper printed with a grid of ¼-in. squares, each of which represents a square foot. These drawings need not be exact, but they should include all the information necessary for a remodel. Depending on the size of your basement, you may need to tape a couple of gridded sheets together.

Start by drawing the basement's existing exterior walls. Then add the first elements of the remodel—2×4 frame walls that run just inside the existing exterior walls. (See Dealing with Outside Walls on the facing page.) These walls define the available space inside the basement.

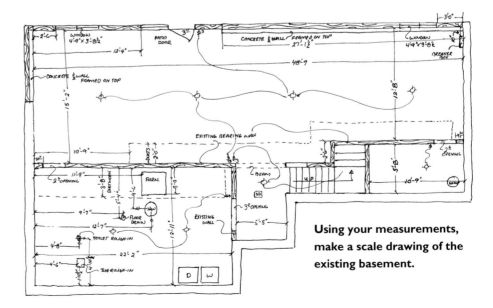

Using your measurements, make a scale drawing of the existing basement.

Dealing with Outside Walls

The exterior wall treatment presented in this book is the one I've used for almost all the basement remodels I've done. Installing full-sized 2×4 framing just inside the existing basement walls allows you to make rooms that are as nicely finished as any in the rest of the house. Where winters and basements are cold, insulating the frame cavity also makes for warmer and quieter basement rooms. Full walls allow you to hide cracked, bowed, or unplumb (but structurally sound) foundation walls. And they make running electrical wire for new rooms easier.

Walkout basements typically have one or more walls in which the upper part is framed and insulated and the lower part is concrete. You can hide the entire wall behind a full-height framed wall. Or you can frame a half-wall to cover the lower, concrete wall, as shown at right. The wide wooden cap on a half-wall serves as a shelf for books or display, or as the bottom shelf of a shelf wall.

Instead of full framing, you can attach 1×2 or 2×2 furring strips to the exterior wall and then drywall onto the strips. I don't do this unless I have to. Furring strips provide less space for insulation, and they offer less scope for correcting out-of-plumb walls. However, there are some framing problems that can be solved with furring strips. Most builders don't space a stairway away from a concrete wall more that the thickness of a flat 2×4. Installing full 2×4 framing at the bottom of the stairs may look odd, so I sometimes continue the wall with 2×2 furring strips. I also use furrings strips where a toilet rough-in is too close to the exterior concrete wall to accommodate a 2×4 wall.

Finally, if your budget is very tight, the simplest way to deal with concrete or block basement walls is to do nothing. Or nearly nothing. Wash the surface with a strong cleaner and let it be, in all its neo-industrial beauty. You can dress up foundation walls with paint (be sure to use a good quality mold- and mildew-inhibiting concrete primer). For a stuccolike look, trowel on a surface-bonding masonry cement, such as Bonsal SUREWALL®, applied about 1/8 in. thick.

A half-wall covers the lower, concrete portion of this exterior wall in a walkout basement.

It's handy to use this bare-bones plan as a master and to make a dozen or so copies of it to use as you determine what your new basement will look like. If you need more copies later, you can make them from the master, rather than having to redraw.

Transforming what you've got into what you want

Everyone brings dreams as well as practical needs to a remodeling project. In theory, almost anything you want to do is possible. I've moved stairways, furnaces, and plumbing fixtures. I've torn out existing basement walls and replaced them.

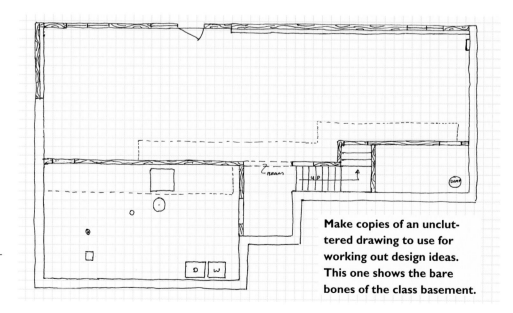

Make copies of an uncluttered drawing to use for working out design ideas. This one shows the bare bones of the class basement.

PRO TIP

Eliminate hallways where you can. Sometimes they're unavoidable, but typically, a hallway just eats up space.

IN DETAIL

Drywall isn't the only option for interior walls and ceilings. If the industrial-structural look appeals to you, there's no reason you couldn't just nail OSB (oriented strand board) on the walls, cover the joints with 1×2 cedar strips, and then varnish the whole thing. Definitely child resistant. Other options include exterior sheet siding like T-111 (commonly called "texture one-eleven") or solid cedar or fir siding. Sheets of thin plywood veneered with a striking wood (or a photographic facsimile of the same) are less popular now than when I was a kid. But if you like the look, such paneling is still available.

I've jackhammered floors and removed bearing walls. But possibilities are always constrained by personal limits of time, space, and budget, as well as by compliance with building codes.

Sometimes designing is simple. What you want falls easily into the space available—a bedroom here, a rec room and bathroom there, with storage space in the unfinished utility room. Sometimes a design is determined by existing features and codes. If you have a walkout basement with two egress-rated windows, it makes sense to incorporate one of those windows into the bedroom and save the cost of cutting through the concrete foundation elsewhere to install a code-compliant bedroom window.

Sometimes what you want may not appear possible—at least at first. If you really want it, don't give up easily. That's what all those plan copies are for. Work and rework your idea until you figure it out. Or until your paper explorations lead you to something that works just as well.

Address practicalities first

Over the years, I've helped many clients and students design their basements by having them answer simple questions. These usually focus on the more practical aspects of the design—what goes where and how it all fits together. Some of those considerations as well as some general discussion of design are covered in the following pages. As you work your way through the design process, refer to Chapters 4 through 10 for more specific information about elements you'll want to include in your design. Each chapter also addresses code requirements.

In addressing practicalities, you will also consider style. I can't help much with style decisions, nor would I want to. Contemporary, colonial, or whimsical, whatever style you like is, of course, a matter of taste. It's your basement. It should look the way you want it to.

Recreation and multipurpose rooms. There are many possibilities for these rooms and very few requirements beyond making sure that what you want fits the space and your budget. To get a feel for how things might fit in various rooms and compositions, some of my students have cut out scale-sized couches, chairs, and tables and moved them around on the plan.

Of course, wet bars, kitchenettes, built-in entertainment centers, special lighting, and so on need plumbing or electrical connections. Be sure to include required services on your plan drawings and in your cost estimates.

Bedrooms. The major requirement here is an egress window, as discussed on p. 13. After you've swallowed that pill, the main question is usually one of size. Is the bedroom just a spare, or will it have a full-time occupant? A room 10 ft. square is small, but you can fit a single bed in it, and a small dresser. Measure the bedrooms upstairs and think about how well they serve your needs.

How about closet space? Standard bedroom closets are 24 in. deep with folding or sliding doors. Or is this your chance to arrange your wardrobe in a spacious walk-in?

When you sketch a bedroom on the plan, be sure to sketch in the bed, too. Unless the room is very large, there are only a limited number of places a bed will fit, particularly queen or king sizes, and you need to make sure those spots will work for you. Add an outlet on both sides of the bed, for convenience. To maximize space for furniture, position the door in a corner, swinging open against a wall.

Bathrooms. Most basements with bathroom rough-ins are plumbed for fixture placement that you've probably seen dozens of times. It's simple, economical, and it works: A door 2 ft. wide swings into a room that is 5 ft. by 8 ft. On the left (or right) is a 3-ft. vanity and then a toilet. At the end of the room is a tub or tub-shower.

Exercise equipment coexists comfortably with an informal work area in this walkout basement (above and right). The photo below shows the other end of the room.

The space shown above was divided by a new wall to become part of a multipurpose room (right) and a bedroom.

This bathroom layout is dictated almost entirely by practical and code considerations. A standard tub or tub-shower requires a rough opening 5 ft. wide by 30 in. deep. By code, a toilet must have 15 in. of free space to each side of its centerline. A standard vanity, with a laminated top 20 in. deep and a drop-in self-rimming sink, can be as narrow as 2 ft. or as wide as 4 ft.

If this is the way your bathroom is roughed-in, it will be economical to leave it as is, although

A basic bathroom rough-in is usually set up for the bathroom layout shown here.

PRO TIP

Pay attention to which way the door opens when you're placing light switches. I've been in more than one house with a light switch behind a door.

TRADE SECRET

If your budget is tight, the best thing to do is to design within the constraints of your existing basement. Leave the furnace, stairs, and heat runs where they are. If you don't have a bathroom rough-in, maybe it really won't be all that much trouble to use an upstairs bathroom.

IN DETAIL

When drawing a bathroom, you need to allow 12$\frac{1}{2}$ in. from framing to the center of the in-floor toilet drain. This clearance is dictated by the dimensions of standard toilets. If the wall behind the toilet is an outside wall, the center of the drain must be at least 16$\frac{1}{2}$ in. from the concrete or block to accommodate a 2×4 frame and drywall. If the drain is closer to the outside wall, adjust the wall thickness. Moving the drain is expensive.

you could increase the overall size without incurring additional costs. But if it is to be your dream bathroom, and you can supply the extra time and money to move the existing plumbing rough-ins, go for it. Put the toilet in a separate space or the tub on a raised platform. Add an 8-ft.-long double-sink vanity or that antique pedestal sink you bought years ago. Install a custom-tiled shower or a whirlpool tub.

Fireplaces. If you want the look and the heat of a fireplace without the mess, gas is much better than wood. The newer, direct-vent, fireplaces don't even need a conventional flue. Because the escaping flue-gas temperature is relatively cool, they just vent through an outside wall.

You can buy a wood-burning fireplace or stove, but you'll need to punch a much larger hole in an exterior wall and build an exterior flue up the side of the house to a point at least 2 ft. higher than any part of the roof within 10 ft. of the flue.

A gas or wood-burning fireplace can be installed along a wall, in a corner, or even between two rooms, if you can vent it. The process can be difficult and, if you're hooking up gas, dangerous. You can have a fireplace installed for you, or you can find a pro who'll let you do whatever part of the work you're comfortable with.

Suspended ceilings. Made of lightweight panels hung in a metal grid, a suspended ceiling provides better sound insulation than a drywall ceiling. It also provides ready access to mechanical installations above. Unfortunately, a suspended ceiling lowers the ceiling height in a room where height is a precious commodity. A suspended ceiling will lose you a minimum of 3 in., which is barely enough clearance to get the panels in and out. For drop-in fluorescent lighting, you'll need at least 5 in. of clearance between the ceiling and the joists. You can also use recessed can lights or surface-mount fixtures.

A direct-vent gas fireplace won't break the budget, though it is a major installation project.

As you work up ideas, get specific. Pick out tile and a color scheme for the bathroom (above) and cabinets and accessories for the wet bar (below).

Low-clearance suspended-ceiling systems have been recently developed that extend only 1½ in. below the existing ceiling or joists. These systems are worth checking out if height is a critical factor in your ceiling selection.

Even in basements with plenty of ceiling height, I install few suspended ceilings. My clients, I think, feel they look more commercial than residential. Suspended ceilings are more common in a bathroom (or below a ground-floor bathroom), where access to pipes may be desirable. If you want a suspended ceiling, installation is straightforward and usually nicely spelled out by the manufacturer in the literature accompanying the pieces and parts.

Doors. In general, I use the widest door I can fit into a room, to make it as easy as possible to move people and furniture in and out. Typically, bathroom doors are 2 ft. or 2 ft. 4 in. wide and bedroom doors are 2 ft. 6 in. wide. Utility-room doors should be at least 2 ft. 8 in. wide to accommodate the installation of a washer and a dryer. A pocket door, which slides into a space that has been framed into the wall, can be bought in the same sizes as other doors. Bifold doors are good solutions for closets; they're commonly available to fit openings from 2 ft. to 6 ft. (using multiple panels). If you need to accommodate a wheel-chair, make all the doors 3 ft. wide.

Posts. In some basements, floor joists are supported by a beam and steel posts rather than a frame wall. This creates an open basement and provides flexibility for wall placement. But it poses the problem of what to do with the posts.

The simplest solution, of course, is to leave them exposed. This can work for informal or utilitarian rooms such as rec rooms or laundry rooms. But more-finished rooms need more-creative solutions. If possible, incorporate the post into a larger feature such as a wall or bookcase, rather than just cladding it in drywall. For example, I

Tips for Drawing Plans

If you're doing all the work on your basement, your drawings don't have to make sense to anyone but you. But you'll need to produce at least one version intelligible enough to pass muster for a permit application. And if you want professional help with some of the work, a drawing that the subcontractor can understand is essential. You don't need professional blueprints to satisfy inspectors or contractors. The tips here will help you produce a drawing that is useful and simple. Just remember that the single most important quality for any construction drawing is neatness and legibility.

- **Draw your plan to scale.** You can go woefully wrong guestimating the relative sizes of rooms and the stuff in them. Graph paper with ¼-in. squares, each square representing 1 ft., works well for most basement remodels.

- **Give the walls you draw some thickness.** Finished interior walls are 4½ in. thick. That's 3½ in. for the 2×4 frame and ½ in. each for the drywalled faces. On my ¼-in. graph paper plans, I make walls about half of one square thick. Drawn this way, walls give the spaces a more realistic feel. You'll also be less likely to forget to deduct wall thicknesses from the room size when figuring dimensions.

- **Use standard symbols where possible.** Architects and builders use dozens of conventional symbols to represent various electrical outlets, plumbing hookups, and just about everything else that goes into a house. The few shown here should cover most elements of your remodel. Using them will make your drawing neater (by reducing the number of labels you need) and easier for inspectors and subcontractors to understand.

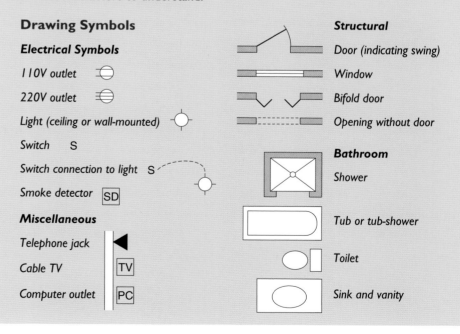

Drawing Symbols

Electrical Symbols

110V outlet

220V outlet

Light (ceiling or wall-mounted)

Switch S

Switch connection to light S

Smoke detector SD

Miscellaneous

Telephone jack

Cable TV TV

Computer outlet PC

Structural

Door (indicating swing)

Window

Bifold door

Opening without door

Bathroom

Shower

Tub or tub-shower

Toilet

Sink and vanity

TRADE SECRET

You may not save money if you hire a subcontractor to install the cheapest materials or fixtures you can buy at a discount store. Cheap stuff is harder to work with, so the sub will probably charge you more to install it.

once encased a post in oak 1×8s and connected it to the wall with a low, room-dividing bookcase. To make the installation symmetrical, I attached a 1×8 structure that looked like the enclosed post to the wall-end of the bookcase. The photo at right shows another post solution.

Angled and curved walls. Breaking out of the flat, right-angle configuration of most floor plans adds some flair and fun to a room. It also adds some work and, if you're too adventurous, a headache or two. If you want angled walls, stick to 45-degree angles if you can. They're much simpler to lay out and build—circular saws, for example, can easily be set to cut at 45 degrees.

Curved walls are more challenging. To make a curved wall, I nail studs to curved top and bottom plates (cut from wide lumber or 3/4-in. plywood) and bend drywall to the curve. The tighter the radius, the more studs are needed to ensure a smooth bend in the drywall. For curves tighter than about a 4-ft. radius, even 1/4-in. drywall will break rather than bend. So, I use larger radii and make gentler curves.

This oak column masks a steel support post. The angled wall ties the post into the floor plan.

Lighting. People often overlook the impact lighting can have on a room. In a basement, where natural light can be scarce, giving some extra thought to lighting can make a big difference in the comfort and function of a room.

There are a number of artful alternatives to hanging a fixture in the center of the room,

Identifying a Bearing Wall

A basement bearing wall supports the floor joists and structure above it. Most basements have at least one bearing wall (or a steel beam and posts) running down the center because houses are generally too wide to be spanned by joists with no intermediate support. It's fairly easy to punch a doorway into a bearing wall, more difficult to remove a larger section, and very difficult to remove the wall entirely.

How do you know if the center wall (or another wall) is bearing? The wall is bearing if the joists in the basement ceiling extend from the outside walls only to the center wall. Newer houses may have joists that run from outside wall to outside wall without a break. These TJI joists, which look like small wooden I-beams, still depend on the center wall for support. Walls alongside stairways are usually bearing. Be sure to install a beam or header if you replace a stairway wall with a half-wall or baluster and rail.

The safe bet is to assume the center wall is bearing. If you're unsure and want to verify, find a contractor or inspector who can check it out for you.

To make an opening in a bearing wall, you must install a header to distribute the load.

Instead of light fixtures that hang from the ceiling, consider alternatives like this wall sconce.

although that is sometimes the simplest and best solution. Recessed lights are well suited for basements. Set inside the ceiling, they don't take up any headroom. Lined up over a work area, they provide useful task lighting. Directed "eye-ball" cans attractively highlight artwork, bookshelves, or wall niches.

I've built troughs containing fluorescent lights around the perimeter of rooms; shining up on the ceiling, they have a pleasing, indirect effect. Sconce lights along a wall also give a warm feeling to a room. In bedrooms, floor or table lamps attached to switched outlets are an attractive alternative to overhead lighting.

Planning

As you make design decisions, amend your critical-path chart to plan the work flow. The chart lists all the major steps already, so now add the wet bar, study niche, or built-in entertainment center under the proper heading. You might chart a separate critical path for a big project, such as an entertainment center, to plot out the

sequence of construction just as you've done for the remodeling as a whole.

Don't worry if you don't have the complete design and exact details worked out after a number of sessions with pencil and graph paper. You can plan your work schedule, obtain a building permit, and begin your project with some decisions still pending.

As you build, you'll continue to work out design details. And you'll change plans you thought were final. For example, as a room takes shape in three dimensions, you may discover that it is too small or too large. Well, change it. It's your basement, your plan, your schedule. You're the boss.

That said, remember that figuring out the design and planning the work beforehand helps you avoid costly mistakes and irritating delays in scheduling. If you're hanging drywall and decide you want a fireplace in the corner after all, you'll have to tear out some of your own handiwork to make it happen. And if the fireplace isn't in stock, the whole project grows cold while you wait for something not in the plan. That's still okay if it's what you really want. But the more you plan ahead and the less you change your plans, the smoother the remodeling process will be.

Working with subcontractors

As you work through the design and planning process (and read through the rest of this book), you'll get a pretty good idea of what's involved in your project, how much of it you're comfortable tackling yourself, and how much you might want to contract out.

Over the years, I've been pleasantly surprised by how many remodeling tasks my students have been able to do themselves. Still, most of them have brought in a subcontractor for at least part of the job. People often find they're more com-

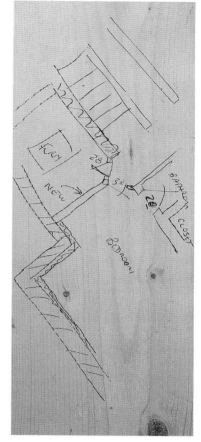

The design process usually continues well into construction. When inspiration strikes, sketch it out on anything at hand.

PRO TIP

As long as it's complete, neat, and legible, a simple sketch is perfectly adequate for a building-permit application.

IN DETAIL

Before launching a basement remodel, check your homeowner's insurance policy to make sure the policy will cover the work you're doing. Each of your subcontractors should also supply you with a copy of their liability insurance. If they aren't insured, you, as the general contractor, could be held responsible for accidents that occur while they're on the job.

TRADE SECRET

Be careful how you label the rooms on the plan you submit for permits. A "family room" may have different requirements than the same room labeled "rec room." Check your community's codes for similar anomalies.

Likewise, be aware that if you are working on an older home, applying for a permit may trigger requirements to upgrade existing systems. In my town, for example, almost any remodeling requires the addition of smoke detectors throughout the house, wired in to the central electrical system (not solely battery-operated).

fortable having a pro tap into existing plumbing lines or hook up new electrical circuits to the service panel. Unless you're experienced in these areas, I recommend you do the same.

You are the general contractor on your basement project, the person responsible for the entire job. If you hire an electrician to wire your basement or a drywaller to tape and finish your walls, he or she is subcontracting to you. You will be responsible for obtaining the general permit on the project. The subs will be responsible for obtaining permits (if necessary) for their work.

Scheduling work. In any construction job, every sub depends on every other sub or the general contractor to get work done on schedule. If one sub lags behind, or the weather throws everyone off, the delays can ripple through dozens of other jobs the subs are working on.

As a homeowner and a one-time general contractor, you are at a disadvantage when hiring subcontractors. Unlike the general contractors that subs work for regularly, you aren't the bread and butter of their business. If push comes to shove on another job, your job could get delayed. It shouldn't happen, but sometimes you just have to go with the flow.

Treat subcontractors professionally, and they will usually respond in kind. If you schedule a plumber for 9:00 a.m. Tuesday, be ready. If you see that you're falling behind schedule, call ahead to make a new arrangement. Don't call on the scheduled day and say, whoops, don't come today. Give a contractor time to reschedule. And when you're rescheduling, don't assume he or she will be able to come the next day. It could happen, but it's not likely. Contractors have to adjust their dozen other jobs, move crews elsewhere, and keep everybody busy and somewhat happy.

Scheduling delays—yours and your sub's—are inevitable. So be sure to include a little "slippage" in your schedule. Even the best contractors fall

behind from time to time, either through their own fault or from any of the hundreds of things outside of their control. If your schedule is too tight you're only building stress into your life.

Getting bids. Conventional wisdom suggests getting three bids for a project, eliminating the lowest and the highest, and going with the one in the middle. Professionals don't always do this, but you should.

As a contractor, I have the advantage of working with subcontractors I've known for years. I trust them and they trust me. If my plumber tells me it'll cost this much to do this job, I respect his bid. I'm no plumber. You don't have the advantage of these professional relationships, so it's wise to get two or three bids for comparison. But don't shop around for five or six bids and try to beat the price down. If you're looking for the cheapest price, you're likely to get the cheapest results, too.

Get bids in writing and sign a contract for the one you choose. The agreement doesn't have to be full of legalese. It just needs to define what's to be done and what's to be left out.

If you want to do some, but not all, of a task, be sure the sub knows this at the time you ask for a bid. Some subs are comfortable with this arrangement, but some aren't. If the sub is willing, carefully work out the specifics of who is to do what and when. And make sure you both know who will buy the materials.

If you hire an electrical, plumbing, or drywalling subcontractor to do the work in its entirety, let the sub supply the materials. He'll know what's needed, based on how he wants to cover the walls or run specific lines. You may decide to buy the electrical and plumbing fixtures yourself (sinks, faucets, lights, and so on). If you want the sub to buy these items, be sure to supply the brand names and model numbers.

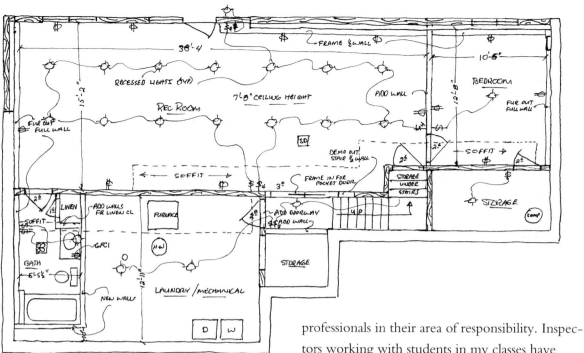

This is the plan submitted for the class basement project. On it, we showed:

- Walls, existing and new
- Doors and windows
- Function and overall dimensions of each room
- Smoke detectors
- Lights, switches, and outlets
- Electrical service panel
- Furnace
- Bathroom fan, sink, toilet, and tub-shower
- Note that ceiling heights, also required for the permit, were listed elsewhere.

Building Codes and Permits

Almost every community has building codes that set standards for all the basic components and structures in a house. Local codes once varied widely, but today most codes conform to the Uniform Building Code (UBC), sometimes called the "national building code," though there are many local variations. Code books are thick and dense. But, happily, for basement remodeling only a fraction of them apply.

Why bother with codes and permits? Most of us know someone who has fixed up a basement without taking out a permit. It's easy to do—you can't see a remodeled basement from the street. But codes and inspections are there for your protection and safety. Without some form of control, you have no legal recourse against shoddy work from unscrupulous subcontractors.

Codes also offer benefits if you're doing the work yourself. For the small cost of a permit, you engage the services of inspectors who are, usually,

professionals in their area of responsibility. Inspectors working with students in my classes have helped them sort out wiring and plumbing problems, structural issues, and heating and ventilation questions. They'll help you, too, if you just ask. And when your plumbing and wiring pass inspection, you know you've done it right.

If you're still tempted to bypass permits, remember that in most jurisdictions obtaining proper permits is the law. If you're caught without them or you avoid an inspection, you may have to uncover whatever they need to inspect. That could be expensive. And, having earned the enmity of the inspectors, you'll be viewed with a jaundiced eye during the remaining inspections.

Applying for permits

Permit procedures vary by community, but in my city at least two copies of the remodeling plans must be submitted for approval. Officials stamp both copies and keep one on file. The other must be on the job site for the inspectors' reference. I always make several copies, one to serve as the "working copy" on the job, and a copy for each subcontractor. My city also requires an estimate of the overall cost of the project, which is used to calculate the cost of the permit.

Demolition and

CHAPTER FOUR

Repair

1 Demo, p. 38

2 Basic Structural
Repairs, p. 46

It's always fun to jump into a new project and start building walls, but sometimes before you can begin with the new, you have to remove the old. This can be strenuous and dirty work. But there is an undeniable satisfaction in standing back and surveying your basement stripped of all that stuff you've been dying to be rid of for years.

What remains may then need fixing. When you assessed your basement as described in Chapter 1, you may have found cracks, leaks, or bulges. In this chapter I'll show you how to fix them.

If your plans call for opening up a stairwell or adding a doorway in a bearing wall, now is the time to do so.

This chapter will help you make decisions about which tasks you want to do, which ones you may not want to do, and when to call in the professionals.

IN DETAIL

A reciprocating saw is an ideal demolition tool. The compact tool can fit into awkward nooks and crannies and cut just about any material. It consists of a narrow blade 4 in. to 12 in. long that moves rapidly back and forth (reciprocates) in front of the torpedo-shaped motor and handle. Blades are easily changed, relatively inexpensive, and can cut wood, metal (nails, pipe, ductwork), plaster, or drywall. You can rent a reciprocating saw, or buy one for as little as $40. If you're tearing out a lot of walls and pipes, it will be money well spent.

Demo

The best basement to work in is an empty basement. Of course, you won't throw out everything. What you decide to keep you can move to a storage area where it's out of the way (the garage, for example) and cover it with sheets or lightweight plastic to keep dust off. If you have large equipment or furniture that you can't easily store elsewhere, find a spot in the basement to consolidate it. Cover it with some heavier plastic (4 mil) and tape the plastic to seal the pile—you'll appreciate this dustproofing when you start sanding drywall. And yes, this pile will be a pain to work around, and yes, you will have to move it at least once, perhaps more, before you're finished. (For more on containing the mess, see the sidebar on the facing page.)

If you're remodeling an unfinished basement, there may be more to clean up than to demolish ("demo") in preparation for remodeling. Redoing an existing finished basement may require undoing just some or all of the previous work. I'll discuss demoing everything in a previously finished area of a basement; you can do the parts that apply to your project.

Trim and drywall demo

Demolition is just reverse construction—you work from finish to framing. Start by prying off the trim (baseboard and casing around doors and windows). If you want to reuse trim, remove it by prying with a flat bar slipped between the trim and the drywall. Remove nails by pulling them from the back side with pliers or sidecutters —this will avoid damaging the trim face. Take the doors off the hinges, and pry the door jambs out. Or sever the nails between the jambs and the studs with a reciprocating saw or a hacksaw.

Many towns and cities have "eco stores" that recycle used building materials such as doors and trim. Recycling extends the life of a town landfill

Begin demolition by removing doors, door jambs, and any trim.

Strip paneling off drywall backing, then remove the drywall.

and provides inexpensive materials to those who need them.

To remove carpet, use pliers to pull up a corner and just keep pulling. Cut the carpet into sections so it is manageable to haul out of the basement. Pry off the carpet tack strip that is

To remove drywall from a frame wall, punch a hole in it, grab the drywall through the hole, and pull off chunks with your hands, a claw hammer, or a prybar.

A prybar helps remove drywall that has been glued to concrete block.

glued or nailed to the concrete around the room edges. Wear gloves; the little tacks can be vicious.

Removing drywall is fairly easy if you can get behind the wall. Just knock it off with a hammer. If you need to pull it off from the front, use the hammer to punch a hole in the drywall. Then

Protection: Isolating the Mess

You're going to make a mess in your basement, but that doesn't mean the rest of your house has to join in. "Protection" is the professional term for isolating that mess. The main problem is dust, which can float up a stairwell, get sucked up into your heating and cooling system, or ride up on your clothes and feet. The last problem is easiest to deal with—leave your work shoes in the basement and dust or vacuum yourself before going upstairs.

If you have a door at the top or bottom of your basement stairs, place a damp towel at the base of the door to trap dust. If you have an open stairwell with no door, the simplest way to block it off is with 2-mil plastic and blue, easy-release tape. Rather than rip the tape off every time you enter or leave the basement, you can easily make an entry with a stick-on zipper. These little gems are simply long plastic zippers with adhesive on the cloth side strips. Stick them on to the

Make a doorway in your protective plastic wall with a stick-on zipper. (See Resources on p. 167.)

plastic, open the zipper, cut the plastic, and you have an instant door. Nice.

If your stairs are carpeted I do not recommend tarps or loose plastic for protection. It's difficult to lay tarps without foot-grabbing folds, and loose plastic is very slick. The best solution for carpets in general, and stairs in particular, is an adhesive-backed plastic that won't slide around on the carpet, yet pulls free easily when you're finished. You'll need to replace the plastic a few times during the life of the project, but it safely keeps the carpet clean.

Your furnace may have a return-air grill in the basement. This is the part of the HVAC system that pulls air from the room to condition and return it. Unfortunately, it will also do a fine job of spreading construction dust throughout the house. The drywall and paint/stain phase of construction can also be hard on blower motors. So tape a plastic cover over any basement return-air grills for the duration of the project. Blocking off return-air vents generally poses no danger, but in the summer there is a slight chance it could cause the air-conditioning coils to freeze up. If that's a concern, talk with an HVAC professional first.

IN DETAIL

A circuit tester makes it easy to determine which electrical fixtures are live. Mine is a small rectangular rubber block with a three-prong plug on one end and three lights on the other. When you plug it in an outlet (as shown below), the three lights on the other end let you know if it's wired correctly. A trouble-shooting guide is printed right on the tester, so you will know if something in your wiring is amiss.

TRADE SECRET

Buy the better quality dust masks for demolition work. They have two rubber straps to hold them to your head. When you take the mask off and look at all the stuff collected on the outside, you'll be glad you did.

hook the claw on the exposed edges and tear off hunks. Be careful to look for concealed wiring and plumbing as you punch and pull off the first pieces. After several pieces, you'll be able to see what's in there and avoid wires and pipes. To keep the mess to a minimum, I like to pull off the largest pieces I can. You may have to break up some of these pieces to get them out of the basement or into your disposal bin. Whether attached to studs or drywall, paneling is usually easy to remove, though if it has been glued the task is more strenuous.

If you're planning to reuse studs, rip off the drywall and, using a hammer, flat bar, or prybar, pull the nails or drywall screws left behind. That's right; pull the screws. They're short enough to pull fairly easily and it's much faster than un-screwing them all.

If you're keeping part of a wall in your project, you'll need to cut the drywall you're removing from the part that stays. You can make the cut with several passes of a utility knife, or you can use a drywall saw or reciprocating saw. If you use a saw, first punch some holes in the demo area of the drywall to check for wires and pipes you might inadvertently cut. If you find some, use the knife. Reciprocating saws can cut wiring and plumbing. When it's unintentional, it's both messy and dangerous.

If you have an older home with plaster-and-lath walls, the demolition technique is similar to that for drywall—except the plaster is much harder, the dust more obnoxious, and the mess is, well, just more.

It's easy to remove ceilings. Just pull drywall or old ceiling tiles off the joists or 1×2 furring strips. Check for wiring and plumbing as you go. Pop out the panels of a hanging ceiling and dismantle the metal frame. The worst part about taking down a ceiling is getting showered by many years of dust—wear a mask, goggles, and a hat.

Removing wires and pipes

Before removing any wiring, go to the service box and cut the power to that circuit. Breakers aren't always labeled (or labeled accurately). If you're uncertain, plug a light into an outlet on the circuit and switch off breakers until the light goes off. Or check with a circuit tester—insert the tester's plug or wires into an outlet and see if the tester's light goes on.

When the circuit is dead, pull the outlet or switch out of its box and detach the wires. Remove the box and wire staples, and pull the wire through the studs back to the next junction box, outlet, or switch. If this is also to go, repeat the procedure. If it is to stay, wrap electrician's tape on the ends and tuck the wires out of the

After shutting off power at the service box, disconnect and pull wires from the walls to be removed. If you're tearing out only part of a wall, wrap the ends of the wire with electrician's tape and pull it back into the studs that are to remain.

+ SAFETY FIRST

Use gloves for demolition work. You get a better grip and protection from sharp objects. Safety glasses will protect you from the inevitable flying shards and from at least some of the dust. A dust mask can be a nuisance, but the dust you encounter in demolition can be downright unhealthy.

way. Do the same for any ceiling fixtures. You may remove some circuits back to the service panel. For now, snip the wires off outside the panel and tape the ends to cover bare wire. Be sure to leave the breaker off for any removed circuits. (I'll discuss the service panel in Chapter 6.)

Plumbing lines and drains need to be cut and capped, and then removed. If you're removing plastic fittings, you can easily do the job yourself. Shut off the water line (or the service coming into the house) and drain the pipe by opening a faucet at the lowest point you can find on the line. Disconnect the pipe at the sink, tub-shower, toilet, or appliance and remove the fixture if it is part of the demo. At the point where you want to remove the pipe, cut it with a hacksaw, pull the sections apart, and glue a plastic cap to the end of the "live" pipe. (See p. 83 for gluing plastic pipe.) Pull all the "dead" pipe out of the walls; you may need to cut it into a number of pieces to do this. Capping iron, copper, and cast-iron drain lines is more difficult. I suggest you have a plumber cut and cap the lines, then tear the dead lines out yourself.

Framing demo

Most basement walls are standard 2×4 framing: a horizontal top plate nailed to the joists, a bottom plate nailed or bolted to the floor, and vertical studs nailed to the two plates. If you're removing only part of a wall, start by cutting through the top and bottom plates with a handsaw or reciprocating saw to separate the framing you're keeping from the framing you're removing. (Concrete isn't friendly to saw blades; use an old blade to cut the bottom plate.)

To demo framing, start with the studs. I find it easiest to knock the bottom of the stud sideways with a hammer to free it from the plate nails, and then pull the stud free from the top plate. This can require considerable pounding and an

To remove wall framing, knock the studs free of the bottom plate. Pull the stud free of the top plate. Bend protruding nails back and forth to break them off flush with the plate.

attitude. It's a great way to relieve frustration. After removing a stud, you'll have nails sticking straight up out of the bottom plate. Either pound them down flat or bend them back and forth with pliers until they break off. Do this right away. When you're wrestling with the next stud, it's way too easy to forget that the nails are there. Stepping on one is an unpleasant experience.

WORKING ON BEARING WALLS

A bearing wall helps support the house above it. If you're removing a bearing wall or creating an opening in one, you must install a header to carry the load. Whether for long spans or for a single door, headers can be made of dimension lumber, engineered lumber, or steel. Your lumber supplier, your codes department, or, as a last resort (because of cost), an engineer, can specify the proper size.

To install a header, you need to provide temporary support for the joists above. To do this, I build two 2×4 frame walls, one on each side of the bearing wall, placed about 2 ft. out from the wall and extending a joist or two beyond the intended opening. To build the walls, lay a 2×4 plate on the floor (no fasteners—the wedged studs will hold it in place), and tack one to the joists above. Then cut and wedge a stud under each floor joist, between the plates. Cut the studs a good 1/16 in. too long, so that you have to hammer them tightly in place. This

will transfer the load from the bearing wall. With both support walls in place, knock out the bearing studs, as described in this chapter.

As shown in the drawings, each end of the header butts against a 2×4 called a king stud and rests on a 2×4 called a trimmer. (Long headers may need two trimmers at each end; ask your structural consultant if you need them.)

To prepare for installation:

1. Cut two king studs to fit between the top and bottom plates on each side of the opening.

2. Cut the trimmers to the height of the opening minus the height of the header.

3. Cut the header to length. Because it will rest on the trimmers, be sure to cut it 3 in. longer than the desired width of the opening (6 in. longer for double trimmers).

The photo sequence and drawings show how to install the header.

To support the floor above, build a temporary wall on each side of the bearing wall (above, left). Wedge studs between top and bottom plates (center). The temporary walls carry the floor load, allowing the removal of studs in the bearing wall (right).

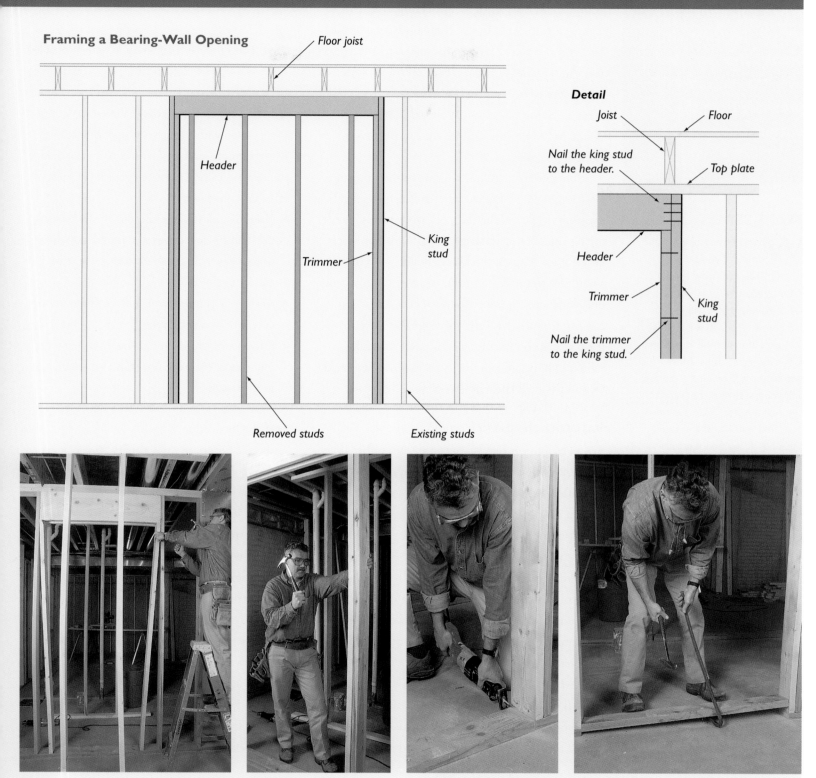

Framing a Bearing-Wall Opening

Floor joist

Header

Trimmer

King stud

Removed studs

Existing studs

Detail

Joist

Floor

Nail the king stud to the header.

Top plate

Header

Trimmer

King stud

Nail the trimmer to the king stud.

Lift the header in place between the king studs. Slide the trimmers under each end of the header to support it. Nail the king studs to the header (left). Then nail the trimmers to the king studs (right).

Cut the bottom plate along the line of the trimmers (left). Then pry the plate free with a long crowbar (right).

PRO TIP

When you knock out a stud, immediately break off or pound over the nails that protrude from the bottom plate.

TRADE SECRET

When I buy caulking compound, I've found it's largely irrelevant how long the tube claims the caulk will last. I'm sure most of it will survive intact in the landfill for at least 50 years after it pulls loose and falls out of the crack. More important is how long the caulk will adhere to the concrete. I've had the best luck caulking concrete with urethane caulk. I use NP-1® by Sonneborn. Avoid pure silicon caulks, which aren't paintable.

If you want to save the studs, or don't want to pound them out, use a reciprocating saw with a metal-cutting blade to cut the nails between the stud and the plates. This saves material, energy, and time, and is a great excuse to buy a reciprocating saw. If you plan to reuse these studs, mark them to remind you that there are 2-in. lengths of nail hidden in the ends. You can ruin a sawblade if you forget.

After the studs are gone, remove the bottom plate by driving a flat bar or crowbar underneath it and prying it off the floor. Bottom plates are usually attached with fasteners that will stay stuck in the floor. Knock the fasteners side-to-side with a hammer to break them off. Most of them won't pull without removing divots of concrete. You can pry top plates off the joists with a crowbar or flat bar. Or you can use a cat's paw nail puller, which will dig into the wood under the nail head to pull the nails through the plate.

Rubble disposal

A quick note on removing rubble. If you're doing a lot of demolition, it makes sense to rent a dumpster, especially if you don't have access to a pickup or trailer. Dumpsters range in size from 6 cu. yd. to 20 cu. yd. and you'll need to find a place off-street to place it. You'll pay a fee to have it dropped off and picked up, a weekly charge if you have it for long, and a dumping charge based on weight. But it'll save you time and some wear and tear on your equipment and your back.

For most of the other debris you'll generate in general basement remodeling, you might check with your local refuse company. Give them a call, or talk to the guys on the truck, and see what they would be willing to haul away with your regular trash or for an additional fee.

I've had good luck with local haulers picking up some extra, especially if they are running a bit

WATER PROBLEMS

Probably the most common basement problem is water. Your basement is not a submarine; it will leak if given the chance. There are a number of sealant systems that coat the exterior face of a foundation with a tough waterproof material. These systems can be expensive to install. Before you commit to one, consider the simpler measures described here:

- Make sure all surfaces abutting the foundation of the house—soil, driveways, patios, sidewalks—slope away from the foundation by at least 1 in. per foot.
- Keep your gutters clean and your downspout extensions on and open.
- Place plants and shrubs at least 2 ft. from the foundation. (Rotted roots can be a conduit for ground water.)

If the grade around your home slopes away from the foundation and you're still getting surface water infiltration, you can install a simple, inexpensive fix, shown in the drawing at right. It employs bentonite, an expansive clay used to seal well casings and farm ponds.

Dig a trench alongside the foundation 1 ft. deep and 2 ft. wide. The bottom of the trench should be level or sloping away from the house, not toward it. (To make cleanup easier, lay 4-mil plastic on the grass where you throw the dirt.) Over the bottom of the trench, carefully sift a ½- to 1-in. layer of finely powdered bentonite, which has the consistency of talcum powder. Then shovel in about ½ in. to 1 in. of granular bentonite to help hold the powder in place. Next, add pulverized nonpercolating clay soil to within a few inches of the top of the trench. Add it in 4-in. layers, tamping down each layer with your feet before adding the nest.

(Check with landscape contractors for sources of these materials.)

Repeat the process—layers of fine bentonite and soil—until you're near the top of the trench. Then fill in with topsoil and sod, making sure you slope the surface away from the house by at least an inch for every foot. Surface water will penetrate into the topsoil and is absorbed by the bentonite and clay, which will swell and seal the ground around the foundation.

I learned this technique from Dave Carter, of St. Mary, Nebraska. He discourages landscape plantings over the sealed area to avoid having roots puncture the bentonite. Plant grass if you must, but Dave prefers decorative rock.

Ground Water

Surface water isn't the only culprit in wet basements. A high water table or other sources of subsurface water (or ground water) may be the problem. If so, a sump pump is the solution. Most newer homes have a pump and its attendant drain tile and sump pit because they are relatively inexpensive to install during initial construction, and they save the contractor from unpleasant confrontations in soggy basements.

Installing a system in an existing basement is more costly, because you'll need to jackhammer out some concrete, dig along the footing, install tile and a pit, lay in gravel, and then re-concrete. But if you need a sump pump, now is the time to have a professional install it. Doing it after pulling up wet carpet and cutting back soggy drywall is frustrating and even more expensive.

Bentonite Foundation Seal

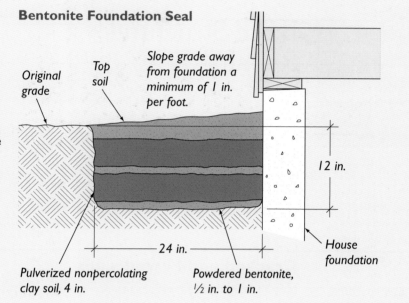

Original grade

Top soil

Slope grade away from foundation a minimum of 1 in. per foot.

12 in.

24 in.

House foundation

Pulverized nonpercolating clay soil, 4 in.

Powdered bentonite, ½ in. to 1 in.

Zapping Mildew and Mold

If your basement walls have mildew and mold in places, locate and correct the source of dampness and treat the existing mildew and mold before adding new walls. Strip off and discard any affected drywall. Then clean the block or concrete wall with a steel brush and a mixture of TSP (trisodium phosphate, a strong cleaner available in most paint stores) and bleach. Mix the TSP according to the instructions on the package. Wear rubber gloves and eye protection because the solution is caustic. I also like to get some outside air in there when I'm working with bleach and TSP. If caustic materials are problematic for you, you can use a cleaner containing borax. Some folks might want to use an air-filtration mask for the mold. If mold is a problem for you, buy a rubber mask with replaceable filters; the inexpensive paper ones won't be much good for microscopic mold and mildew particles.

TRADE SECRET

If you're relocating the bathroom or moving the toilet, it's simpler to cut out the concrete, lay in the new drain pipe, and repour the concrete now than later. It's possible to do this after you've framed walls, just more difficult. I recommend you hire a plumber to do this work or to supervise the tasks that you're doing yourself.

IN DETAIL

To repair wall cracks wider than ¼ in., fill the crack with backer rod before caulking. Backer rod is a compressible and flexible polyethylene foam available in diameters of ⅜ in. and up. Buy backer that is thicker than the width of the cracks.

light that day. Just don't overdo it; and even if they don't charge extra, a tip is nice.

Basic Structural Repairs

When you planned your project you evaluated the basement's basic structural condition. Now is the time to fix problems you discovered then— or that may have revealed themselves when you started tearing things out. It is also the time to install egress windows, if necessary, as discussed in Egress Windows on p. 13.

Cracked and bowed walls

Not all cracks and bows need to be repaired. If you and your structural consultant have decided to make repairs, be sure first to address the underlying cause of the defects. Most often the problem is water. When the soil adjacent to the wall is wet, it expands and exerts considerable pressure (called hydrostatic pressure) against the wall. Likewise, when water in the soil freezes, the water itself expands as it turns to ice and exerts additional pressure; this is called "frost heave." So, before you fill cracks or straighten bows, check for drainage problems around your foundation. (See Water Problems on pp. 44–45.) If you're uncertain about whether you have a drainage problem or don't know what to do about one you have, the opinion of a landscape or grading contractor is worth the cost.

Filling cracks. As mentioned in Chapter 1, filling cracks in the foundation keeps out bugs and prevents seepage. Large cracks and deteriorating mortar can be filled with fresh mortar in a process is called "tuck pointing." Some skill is required to make and apply the mortar. Mortar dries hard and will itself crack with the inevitable movement of a freeze-thaw cycle. If your cracks are bad enough

Fill wide cracks with backer rod before adding a good-quality urethane caulk.

☑ **According to Code**

Your codes department will want to inspect any framing you do, on bearing walls in particular, before you insulate and hang drywall. Egress windows must be installed in bedrooms (see Egress Windows on p. 13). Stairs to the basement must have a handrail the full length of the stairs at a height of 36 in. to 38 in. plumb above the nosing of the stair tread. A half-wall is not considered a handrail, unless it has a handrail-shaped grip on top.

to need tuck pointing, I recommend hiring a professional to advise you or to do the work.

You can repair small cracks with a tube of caulk and a simple caulking gun. A good urethane caulk rated for concrete adhesion will fill the crack and will flex with the freeze-thaw movement. To apply caulk, clean out the crack, removing loose material. Cracks wider than ¼ in. can suck up a lot of caulk. Push backer rod into these cracks before caulking. Cut the nozzle on the tube to about the size of the crack and squeeze in the caulk with steady, even pressure. With a damp finger, press the caulk in and smooth it out. Keep a glass of water handy to dip your finger, and a rag in your back pocket to wipe off the excess gook.

Straightening a bowed wall. If the wall requires repair or you want to straighten it for some other reason, there are two basic alternatives. The wall can be rebuilt or it can be pulled straight. Rebuilding is a considerable undertaking involving the structural integrity of your entire house—have it done professionally.

Straightening a wall is no small task, either. I recommend having a pro do it and saving your time and energy for the parts of the remodeling you'll see and use.

Repairing floors

As we discussed in Chapter 1, few basement floors need extensive repair. Depending on your choice of floor treatment, you may want to do some repair. Carpet and pad will hide minor defects in the floor, but defects will telegraph through linoleum or tile. You can hire someone to remove high spots with a floor grinder. (These tools can be rented, but I don't recommend doing this job yourself.). You can fill low spots with a floor-leveling compound feathered out with a trowel. To avoid damage to the leveling compound, it's best to do these repairs just before laying the flooring. (See Chapter 9.)

Opening Up a Stairwell

If the stairwell to your basement is enclosed, a good way to give the basement a more open feel is to replace one of the stairwell walls with a half-wall or a handrail supported by a newel post and baluster. This provides a much more inviting entrance to the basement and simplifies moving things up and down the stairs.

Opening up a nonbearing enclosed stairwell wall is relatively easy, as shown in the drawings. If the wall is load bearing, or if you're not sure whether it is, have a professional look at it. It's still possible to open up the wall, but adequate structural supports will be necessary and can be complicated. To conform to code, the top of the finished half-wall or baluster handrail should be 36 in. to 38 in. above the stair nosings. A half-wall replacement is shown here. For a baluster and newel post, use the same framing procedure, but cut the existing wall down so the new top plate will be even with the ends of the treads. Then install a newel post, balusters, and a handrail when you're trimming out the basement.

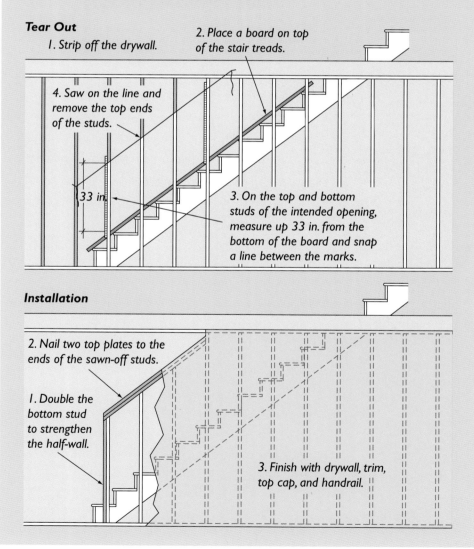

Tear Out
1. Strip off the drywall.

2. Place a board on top of the stair treads.

4. Saw on the line and remove the top ends of the studs.

33 in.

3. On the top and bottom studs of the intended opening, measure up 33 in. from the bottom of the board and snap a line between the marks.

Installation

2. Nail two top plates to the ends of the sawn-off studs.

1. Double the bottom stud to strengthen the half-wall.

3. Finish with drywall, trim, top cap, and handrail.

Framing

CHAPTER FIVE
Walls

Top plate

Header

Now you're ready to build walls. Here is where it starts getting exciting; the alpine smell of fresh-cut pine, the sense of accomplishment in seeing rooms take shape. And though the framing is all eventually hidden, it is the skeleton upon which everything else hangs, so it's important to do it carefully.

As discussed in Chapter 1, I think full 2×4 framing makes the best basement walls, so that's the method presented here. We'll cover layout and framing of exterior and interior walls, framing doorways, framing around windows, electrical breaker boxes, HVAC ducts and plumbing lines.

These are the main tasks you'll encounter when framing your basement. With these common techniques you'll also be able to tackle framing problems specific to your basement.

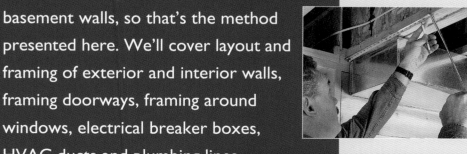

PRO TIP

When checking walls for plumb, extend your level's length by placing it against a straight stud to ensure an accurate reading.

IN DETAIL

Even if you've never hammered a nail, you're probably familiar with construction lumber: 2×2s, 2×4s, 2×6s, and so on. These names designate the "nominal" cross-sectional measurement of the pieces, not the actual dimensions. (See the chart below.) While you order framing lumber using nominal dimensions, it is important to use actual sizes when laying out walls and other framing. Lumber mills typically cut construction lumber a little longer than its nominal length. If you need an 8-ft.-long piece, don't assume an 8-footer will fit—measure first. And don't assume the ends are cut square at the mill. Often as not that's up to you, the framer.

Examples of construction lumber

Nominal size:	Actual size:
1×2	$3/4 \times 1^{1}/_{2}$
2×2	$1^{1}/_{2} \times 1^{1}/_{2}$
2×4	$1^{1}/_{2} \times 3^{1}/_{2}$
2×6	$1^{1}/_{2} \times 5^{1}/_{2}$
2×8	$1^{1}/_{2} \times 7^{1}/_{8} - 7^{5}/_{8}$
2×10	$1^{1}/_{2} \times 9^{1}/_{8} - 9^{5}/_{8}$
2×12	$1^{1}/_{2} \times 11^{1}/_{8} - 11^{5}/_{8}$

Anatomy of a Wall

A good framer, like a good doctor, knows the names and functions of the "bones" that make up a wall's wooden skeleton before starting to saw away at them. Fortunately, the structure of a wall is much simpler than that of a body, as the drawing shows. At its simplest, a wall comprises vertical pieces, called studs, nailed between horizontal pieces, called plates.

In a basement, a wall's top plate is attached to the overhead floor joists and the bottom plate is fixed to the concrete floor. The plates provide fastenings for the studs, and the studs provide support for the drywall or paneling that forms the finished surface of the wall.

Openings for doors, windows, and similar elements are defined by a variety of shorter horizontal and vertical members called trimmers, cripples, and headers. Blocking provides attachment for top plates that run parallel to floor joists. Backing provides support for drywall and paneling where other frame members don't.

In addition to walls, framing includes soffits, which hide ventilation ducts, pipes, wiring, and whatever else extends below the floor joists. Soffits have a slightly different anatomy than a wall, as shown on p. 67.

If you've watched framers assembling a wall for a new house, you'll know that they usually lay the plates and studs on the floor and nail them together, and then raise the assembled wall into position. This works fine when the sky is your ceiling, but not when your ceiling is cluttered with pipes and ducts and your floor is slightly undulating. Experience has taught me to nail the plates to the floor and ceiling first, and then cut each stud to fit snugly between them. While this method lacks the satisfaction of seeing an entire wall raised into place at once, it saves time and frustration and, in a basement, makes a better wall.

Framing Basics

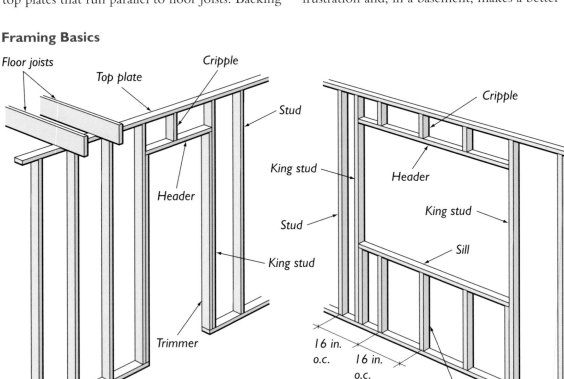

Basic Wall with Door

Rough Window Opening

Layout

When you've estimated and ordered your framing materials (see p. 52), you're ready to lay out the walls. I use a chalk box to snap lines on the floor to position the location of the frame walls' bottom plates. Start with the outside walls (against the concrete or block foundation walls), and then snap lines for the interior ones.

Laying out outside-wall plates

To ensure that the outside frame walls will be plumb and straight, they need to be set away from the foundation walls. This will allow for bulges, bows, and other projections. To find out how much space to allow, I check the foundation wall for plumb with a level held against the edge of a straight stud cut just short of the basement ceiling height, as shown in the photo at right. A shorter level will read only part of the wall. I check at each corner of the foundation wall and several spots in between. If the frame wall doesn't extend the full length of the foundation wall, check for plumb where the ends of the frame wall will fall.

If the foundation wall leans toward the outside at the top, the bottom of the leveling stud will be tight to the bottom of the wall. If the wall leans into the room, the bottom of the stud will be some distance from the bottom of the wall. At each spot you check, hold the leveling stud plumb and mark where the edge of the stud rests on the floor. At the corners (or at the ends of the frame wall) measure the distance from the foundation wall to the marks. Add $1/2$ in. to the larger of the two measurements and re-mark both corners with the new dimension. For example, if one corner measured $3\frac{1}{2}$ in. to the level-stud mark, and the other $3\frac{7}{8}$ in. to the mark, you would re-mark both corners at $4\frac{3}{8}$ in. from the outside wall.

Next, snap a chalkline between the two new marks. Check to see if the chalkline clears the intermediate marks you made along the wall. If it

Begin laying out the bottom plate position with a level and straight stud held plumb against the wall, as shown at left. Then mark where the outside edge of the stud rests on the floor.

Add $1/2$ in. (for clearance) to the measurement that is farthest out from the wall and mark that distance at each end of the wall.

doesn't, move the corner marks out from the foundation wall far enough to clear the intermediate marks and snap the line again. The chalkline indicates the position of the inside edge of the bottom plate, placed so that the frame wall will be straight and plumb, clearing any vagaries in the foundation wall. Snap layout lines for all the outside frame walls in the same manner.

Snap a chalkline from one end of the wall to the other, stretching from the clearance-adjusted marks.

ESTIMATING MATERIALS

Determining how much lumber you need isn't difficult if you've made a reasonably accurate plan of your project, which will include most of the information you need.

Materials for walls include top and bottom plates and full-length studs (2×4s and sometimes 2×6s). You'll need studs to frame corners, intersections, and openings. Soffits require frame members, too (usually 2×2s), as well as oriented strand board (OSB) "skin" to provide rigidity.

Except for bottom plates, all the framing lumber you buy will be designated SPF, for spruce, pine, and fir, the three species used for framing. Because the bottom plates contact the floor, they must be chemically treated to protect them from damage caused by moisture and insects. (See According to Code on p. 55.)

Framing lumber is sold in lengths that increase in 2 ft. increments, from 6 ft. to over 20 ft. Lumber to 16 ft. is generally the same price per lineal foot. Material 18 ft. to 20 ft. long costs more per lineal foot. Anything over 20 ft. costs even more.

Plates

Begin estimating materials with the wall plates. Make a list of the wall lengths on your plan drawing. Do not deduct for doorways; the plates run through those openings and are cut away after the wall is framed. Remember you need an SPF top plate and a treated bottom plate for each wall. Because lengths are in 2 ft. increments, a wall 12 ft. 2 in. long will require

Framing Materials List

Room	Walls: lin. ft.	SPF / ACQ	8-ft. studs (1 per lin. ft.)
Rec room	19 ft. 15 ft. 2 in.	20 / 20 16 / 16	10 (50% for half-wall) 16
Bedroom	12 ft. 8 in. 12 ft. 8 in.	14 / 14 14 / 14	14 14
Bathroom	12 ft. 12 ft. 5 ft. 5 in.	12 / 12 12 / 12	12 12
Storage Stairwell	5 ft. 5 in. 4 ft.	16 / 16 (includes 6 ft. for bathroom)	16
Material ordered:		4 / 4 – 2×4 – 12 ft. 2 / 2 – 2×4 – 14 ft. 2 / 2 – 2×4 – 16 ft.	109 8-ft. studs (1 per lin. ft. plus 15%; 94 + 15 = 109)
Soffits	**Length in lin. ft.**	**2×4s**	**OSB**
Rec room Bedroom Bathroom	28 lin. ft. 12 lin. ft. 52 lin. ft. 12 lin. ft.	5 ft. per 2 ft. of soffit 26 × 5 ft. = 130 lin. ft.	32 lin. ft. of soffit per 4×8 sheet 52 / 32 = 1⅝ sheets
Material ordered:		**11 – 2×4 – 12 ft.**	**2 – 4×8 sheets OSB**
Concrete fasteners		**Framing nails**	**Framing nails**
1 per 2 lin. ft. of wall plate 94 × 0.5 = 46		12d box 10 lb. per 100 lin. ft. of wall	8d box nails 5 lb. per 100 lin. ft.
Material ordered: 50 fasteners		10 lb. 12d nails	5 lb. 8d box nails

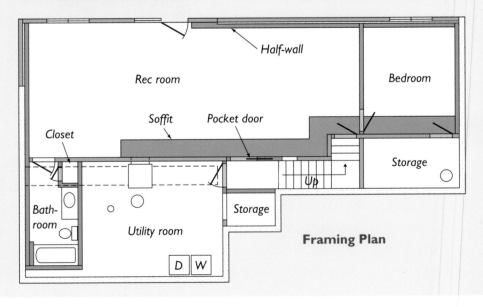

Framing Plan

Half-wall

Rec room

Bedroom

Soffit

Pocket door

Closet

Storage

Up

Storage

Bath-
room

Utility room

D W

14-footers. (You'll probably use the waste for blocking.)

In a basement, plates are the only lumber required in lengths greater than 8 ft. (unless you have higher ceilings). A 16-ft. 8-in. wall could be made with 18-ft. plates. But considering price and convenience, it makes more sense to buy an 8 ft. and a 10 ft. and butt them end-to-end.

After figuring the plates, I often add four SPF 12-footers per 100 lin. ft. of wall, "just because." Because you'll need some backing here and there; because some boards won't be straight enough; because you might need them.

Studs

Next, figure the studs. In conventional framing (the above ground walls of a house), studs are sold cut to an exact length, which will produce an 8-ft. finished room height. But ceiling heights vary from basement to basement, often from spot to spot in the same basement. So, to determine the stud length to buy, you need to measure the ceiling height in your basement, from concrete floor to the bottom of the floor joists. Typically, the height will be between 7 ft. 8 in. and 7 ft. 10 in., so 8-footers will do just fine. And they're cheaper than precut studs. When you see that discount pile of "cheap studs," flee—there are good reasons why no one else wanted them. Steel studs are increasingly available in home stores, but homeowner-remodelers rarely use them, so I won't cover them here.

How many studs do you need? I figure one for every lineal foot of wall plus 15 percent. So, for 100 ft. of wall, order 115 8-footers to use as studs. In the actual walls, studs are spaced 16 in. on center; the extras take care of corners and framing around doors and windows.

Soffits

To estimate material for soffits, measure the lengths of the HVAC duct runs you want to cover (including electrical wires and plumbing pipes nearby). If a duct ends several feet before a wall, I generally measure to the wall. A continuous soffit looks better and is easier to build than one that stops short or jogs around.

Soffits vary, but a basic soffit requires 5 ft. of 2×4 for every 2 lin. ft. of soffit. The soffit "skin" will require one 4×8 sheet of 7/16-in. OSB for every 32 lin. ft. of soffit. OSB is an inexpensive panel made of large wood chips compressed with glue under great pressure. I use a portable circular saw to rip the 2×4s into 2×2s for the soffit frame; these 2×2s are cheaper and usually straighter than those you buy. If you'd rather buy them, order 6 lin. ft. of 2×2 and 2 lin. ft. of 2×4 for every 2 lin. ft. of soffit.

Fasteners

You'll need concrete fasteners to fix the bottom plate to the floor and nails to assemble the walls. (See Framing Fasteners on p. 59.) I figure one concrete fastener per 2 lin. ft. of wall, 10 lb. of 12d box nails and 5 lb. of 8d galvanized box nails per

Having lumber delivered can make a big job much easier.

Moving lumber through a basement window avoids the headaches of negotiating stairway corners in the house.

100 lin. ft. of wall. If you're using a nailer, you'll need a box of 3-in. collated nails (stuck together in strips). There are about 5,000 nails in a box of collated nails.

Purchasing

You could go from lumberyard to home store and buy your materials piece by piece. But it is much easier, and sometimes cheaper, to buy from a single source. Call around to several suppliers and have them give you a quote based on your material list. Ask if delivery is included in the quote. If you can, visit the supplier to check the quality of the material.

TRADE SECRET

To ensure that walls meet at a right angle, you can lay them out using the 3-4-5 rule, as shown in the sketch. Measure 3 ft. along one wall and 4 ft. along the other. Then adjust the angle so that the distance between these points is 5 ft.

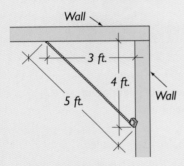

Wall

3 ft.

4 ft.

5 ft.

Wall

An out-of-square room is shown up by many patterns on tiles or linoleum. Where those floorings are to be used, check the room for square by measuring the two diagonals from corner to corner. If the measurements are the same, or within 1/4 in., the room is square. If not, you can re-chalk the interior walls to square that room and throw the out-of-square condition into an adjacent carpeted or unfloored room where it won't show.

Laying out interior-wall plates

Laying out the interior walls is fun because you see your plan beginning to take shape on the floor of your basement.

Start with the interior walls that are defined by specific requirements or existing conditions: walls that need to be precisely located to accommodate plumbing or tub-shower units, or rooms that must be a certain size. Most such accommodations concern wall position. But one requires larger framing material: If there's a 4-in. sewer stack in a wall you're framing, and both sides of the wall will be drywalled, frame the wall with 2×6s. The wider studs provide room inside the wall for the stack and for fittings.

Working from your plan, establish the position of interior walls by measuring from the lines you chalked for the outside frame walls. (You can adjust the angle between the walls as shown at left.) Snap a chalkline for both edges of each interior-wall bottom plate. Chalk scuffs off easily, so at each wall intersection or corner, make a durable X on the floor with a pencil or magic marker. If the chalk lines disappear later, you can just re-snap from the corner marks.

Cutting the plates

With the walls chalked out, cut the top and bottom plates and lay them in place on the floor. Again, I start with the exterior walls, measuring from the chalklines, not from the foundation walls, as shown in the drawing at right. In corners, one plate runs by the other. For the "run-by" plate, measure from the chalkline and add 3½ in., the width of the adjoining plate. For a plate running between two frame walls, just measure from chalkline to chalkline. Pairs of top and bottom plates are the same length. Make all bottom plates from treated lumber. And remember to cut plates the full length of the wall, disregarding doors, windows, and other openings.

Lay out the plates for interior walls by measuring from existing walls or from chalklines for exterior walls. To accommodate the sewer stack, this bathroom wall will need to be made with 2×6s.

Measuring for the Bottom Plate

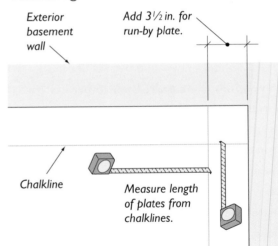

Exterior basement wall

Add 3½ in. for run-by plate.

Chalkline

Measure length of plates from chalklines.

Laying out studs

I mark the position of the studs on the edges of each pair of plates. I use traditional 16-in. on-center (o.c.) spacing for studs in basement walls. The 16-in. spacing provides good support and is the correct spacing for hanging 4×8 sheets of drywall, plywood, and paneling edge to edge. At this stage, I mark a stud every 16 in., ignoring wall intersections and window and door openings. Those are taken care of later.

To mark for studs, place a top-and-bottom pair of plates together on sawhorses. Align the ends of the plates so they're flush. Clamp or tack the plates together so they won't slide. Hook a tape measure over one end and make a mark ¾ in. behind each 16-in. interval (16, 32, 48) highlighted on the tape. The first mark will be at 15¼ in., the second at 31¼ in., and so on. As you go, place an X on the "uphill" side of each mark—toward the 16 in. mark for the first, and so on.

For walls that meet at an outside corner, I measure from that corner. Each corner has "run-by" plates and plates that butt into the run-by plates. When laying out the studs, extend the tape 3½ in. beyond the ends of the "butt-into" plates, and then mark. This ensures that the studs will be spaced to accommodate full sheets of drywall.

When you've marked all the studs, extend the marks across both plates with a try square. Mark Xs on the second plate as you did on the first. Assembling the wall with the 1½-in.-thick studs placed on the X side of each mark spaces them on 16-in. centers.

After you lay out the studs on a pair of plates, reposition the plates on the floor against their chalklines. Place the corresponding top plate on top of each bottom plate. Use a square to mark on the plates all the corners and midwall intersections. These will serve as alignment marks when you attach the bottom plates to the floor and the top plates to the joists.

Measure and mark along the plates for 16-in. o.c. studs.

Mark stud positions across each pair of top and bottom plates.

The X indicates the side of the line to place the stud.

✓ According to Code

Treated lumber, required by code for bottom plates, withstands insects and moisture. The most common treatment, CCA (lumber treated with chromated copper arsenate), was phased out by the EPA. New and less hazardous preservative treatments include ACQ (ammoniacal copper quat), sold as ACQ Preserve® and Natural Wood®. Copper boron azole (CBA) is marketed under the name Natural Select®.

IN DETAIL

It is important to know the exact sizes and requirements of your fixtures before you start framing. Make sure you get the rough-opening dimensions from the supplier. Note also that the wall behind a toilet must be at least 12½ in. back from the center of the toilet-drain rough-in on the floor. It can be an inch or so more than that, but not any less, or you'll have to buy a more-expensive offset toilet.

TRADE SECRET

Use a double bottom plate when framing basement walls, adding an ACQ-treated piece to the plate. For interior walls, this bottom piece is 1-in. wider than its mate and protrudes an equal distance on both sides. (You can rip a 2x6 to 4½ in. wide or simply nail a 1-in. wide strip onto an ACQ 2x4.)

For exterior walls, shift the usual ACQ plate ½ in. into the room. There are two advantages to this system. First, the drywall rests on the additional plate, keeping it from wicking moisture up from the floor. Second, the double thick base plate provides a smooth transition to the floor so the base trim has backing top and bottom.

Laying Out Corner Framing

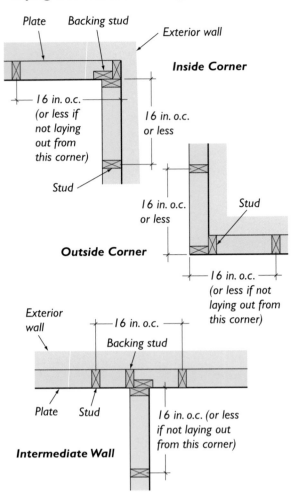

Inside Corner

Plate — Backing stud — Exterior wall

16 in. o.c. (or less if not laying out from this corner)

16 in. o.c. or less

Stud

Outside Corner

16 in. o.c. or less

16 in. o.c. or less

Stud

16 in. o.c. (or less if not laying out from this corner)

Exterior wall

16 in. o.c.

Backing stud

Plate   Stud

16 in. o.c. (or less if not laying out from this corner)

Intermediate Wall

Laying Out Door Openings

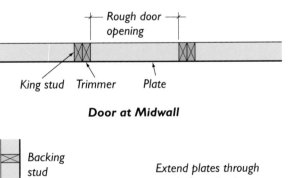

Rough door opening

King stud   Trimmer   Plate

Door at Midwall

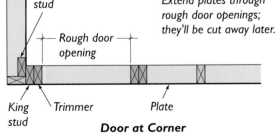

Backing stud

Rough door opening

King stud   Trimmer   Plate

Door at Corner

Extend plates through rough door openings; they'll be cut away later.

Laying out corners

Framing at corners must provide surfaces for attaching the pieces of drywall that meet in the corner. Without a solid corner backing for each sheet, it is difficult to produce a neatly finished drywall corner or one that won't crack over time. The drawings at left show framing for inside and outside corners and corners formed by intermediate walls. There are many ways to frame corners; these have worked well for me.

Mark the positions of the corner studs and backing on the top and bottom plates; use Xs to indicate position as you did for the studs. If a 16-in. o.c. stud you've previously marked happens to fall within ½ in. of the space where these backing studs need to be, eliminate the 16 in. o.c. stud.

Laying out doors

Framing for doorways must create an opening 2 in. wider than the nominal width of the door. This "rough opening" allows for the door, a ¾-in.-thick jamb on each side and a ¼ in. space behind each jamb for shims, to ensure the jambs are plumb. The opening for a "three-oh" door (3 ft. 0 in. wide) should be 3 ft. 2 in. wide; a "two-six" door (2 ft. 6 in. wide) needs a rough opening 2 ft. 8 in. wide.

Each side of the opening is formed by two studs as shown at left. The king stud is usually the height of the wall studs. The trimmer is cut to support the header. (The height of the rough opening isn't important at this stage.) As the drawing shows, framing for a door adjacent to an inside or outside corner should also include king studs and trimmers on both sides of the rough opening. The combination of trimmers and king studs provides solid backing for both the hinge side and the striker side of the door. It also provides backing for a standard 2¼-in.-wide casing.

Working from your plan, measure and mark the positions of king and trimmer studs for all

"Furring" Outside Walls

As we discussed in Chapter 3, you may want or need to strip your outside walls with 1×2 or 2×2 "furring" strips, instead of a full 2×4 frame. You can attach the strips directly to the wall. As shown in the drawing below, a typical furred wall includes a treated 1×4 or 2×4 running horizontally along the very bottom (to provide a nailing surface for the base trim), one strip along the top, and vertical 1×2 strips on 16-in. centers.

You can attach the strips to the masonry with a stud gun, with masonry screws, or other concrete fasteners. Place fasteners about 12 in. from the top and bottom, and put one in the center. I like to use construction adhesive behind 1×2s, along with mechanical fasteners. A stud gun tends to blow 1×2s apart, so use another fastener unless you're willing to lose a few strips. With 2×2s, it is possible to fix the top and bottom plates to the wall and floor, then nail the vertical strips to the plates. But you'll still need to attach the center of the strip to the masonry wall to keep it from bouncing.

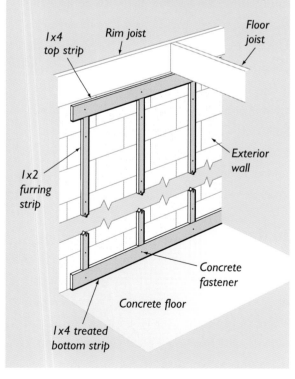

1x4 top strip
Rim joist
Floor joist
1x2 furring strip
Exterior wall
Concrete fastener
Concrete floor
1x4 treated bottom strip

the doors. In addition to the Xs that position the studs, I mark a T where each trimmer will go. The bottom plates run through the doorway openings, which makes construction easier. When you've finished framing, you'll cut them away.

Laying out other openings

The last layout task is for things that penetrate the walls: windows, ductwork, plumbing, and the electrical service box. Fortunately, they're all laid out in about the same way. You could lay out these openings on the plates by measurement. But it's easier, faster, and more accurate to put the bottom plate in position on the floor and plumb down to it from the window or other object.

For a window opening, you'll need a king stud on each side, a bottom sill and a top header, and short studs (cripples) under the sill, as shown in the drawing below. When positioning the king studs, you'll need to accommodate the trim you'll use. If you're going to wrap the opening with drywall (see p. 108), position the king studs (and the rough opening sill and header) ¾ in. back from the inside of the window frame. If you're adding a ¾-in.-thick jamb extension (see p. 126), place the rough opening members 1 in. back from the frame. These positions allow for ⅛-in. trim or drywall reveal. I hold a straight stud and level against the window frame to mark king-stud positions on both plates.

To position studs for a window, plumb down from the edge of the window jamb and mark the plates.

Position the king studs for duct-work or pipes by plumbing down to the plates.

Laying Out Window Openings

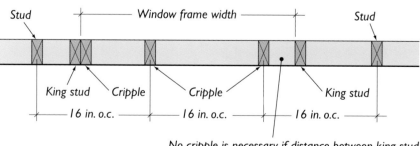

Stud
Window frame width
Stud
King stud Cripple Cripple King stud
16 in. o.c. 16 in. o.c. 16 in. o.c.

No cripple is necessary if distance between king stud and nearest 16-in. o.c. cripple is less than 6 in.

PRO TIP

If you're adding a fireplace, remember that you need to purchase it and frame for it at this stage.

IN DETAIL

When you buy a level, first check that it lives up to its name. Lay the level on something that should be reasonably level, the floor of the store, for example. Move the level around until you find a spot that "reads level," where the bubble is in the very middle of the vial. Turn the level end for end, same edge up. It should read the same. If it doesn't agree with itself (the bubble is off-center), try another level. You can check it for plumb the same way. Hold it against a post or column in the store. If it reads plumb (the bubble is centered), rotate the level 180 degrees, keeping the same end up. It should still read plumb. If it does, you have a good one.

Treat the breaker box like a window opening, but position the king studs 1 in. away from the box on each side. This allows access to the panel during hook up, and it accommodates several finishing options for the breaker box: leaving it as is, wrapping drywall back over the king studs, installing a jamb with trim, or covering everything with a hinged door.

Framing around ductwork or a beam is a little different. The top plate is continuous over windows, doors (usually), and the breaker box, but it has to jog down under ducts and beams. To position the king studs, plumb down from the face or faces of the duct or beam, measure out an inch to give some breathing room, and strike a line on the plate. The king stud will sit behind that line, with the top plate extending below the duct or beam and supported by cripple studs. If there's a 16-in.-o.c. stud from the initial plate layout that is in the way of the king stud, eliminate it.

Often, the water lines run parallel to a duct or beam and a couple of inches out. There, I plumb down an inch back from the water lines instead of the duct, to enclose them in the soffit, too.

Laying Out Other Openings

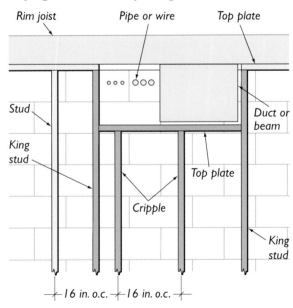

Rim joist
Pipe or wire
Top plate
Stud
King stud
Duct or beam
Top plate
Cripple
King stud

16 in. o.c. 16 in. o.c.

Building the Walls

With layout complete, you can begin to build walls. The sequence is straightforward. First, attach the bottom plates to the concrete floor. Then fasten the top plates to the joists overhead. Cut and fit the studs, trimmers, and cripples in between. Wall frames go up quickly and as they go up it is satisfying to finally see your basement dreams taking shape.

Bottom plates first

Fixing bottom plates to a concrete floor is a daunting prospect to a novice framer. Fortunately, a range of clever fasteners, described in the sidebar on the facing page, makes the task much less difficult than it used to be.

Whatever fastener or combination of fasteners you choose, you should use one about every 2 ft. and one within 3 in. of the end of each wall, including both sides of a doorway. Before shooting or screwing a fastener, make sure the plate is accurately aligned on the chalk layout lines.

Where a doorway is near an adjacent wall, only 3 in. of the bottom plate may remain after the plate crossing the doorway is cut out (see Door at Corner on p. 56). Because a stud-gun fastener driven near the end of a plate can split the plate, I use either a wedged or expanding anchor or a masonry screw to fasten the plate ends that will become short plates. As added insurance, I also smear construction adhesive under the end of the plate (spread after cleaning away the dust from drilling the fastener hole).

Installing top plates

Top plates are attached to the joists of the floor overhead. Where plates run perpendicular to the joists, they can be nailed right to the joists. Where a plate runs parallel with the joists, you must install "blocking" between the joists to have something to nail to, as shown on p. 60.

FRAMING FASTENERS

Framing requires fasteners for attaching wood to wood and for attaching wood to concrete. Framing nails for wood-to-wood connections come in two general categories:

- **For hand work.** I prefer box nails, which are a little lighter, less likely to split the wood, and easier to drive than common nails. Nails are sized in "penny weight," designated by a "d" after the size. You'll need 12d box nails (about 3 in. long) and 8d box nails (about 2 1/2 in. long).

- **For nailers.** Pneumatic nailers use collated nails, special nails stuck together with adhesive in a bandolier-like string. For framing, you'll need 3-in. nails. Buy nails compatible with the nailer you're using.

Concrete fasteners come in a variety of types, three of which I recommend for homeowner use. Don't use hardened concrete nails, which are the least expensive but also the most frustrating for novices to drive.

- **22-caliber stud gun.** The simplest to use, it shoots 2 1/2-in. nails through the bottom plate into the floor, propelled by a gunpowder charge equivalent to that for a 22-cal. bullet. Gun, nails, and charges are sold at many hardware stores. Old concrete (cured for 20 or 30 years) can be too hard and brittle for the stud gun to penetrate well.

- **Concrete screws.** You drill a hole through the plate and into the concrete, and then drive a screw. You'll need a hammer drill, a special bit, and screws. Buy the correct-size bit when you buy the screws. Drill the hole at least 1/2 in. deeper into the concrete than the fastener will penetrate. Power-drive the screw.

- **Wedged and expanding anchors.** Drill through the plate into the floor with hammer drill and cement bit. Then hammer home the fastener; it wedges or expands against the sides of the hole in the floor.

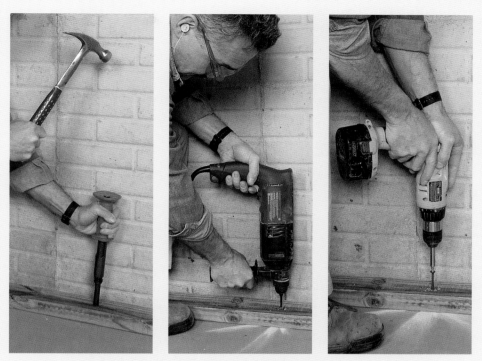

You can fasten bottom plates with hardened nails driven by a stud gun (left). To use a concrete screw, first bore into the floor through the plate with a hammer drill (center). Power drive the concrete screw into place (right).

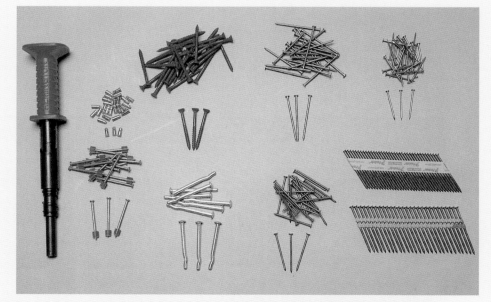

Framing fasteners are shown above. For fixing bottom plates to concrete (left to right, in columns): 22-caliber stud gun; its charges and fasteners; concrete screws and expanding anchors. For nailing together wall frames: 12d box nails and 8d box nails; 6d box nails and collated nails for a pneumatic nailer.

PRO TIP

Don't fasten the bottom plate down in a doorway; it will be cut out later.

TRADE SECRET

Before you nail the plates to the floor, cut halfway through the bottom of the bottom plate each side of a doorway opening. Then, when the wall is framed and you're cutting out doorways, you don't have to cut all the way to the concrete and dull your sawblade.

These 2×4 pieces of blocking are placed wide-face down and spaced 2 ft. on center. The distance between joists varies, so I measure and cut each one to fit its space. Here's how to set a top plate.

1. The edges of each top plate must align with those of its matching bottom plate. To do so, plumb up from each end of the bottom plate to the nearest joist or block above and make a mark.

2. Snap a chalkline across these two marks the length of the wall.

3. Position the top plate along the chalkline, which puts it plumb above the bottom plate. Hold the top plate in place with clamps or wedge it with two studs cut snug to length. Now, align the stud marks on the two plates. I place the straight stud and level on a bottom-plate stud mark and tap the top plate into alignment. When one mark is plumb above its mate below, all the marks will be aligned.

4. Nail the top plate to the joists or blocks. Nailing up into joists with a hammer is hard work, another good reason to rent a pneumatic nailer.

The top plate of a wall running parallel to the joists must be fastened to blocking.

Cut blocks to fit between joists. Nail them in place on 2-ft. centers.

Wedge blocking in places too tight to nail.

Blocking in an Awkward Spot

You may need to block between the last joist and the rim joist on top of an exterior wall, as shown here. The block will sit on top of the sill plate and can be nailed there, if you can get to it with a hammer. Occasionally, it's impossible to nail the block to the sill plate. If so, I cut another block to wedge the first piece of blocking against the floor above. I glue it with construction adhesive.

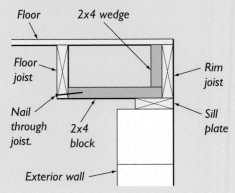

Wedged Blocking

Floor
2x4 wedge
Floor joist
Rim joist
Nail through joist.
2x4 block
Sill plate
Exterior wall

Mark the position of the top plate directly above the bottom plate using a square and straight-edged stud, as shown at left. After marking the top-plate location at both ends of the wall, snap a chalkline to position intermediate studs (above).

With level and straightedge, align the stud marks on top and bottom plates (left). Then, with the top plate in position, nail it (above). A quick-action clamp holds the top plate in place.

Nailing up studs

I've found work goes faster and I make fewer mistakes if I first install all full-length studs (those that extend between bottom and top plates).

1. Because floors and joists are uneven, I measure and cut these studs individually. Again, for efficiency and speed, I measure all the studs for a wall, marking lengths on the wall as I go. Then I mark and cut each stud with a miter saw, and write its length on it. Then I pile them in order, wall by wall.

2. Full-length studs are toenailed to the bottom and top plates. I usually nail the bottom first, because it's easier to do; then I nail the top. Position all bowed edges in the same direction, as described in the sidebar below. Toenailing with a hammer, I use three 8d nails on each end, two on one side, one in the middle on the other. With a nailer, I use 2½-in. nails, two on one side only. For hand-toenailing studs in basement walls, 12d and 16d nails are overkill, and frustrating to use unless you've driven a truckload of them.

3. Assemble and nail corners and wall intersections just as you laid them out on the plates. In addition to toenails top and bottom, nail adjacent pieces together about every 16 in.

Framing windows

Framing for windows, doors, and other openings is similar. As discussed earlier, full-height king studs form the sides of window openings. You will have installed the king studs with the rest of the full-length studs. Adding a header above and a sill below encloses the opening. Cripples nailed in the spaces above and below the opening provide attachment for drywall.

Selecting Studs

As you dig through your lumber pile for studs, you'll be sorting them for quality. Some will actually be dead straight. Most will have a slight crook, bow, or twist, or a "waney" edge, which includes some of the curved outer surface of the tree.

For studs, a bow of up to about 5/16 in. is usable, as is a stud crooked no more than about ½ in. You can run a string down the board to calibrate your eye, but you'll soon be able to judge an unacceptable board just by sighting down it.

Save the straightest studs for walls behind cabinets. Align bowed boards so they all bulge into the room. (When selecting studs, I mark an arrow on the stud showing the direction of the bow.) Setting the bows all the same way produces a continuous curve to the wall, which looks flatter than a wavy wall. Crooks are lost in the wall and can, to an extent, be straightened when you hang the drywall. Waney studs are problematic only if the waney edge limits the nailing surface.

Twisted studs are more of a problem. They tend to move more as they dry out, which can cause nail pops in drywall. A slight twist is okay, but if I lay a stud on the floor and one end pops up more than about 5/16 in., I don't use it. Studs you reject for full-length use can be cut up for backing and soffits.

Defects in Studs

Edge

Face

Crook   Bow   Wane   Twist

Measure each stud to ensure a tight fit between plates.

Align studs with marks on the plates. A well-placed foot keeps the stud from moving while toenailing.

After the bottom of the stud is fixed, toenail the top end to the top plate.

Toenail corner pieces into top and bottom plates. Then nail adjacent pieces together on 16-in. spacing.

TRADE SECRET

Not all basement doors can be full height. For a door beneath a beam or duct, you have to frame the rough opening as high as you can, and then cut the door jamb and door to fit. The king stud extends from the bottom of the beam or duct to the bottom plate. Nail the header to this short king stud first. Then fix them in the opening and nail in trimmers.

1. Determine the length of the sill by measuring between the king studs at the bottom plate (this avoids errors produced by crooked studs). Cut the sill, place it on the bottom plate between the kings studs, and transfer 16-in. centerlines for the cripples from the plate. If the end cripples fall more than 6 in. from the king studs, add a cripple next to the king stud.

2. Mark the position of the sill on the king studs and nail it in place through the king studs. Measure and cut cripples to fill between the sill and bottom plate and toenail them in place.

3. In basements, the wall's top plate often serves as the header over a window or other opening. If the top of the opening is lower than the plate, you'll need to add a header. Lay it out and install it, along with any cripples, as you did the sill plate. For openings wider than 3 ft., I double the header and sill, making each out of two 2×4s installed face down. (See p. 57 for how to position the sill and header for a drywall wrap or jamb extension.)

4. Other than doors, most openings in walls (electrical service box, ductwork, meters) are framed the same as windows.

+ SAFETY FIRST

Miter saws and pneumatic nailers do not distinguish between wood and bone. The saws are very safe to use, but all the safety devices in the world will not protect you from carelessness. When you are cutting, that's what you need to focus on. Do not pull boards out from under the blade or look away while the blade is still spinning. Nailers have safety guards to prevent accidental discharge. But when shooting, keep track of who's near you, and what's on the other side of the board.

The king studs for a window opening are installed with other full-height studs. Here, the studs forming the sides of the opening for the ductwork are being installed.

1 Cut the sill to length, lay it on the bottom plate, and transfer the stud spacings onto the sill.

2 Nail the sill between king studs.

3a Nail through the king stud into the header.

3b A header and cripples frame out the opening above this window.

4a Here is the completed framing for a window opening and an opening around ductwork.

4b Frame an electrical service box as you would a window.

TRADE SECRET

To make 2×2s that are cheaper and usually straighter than those at the lumberyard, I rip 2×4s in half with a portable circular saw. Most circular saws come with an edge-guide for ripping. For safety, clamp the 2×4 to sawhorses, moving the clamp and board to accommodate the cut.

Framing doors

Door openings are framed by king studs and trimmers, the trimmers supporting a header above the door. With the full-length king studs in place, you need only add trimmers and headers to finish the door openings.

For standard full-height (6 ft. 8 in.) doors, I cut trimmers 81¼ in. long. When the bottom plate upon which the trimmer rests is cut out of the doorway, the rough opening (concrete floor to header) will be 82¾ in. Allowing for jamb and shims, this will leave about 1¼ in. below the bottom of a standard interior door. This clearance allows for the door to swing comfortably over carpet and wood floors. This leaves a larger, but acceptable, gap over linoleum. Using trimmers of the same length also sets the top trim for all the doors at one height, for a uniform appearance.

Nail the trimmers to the king studs. I use a couple of 12d nails for top and bottom and every 16 in. or so in between. For doors in nonbearing basement walls, headers haven't much structural importance. They're basically backing for drywall and trim. If the rough opening is for a door up to 3 ft. 0 in. wide, I use a single 2×4 for a header, nailed face down. For wider doors, I nail two 2×4s together to strengthen the opening, and install them face down, too. Cut the header to fit snugly between the king studs. Position it on top of the trimmers and nail through the king studs into the ends of the header.

If the opening between the door header and the top plate is larger than 4 in. to 6 in., toenail short cripples on 16-in. centers to provide backing for drywall.

Building Soffits

The final major framing task is building soffits to enclose all those pipes, ducts, and beams cluttering the ceiling. There are lots of ways to build soffits. The one I'll describe here is simple and solid and can be built fairly quickly.

As the drawing below shows, a soffit consists of 2×2s and a face of oriented-strand board (OSB) nailed to the joists on one or both sides of the duct, beam, or pipes. If the duct runs next to a wall, an OSB face on one side is connected with 2×4 "lookouts" to a 2×2 ledger attached to the wall. (If the duct is in the middle of a room, there are OSB faces on each side of the duct.) The OSB and lookouts provide rigidity and nailing surface for the drywall that covers the soffit.

Ducts often run next to a wall, so I'll describe building a soffit for that situation.

Framing a Tub-Shower

On standard tubs and tub-showers, the flange comes out about 30 in. You need a stud there as backing for the fixture-drywall intersection. I like to use a 2×4 flat, centered at 30 in. to provide a bit more surface for nailing.

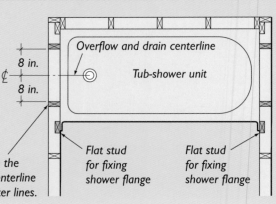

Overflow and drain centerline

Tub-shower unit

8 in.

₵

8 in.

Flat stud for fixing shower flange

Flat stud for fixing shower flange

Place studs 8 in. from the overflow and drain centerline to allow room for water lines.

1. Start by positioning the 2×2 ledger on the wall. Its bottom edge should be 2 in. lower than the low point of the duct run. Measure down from the joists in several places to find the low point. Mark that dimension at each end of the duct run and snap a chalkline on the wall between the marks.

Next, establish the position of the 2×2 ledger on the joists. It should be 2 in. away from the face of the duct (or from any included pipes). Measure from the wall to the face of the duct to find the dimension, add 2 in., and mark this distance on joists nearest each end of the duct. From these marks, snap a chalkline on the bottom of the joists. (On the rare occasions that a duct runs parallel to the joists, install blocking between the joists on 2 ft. centers, and snap a line on the blocking).

2. Cut a pair of 2×2s the length of the soffit run. Nail one above the chalkline on the studs and the other on the duct side of the line on the joists. Where the duct penetrates a wall, nail a 2×4 backing block between the studs that bracket the joist chalkline; center it on the wall chalkline.

2a

Begin the soffit by nailing a 2×2 ledger to the studs, positioned 2 in. below the ductwork.

2b

After marking out from both ends of the duct, snap a chalkline along the joists and nail a ledger in place.

1

Mark the position of the ledger for the joists 2 in. away from the duct.

Anatomy of a Soffit

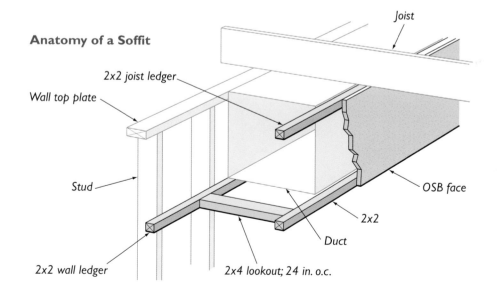

Joist

2x2 joist ledger

Wall top plate

Stud

OSB face

2x2

Duct

2x2 wall ledger

2x4 lookout; 24 in. o.c.

PRO TIP

When toenailing a lookout, set its end on the floor and drive the nails so the points just poke out of the wood. This makes it easier to fix to the wall ledger.

TRADE SECRET

If you're nailing a soffit's OSB face to the joist ledger with a nailer, remember to check for nearby water lines before you pull the trigger. A 3-in. nail will protrude about an inch beyond the OSB face and the 2×2 ledger. As an added precaution, know where the water shutoffs are.

3. To make the OSB face, cut strips of OSB ¼ in. less in width than the measurement from the bottom of the joists to the bottom of the wall ledger. Nail a 2×2 on each OSB strip, flush with the straightest edge.

To support the OSB face during installation, clamp or nail a scrap 2×4 to the wall at each end of the duct run. Position the support level with the bottom of the wall ledger. (Hold a level against the ledger and draw a line on the backer block in the wall.) Also using the level, plumb down from the chalkline on the joists and mark a vertical line across the backer block. This line will help you plumb the OSB face later.

4. If you don't have an assistant, you can attach the OSB face by yourself with help from a quick-release clamp or other one-handed clamping tool. Rest one end of the OSB face on the scrap clamped to the end wall. Lift the other end and clamp it to the joist ledger, leveling it by eye with the bottom of the wall ledger. Move back to the end wall and nail the OSB face to the joist ledger.

5. Return to the end clamped to the joist ledger. Align the OSB face using a level stretched from the wall ledger to the OSB, adjusting the clamp as necessary. Tack or screw the OSB face to the joist ledger to hold it in place. If you have a helper, he or she can hold the OSB level while you nail.

If the soffit run is less than 16 ft., repeat the OSB installation for the second piece of OSB, cutting it to fit about ¼ in. shy of the space to fill, so it will fit in easily. If the run is longer than 16 ft., simply clamp a scrap piece of 2×4 from the wall ledger to the end of the first 8-ft. run, rest the next 8-ft. run on the scrap, and proceed as before.

6. With the OSB face attached to the joist ledger, you need to plumb and fix the face to the end walls. Align the back face of the OSB with

Mark the position of the wall ledger on the 2×4 backer nailed in the end wall.

With the OSB face supported on a 2×4 scrap clamped to the backer block, nail the face to the joist ledger.

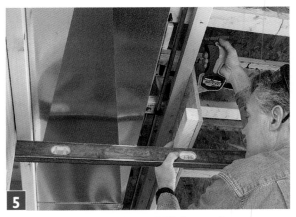

At the other end, level the OSB face, using a clamp to hold it in place. Then nail the face to the joist ledger.

the plumb line you drew on the end-wall backer. Measure and cut a 2×2 to fit between the wall ledger and the 2×2 attached to the OSB. Rest it on top of the 2×4 scrap support and nail it to the wall. Then nail the OSB to it. If the soffit ends before a wall, cut and nail similar 2×2s at the top and bottom of the soffit.

7. With each end of the soffit plumb, level, and solid, stretch a taut string line from wall to wall just behind the 2×2 attached to the lower edge of the OSB. Double-check the leveling of the soffit face against this line. It's easy to misread a level. The string will allow you to fine-tune the height of the OSB face. When you're satisfied the face is level, fasten it to the joist ledger about every 8 in. with 5d nails or 1½-in. staples shot with an air gun.

8. Now mark the positions of the 2×4 lookouts on the OSB face and wall ledger. Place them on 2-ft. centers, measuring from the wall that begins the soffit run, to ensure there is a lookout at all the OSB joints.

As for studs, I measure the length of each lookout from the wall ledger to the taut string. Pulling the OSB face to the lookouts ensures a straight soffit. The string is straight; the OSB is not. Toenail each lookout first to the wall ledger with 12d nails. Then drive a couple of 12d nails through the OSB face into the end of the lookout. The soffit is now ready for drywall.

Framing Check

So, the walls are up, the doors and windows framed in, the soffits are up. All that's left to do is to double-check your work. In particular, make sure that you have installed backing to accommodate all drywall and fixtures.

In the bathroom, check framing around the tub. (See Framing a Tub-Shower on p. 66.) If

If the soffit ends in the middle of a room, add 2×2 end pieces top and bottom to support the drywall.

To support the drywall on the bottom of the soffit, nail 2×4 lookouts on 2-ft. centers to the wall ledger and the OSB face.

you're installing grab bars by the tub or toilet, measure them and nail 2x4 backing between studs in the appropriate places; the backing will provide solid attachment for the grab bars.

To make sure there is backing for the drywall, inspect each inside corner, wall-to-wall and wall-to-ceiling. Imagine you're nailing up a sheet of drywall: Is there something in the corner to nail it to? Where there is a void, nail or screw in some backing.

FRAMING A HALF-WALL OR PARTIAL-HEIGHT WALL

In many basements, one or more exterior walls are combinations of frame and concrete construction—the upper part is framed and insulated, the lower part is concrete. If you've chosen not to hide the entire wall behind a full-height framed wall, you'll want to build a half-wall to cover the lower, concrete wall.

A half-wall is laid out just like a full wall. Measure and snap lines on the floor to position it. Measure, cut, and lay out 16-in. centers for studs on a treated bottom plate and SPF top plate. The height of the half-wall should be 2 in. more than the distance from the top of the concrete wall (at its highest point) to the floor.

It is easiest to nail a half-wall together first, and then stand it up in place. Lay the plates on edge on the floor, place the studs in between, and nail through the plates into the ends of the studs, using 12d nails. Stand the wall up and align it with the chalkline on the floor, tack or clamp it in place temporarily, if necessary.

Sight down the top plate from one end to detect humps or dips telegraphed up from the floor. If the top plate is straight or dips lower in the middle, fix the bottom plate to the floor at both ends. To eliminate a dip, wedge wooden shims between the floor and the bottom plate. Then fix the plate to the floor at 2 ft. intervals. If the wall is high in the middle, fix it to the floor there. Then shim as necessary from the center to the ends and complete fixing it to the floor.

For stability, the upper portion of a half-wall must be firmly anchored. First, fix the ends of the wall. If the half-wall butts into or runs along a frame wall, plumb the end of the half-wall and nail into blocking in the adjoining frame wall. Where a half-wall butts into or runs along a concrete wall,

glue and fasten a 2-ft.-long piece of treated blocking to the concrete wall. Then plumb and fix the half-wall to the blocking. To ensure a straight wall, fix blocks to the concrete every 4 ft. Then stretch a string from end to end along the top plate. Pull the top plate to the string and nail the studs to the blocks as you move down the line.

If the half-wall's top plate is more than 2½ in. from the exterior frame wall, you'll need to provide support for the wall cap or drywall wrap by nailing a 2×2 in. backing to the exterior wall, flush with the top plate of the half-wall.

Here, the exterior wall of a walkout basement is framed on top of a partial concrete wall. The half-wall will hide the concrete.

Drive shims under the bottom plate to straighten the top plate of a half-wall.

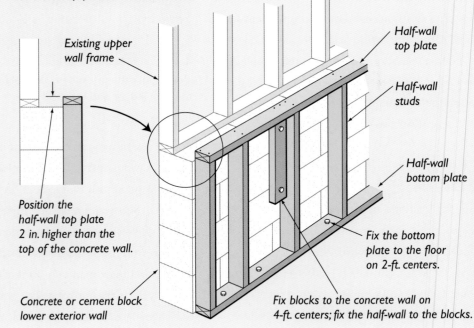

Existing upper wall frame

Position the half-wall top plate 2 in. higher than the top of the concrete wall.

Concrete or cement block lower exterior wall

Half-wall top plate

Half-wall studs

Half-wall bottom plate

Fix the bottom plate to the floor on 2-ft. centers.

Fix blocks to the concrete wall on 4-ft. centers; fix the half-wall to the blocks.

Adding an Egress Window

As I discussed in chapter 1 (p. 13), if your basement remodel includes a bedroom, building codes require that room to have an egress window—that is, a window large enough to permit escape and rescue (by someone in bulky gear) in an emergency. Any project that requires punching a hole through a foundation wall is going to be demanding of both effort and expertise. Both demands can be met by hiring a professional to do the job. But there is much you can do yourself, even if you don't do all the work. The discussion here provides the basic outline of the task. If you decide to tackle some or all of it yourself, you can save a considerable amount of money. But, I suggest seeking a professional's advice before and during construction to avoid costly or dangerous mistakes.

Installing an egress window requires a number of separate purchases: You'll have to buy a specially designed egress window well in addition to an ordinary, but code-compliant,

✓ According to Code

To qualify as an egress window, the location, size and window-well dimensions must meet specific requirements generally based on those of the International Residential Code (IRC). Code specified minimums are 24 in. tall and 20 in. wide. Most window styles can be used for egress, as long as they meet code. In addition to the specific window and window-well requirements, you must also satisfy code requirements for lot lines and zoning setbacks. For example, an egress window well will project at least 3 ft. from the building wall, and in some neighborhoods that might be too close to a lot line.

window. You'll need gravel for backfill, window trim and a variety of fasteners, caulk, ready-mix concrete and lumber for bracing.

Window wells vary depending on aesthetics and cost. The Bilco® ScapeWEL unit shown in the photos cost about $500; some units are available for less than $200. Other options include precast concrete, interlocking landscape stones, even railroad ties, as long as the code requirements are met.

Digging the hole

Before digging, call to have someone come to locate buried utilities that might be in the area. Our local One Call service responds quickly, as do most. You can also call the national Call Before You Dig hotline (811).

You can use the window well itself to layout the size of the hole. You'll need to allow for fill around the unit, too. The ScapeWEL required 1 ft. of river rock or pea gravel fill all around to provide adequate drainage. So, you're going to be digging a large hole and removing a lot of dirt. On one of the first egress windows I installed I thought I'd save money by digging with a shovel and hauling the dirt away in my pickup. My first load weighed in at 3,000 lb.; the second hit 3,500 lb. What I saved in dumpster fees I spent on back massages.

Installing the well

Once the window-well hole is dug, you can either cut the hole in the basement wall, then install the window and the window well or install the well then cut the hole. Typically, I cut the hole first, because it gives more room to maneuver the equipment necessary to cut through the block or concrete. However, sometimes installing the well first is the best choice. The job shown in the photos is an example. With bad weather looming and the window on back

Wedge bolts drive with an impact drill fix the well flanges firmly to the foundation.

Gravel and rock backfill keeps the well firmly in place and enhances drainage.

PRO TIP

Don't even draw an egress window plan until you've checked with your local codes department for exact requirements in your area.

IN DETAIL

The advantage to mounting directly to the block is that no exterior trim is then required. Just caulk between the window and block or concrete and you're done. However, if the opening is rough, it can be difficult to attach to as well as unsightly. Installing framing and trim is often the best method, though it takes more time and a bit more money. Frame with 2-in.-thick dimension lumber wide enough to cover the block. (Pieces that frame a masonry opening like this are called "bucks.") Make sure to order the window sized to fit in the framed opening, with allowance for fitting.

order, I installed the ScapeWEL first, knowing I could cut out the block with a diamond blade on a circular saw within the limitations of the installed window well. Regardless of your sequence of installation, the processes are the same.

Before installing the well, clean off the wall and fill cracks that won't be cut out of the wall. Chip off protrusions from the wall above and below grade so the well flange will rest flush against the wall.

The ScapeWEL assembles in four parts: two side pieces attach to the foundation with flanges and two back panels snap onto the side pieces to create a step. To attach the flanges, I used ⅜-in. diameter, 2 in. long wedge bolts (sometimes called expansion-sleeve anchors). Some contractors use masonry screws or powder-driven nails, but these fasteners don't have the pull-out or shear load strength I prefer. I also like the way the wedge bolts suck in tight when torqued with an electric impact driver. If the well flange holes are too small for the larger fittings, just bore them out.

After snapping back panel to the side walls, I cross braced the unit on the inside with dimension lumber so it wouldn't deform when I backfilled with gravel. You can shovel the backfill rock and gravel by hand, as I did here (all 6,500 lb. of it) or hire a skid loader to do the job.

Cutting through the foundation

You can hire someone with a water-cooled concrete saw large enough to cut all the way through most block or concrete walls. Paying by the lineal foot of cut, with an additional charge for hauling away the concrete chunks, a cut-out usually runs $400 to $600.

You can also cut through the foundation yourself, as shown above right. This is a difficult and dusty job (wear a face mask or respirator), but it is less expensive than hiring a professional. Using an electric saw with a masonry blade, you'll have

A heavy duty circular saw with a masonry blade cuts partway through the foundation wall from both sides.

A sledge hammer and rotary hammer help complete the opening.

Fit ACQ-treated lumber, or "bucks," into the opening.

Nail the window flange to the bucks using galvanized roofing nails.

Finish the exterior by fitting the trim and caulking between it and the concrete or block foundation.

to cut from both sides of the wall and then punch out the remainder with a sledge hammer. Smooth the rough edges with a chipping hammer or an electric rotary hammer and fill the cores of the remaining bottom blocks with bag-mix concrete.

Setting the window

There are two ways to attach a window to a masonry opening. One is to attach directly to the block through the side jambs of the window. The other is to frame the opening with ACQ treated lumber and attach the window to the frame.

Flanged windows are easy to install (provided the opening has been sized correctly). Position and level the window, then nail the flanges to the bucks. I also like to build up a sloped concrete sill on the bottom below the new window, because this is where water will tend to accumulate. I cut the side and top trim to fit the space between the window and the block and lintel

and caulk where the trim meets the window and the block and lintel.

Ordinarily, this would finish the installation, but things are seldom ordinary when remodeling. The foundation shown in the photos had some cracks, and though the wall wasn't badly bowed, cutting deeply in a block wall raised concerns about its long-term structural integrity. I installed a 4-in. steel I-beam on the inside of the wall on each side of the opening as insurance.

Drainage

Like any hole in the ground, a window well accumulates water. If possible, I tie into an existing sump-pump and drain-tile system around the house foundation, running drain tile of my own down from the well's gravel fill. If there is no drain tile system, buy or make a cover for the well. And make sure you create a positive slope away from the well in all.

Mechanicals

CHAPTER SIX

1 HVAC, p. 76

With the framing in place, you now have a skeleton on which to hang heating, ventilating, and air conditioning (HVAC) runs; plumbing lines; and electrical wiring. Collectively, these three systems are referred to as the "mechanicals." Typically, professionals in these areas are more regulated than in others. But in your own home, codes allow you to do all the mechanical work yourself.

This chapter will give you an overview of the mechanical requirements for a typical basement remodeling. It will help you decide how much or how little you want to do yourself, what the processes should look like if you hire a professional, and where you might be able to work with a professional in doing at least part of the work yourself.

HVAC ducts are big and bulky, and they're harder to snake through small spaces than are plumbing or wiring. So I do the HVAC first, then the plumbing, and the wiring last. That's the order in which we'll cover them here.

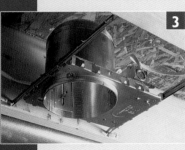

2 Plumbing, p. 82

3 Wiring, p. 87

IN DETAIL

It's amazing how sensitive the human body is to temperature. If a basement is just 3° cooler than the upstairs (and that's typical), it will feel too cool for most people to sit in comfortably. If you can't provide supplemental heating, you can run the furnace fan continuously to help even out the temperature differential between the basement and the rest of the house.

TRADE SECRET

Costs will vary from area to area, but generally an HVAC contractor will have a flat fee for each duct extension and for the return air. Get a bid, and realize you'll save about half that doing it yourself. Of course, that doesn't include the cost of the tools you'll need and the Band-Aids®. The pros will be in and out in about half a day. You'll spend that much time just going to the store two or three times. But you'll have the satisfaction of doing the job yourself and saving some hard cash.

HVAC

Basements are almost always cool. This can be a blessing in the heat of summer. In the dead of winter, even where winters are mild, it is not. No matter how nice your new basement rooms are, if they're uncomfortably cool, you won't enjoy them. Basement air-conditioning isn't an issue in many parts of the country. But where I live, it's so hot in the summer that basement living space often needs to be cooled, too.

So the first HVAC consideration for a basement remodel is providing adequate heating and cooling to the new spaces. The second consideration is less obvious, but very important for safety. You need to make sure your newly

Codes for Mechanicals

We'll discuss specific code requirements as they arise in this chapter. In general, each of the mechanical systems (HVAC, electrical, plumbing) will require a separate permit and inspection to ensure the work complies with codes and is correctly installed. This is where local building inspectors can really help you out, because incorrectly installed mechanicals can be dangerous, even deadly.

If you hire your mechanical work done, the contractor is responsible for the permit in that area of work, and for complying with codes, even though you have the permit for the general remodel. If you're installing one or more mechanical systems yourself, you must take out the appropriate permits and you must schedule all the required inspections. When you show your local permit department your plan, you can find out if there are any local variations from the national codes we'll discuss here, as well as other useful information. Don't be afraid to ask questions.

HVAC Codes

Bathrooms must be vented to the outside, with a 4-in. minimum diameter for ducts longer than 2 ft. Gas furnaces require adequate combustion air. (See Helping Your Furnace Breathe on p. 80.) Local codes can exceed national codes, so check with your codes department.

reconfigured basement will provide enough air to the furnace for combustion (enough air for it to "breathe," as it were). Lastly, codes require that you vent the bathroom to the outdoors.

Fortunately, HVAC systems in many homes were sized at installation to handle the whole house, including the basement. If you are uncertain about your system's capacity, a consultation with an HVAC professional will be money well spent. Not all systems can be easily or inexpensively altered for a basement remodel. Radiant and baseboard heating systems can service all or part of a basement. See the sidebar on p. 78 for information about these options.

Adapting your HVAC system

On the main floors of your house, vents for heated and cooled air are located along the outside walls, preferably in front of doors and windows, which are the areas of greatest heat loss or gain. Air to replenish the supply for conditioning is drawn (or "returned") from more central interior locations.

If an unfinished basement is heated or cooled at all, it is usually through a vent or two cut directly in the trunk supply line that feeds the main floors. For more effective and efficient heating and cooling in a finished basement, those vents should be blocked off and ductwork extended to the outside walls. Return-air grills to replenish the supply of air for conditioning should be installed in interior walls and connected to the existing return-air ducts.

To determine how many duct runs you need, an HVAC professional would do a load calculation, including window and door sizes and locations, type and depth of insulation, and room sizes. However, on a practical level, the number of runs is up to you, based largely on what you intend to do in the space. An exercise area doesn't need as much heat as a computer or TV room. Extra duct runs are easy to install now, before drywalling, while everything is open. The drawing at right shows the HVAC alterations done in our class basement.

Extending supply ducts. The best way to add ductwork for heating and cooling is to tap into an existing and nearby trunk supply line (the rectangular metal ducts). The process involves cutting a hole in the top of the supply duct, installing a 90-degree elbow, connecting pipe sections to where you want the air, and finishing with a 90-degree 4-in.-by-10-in. boot that diverts the air down toward the floor.

Cutting the hole in the top of the supply duct is the only tricky part. There are two ways to do it. The low-cost, low-tech solution is to punch a hole in the top of the duct with a hammer and screwdriver. Then, with tin snips, cut out pieces to make the hole at least 8 in. wide. There's little room between the duct and the flooring overhead, so you'll have to twist and turn to maneuver the snips. The hole will be pretty ragged.

Heating and air-conditioning systems in newer homes are often sized to serve a finished basement as well as the main floors of the house.

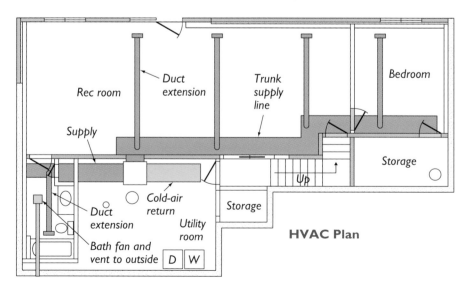

HVAC Plan

+ SAFETY FIRST

Fresh-cut tin is as sharp as a razor. I have bled freely on too many jobs when I didn't take the time to use gloves. Leather ones are helpful; the HVAC guys usually use Kevlar® gloves, the same material used for lightweight bulletproof vests.

SUPPLEMENTAL HEAT

If you can't extend your furnace's ducts to areas of your basement you'd like to be warmer, or if you just want to add a few degrees to a room, you might consider installing one or more of the following types of supplemental heating.

Radiant Heaters

I discovered the wonder of radiant heat a few years back in my own basement. It was always cold down there, and one particularly cold winter I grabbed a radiant heater from my shop and hung it from the ceiling. It was an amazing transformation. The electrical elements in radiant heaters don't heat the air, they heat objects in the room. (Think of the difference between standing in the sun and in nearby shade. The air temperature is about the same in both spots, but the sun's radiant heat makes you much hotter in the sun.) So the room air didn't feel warmer, but the chair was warm, the carpet was warm, and after I sat there for a bit, I felt warm too.

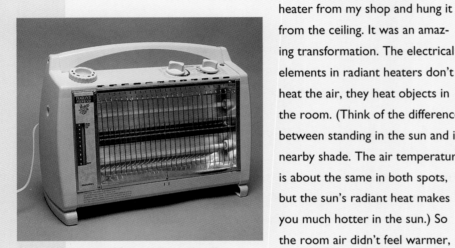

A portable radiant heater like this offers flexibility in supplementing heat. Permanently installed radiant heaters are also available.

Portable radiant heaters are common. Cove units mounted near the intersection of ceiling and wall direct the heat down, without taking up floor space or blowing air around. They're great for heating specific areas.

Baseboard Heaters

These heat by convection. That is, they warm the air, which rises and is replaced by cooler air, which is heated and also rises. The result is a convection flow and a room full of warm air. Baseboard heaters are relatively inexpensive, can be run manually or off thermostats for zone heating, and are easy to install. Run the wiring for cove

This electric baseboard heater is wired directly to a circuit and thermostat.

and baseboard heaters now (some may require 220-volt service). The units themselves are installed after the walls are painted and carpet laid.

In-Floor Heaters

These simple systems consist of electric heating mats or wire runs that can be installed under carpet, wood, and ceramic tile floors. They're more expensive than the other options, but a warm floor under cold feet is hard to beat, particularly in a bedroom or bathroom. I've installed a mat system, and with the help of an accommodating supplier, installation went fairly smoothly. Mats are safe even in bathroom floors, since the mats use a low-voltage DC current to provide a slow steady heat.

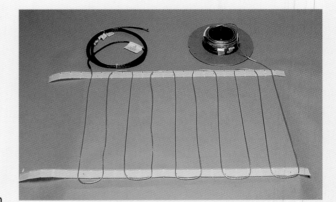

This in-floor heating system consists of copper wire stretched between plastic strips. Heat output is controlled by a thermostat. In use, the wire is covered by mortar and floor tile.

Next, make a flange by cutting a flat piece of tin several inches larger than the hole. In the center of this piece cut a neat 6-in.-dia. hole and attach the 90-degree elbow. Screw the flange over the hole in the top of the duct and seal the joints with silver tape. The rest involves simply connecting and taping pieces of duct pipe together.

Return-air. The return-air part of your system draws air into grills at floor level and up through the space between two wall studs to a return-air duct connected to the furnace. The number of return-air runs and the size of the grills depend

Extending HVAC Supply Duct

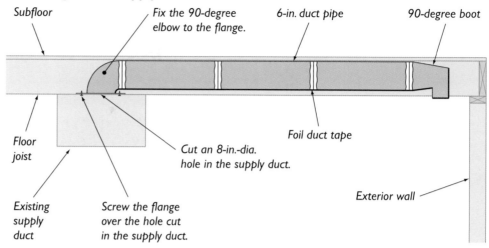

Subfloor

Fix the 90-degree elbow to the flange.

6-in. duct pipe

90-degree boot

Foil duct tape

Cut an 8-in.-dia. hole in the supply duct.

Floor joist

Existing supply duct

Screw the flange over the hole cut in the supply duct.

Exterior wall

After connecting to an existing HVAC supply line, run lines as needed, ending in a 90-degree boot.

Seal HVAC joints with foil tape to increase your system's efficiency.

HVAC Materials

The most common HVAC job in basement remodels is extending supply ducts. Ductwork is made of relatively lightweight galvanized metal. To extend each run, you'll need 6-in.-dia. duct, one 90-degree elbow to connect to the trunk supply, and a 90-degree, 4-in.-by-10-in. "boot," which connects to the duct and is covered by a grill. Duct is often sold unrolled in 2-ft. lengths. (The edges snap together to create a cylinder. If you have to cut a section to length, do so before snapping it into a cylinder—it's easier to cut when flat.) You'll need two hex-head, self-tapping metal screws to fix each section joint. Each joint on a duct run should also be sealed with foil tape. You'll need about 2 ft. per joint on a 6-in.-dia. duct. Buy a roll of metal strapping to support the duct along the length of long runs. It makes a stirrup around the pipe and attaches to the floor joists.

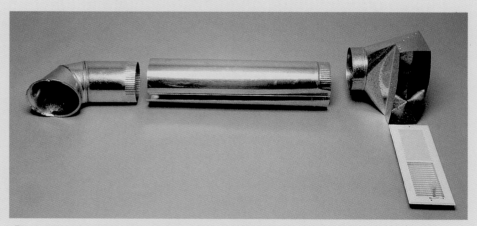

Duct extensions are assembled of lightweight galvanized metal parts. You may need several sections of 6-in. pipe.

PRO TIP

Duct tape may have thousands of uses, but taping ducts is not one of them. It deteriorates in the heat and dry air. For ducts, you need to use foil tape.

TRADE SECRET

If the joints in your HVAC system have not been taped (supply ducts, trunk lines, return-air ducts), you can increase the efficiency of your HVAC system by 10 to 15 percent by taping all the joints with foil tape.

IN DETAIL

Two good pairs of tin snips are needed for cutting ducts to extend supply lines. You'll need a pair that cuts straight, and a right-cutting and/or left-cutting snips that cuts circles without getting in its own way. Instead of snips, you can use a circle-cutting attachment for an electric drill. (An attachment costs about $70.) You may also need a right-angle attachment for the drill.

Helping Your Furnace Breathe

Gas furnaces need air to fuel their fires. Installed in an open basement, they have a lot of air to draw from. When you divide your basement into rooms, you're reducing the air easily available to your furnace (and gas water heater) for combustion. You need to make sure you take steps to provide that air. An HVAC specialist can figure out how much air you need and how to get it.

Or you can figure it out yourself. The BTUs required by a furnace or water heater are listed on their specification plates. To find the cubic feet of air they require, divide the total BTUs by 20. In our class basement, the furnace was 70,000 BTUs and the water heater 40,000 BTUs. Dividing the total of 110,000 BTUs by 20 indicated that the furnace needed 5,500 cu. ft. of available air. The room housing the furnace and water heater was 15 ft. by 16 ft. by 8 ft., for 1,920 cu. ft., so we needed access to 3,580 additional cu. ft. of combustion air. The adjacent rec room was 14.5 ft. by 48.5 by 8 ft., or 5,626 cu. ft. Accessing this air required the installation of only two louvered grills in the common wall between the rooms.

Code requires, at minimum, two grills that have 100 sq. in. of free area each, one within 1 ft. of the floor, one within 1 ft. of the ceiling. (Free area is the actual air space in the grill, after deducting the frame and grates.) Code also requires that grills have 1 sq. in. of free area per 1,000 BTUs of the appliances they service. (These grill requirements are not additive; use the larger of the two.) For 110,000 BTUs, we needed a total of 110 sq. in. of free area in two grills, or at least 55 sq. in. of free area per grill. So, just keeping with the minimum required size (100 sq. in. of free area per grill) satisfied the code.

Another option for pulling in combustion air is to install a louvered door to the mechanical room, again figuring free area for venting, and meeting the code minimums.

Note that local HVAC codes may vary. In my town, for example, we're not allowed to pull combustion air from a bathroom, nor can we access the mechanical room through a bathroom. Be sure to check your codes before proceeding.

Metal flashing defines the opening for a grill that will allow the movement of combustion air from the rec room into the furnace room.

on the amount of conditioned air delivered to the room. The air being pumped into the room must equal the air being pulled back to the furnace.

Here's how you figure out the return-air requirements for a room. To size it, figure the cross-sectional area of each supply duct you add to the room and add these together. The return-air grill you use must have as much free area (unobstructed by flanges and grates) as the total area of the ducts supplying air to the room.

Return-air grills fit into metal frames attached within 1 ft. of the floor to the wall studs. Install the frames now. If the wall won't be drywalled on the back side, enclose the return-air space by fixing sheet aluminum or foil-covered cardboard made just for return-air ducts to the studs. Connect the between-studs ducts to the furnace return-air trunk line with lengths of round ductwork. The cross-sectional area of the runs back to the trunk line must also equal the square inches of supply dumped into the room.

Combustion air. If you have a gas furnace, codes require that it have sufficient "combustion" air to feed the burner. See the sidebar on the facing page for more information. Note, this is not optional; asphyxiating your furnace could produce a dangerous gas buildup in your home.

Bath fan. If you're adding a bathroom and doing your own HVAC work, now is the time to install a fan. If you're subcontracting, make sure bath-fan venting is in your HVAC bid—it's easy to overlook. Codes require that the bath fan be vented to the outdoors. If the vent is longer than 2 ft., it must be a minimum of 4 in. in diameter. Otherwise, its size can vary according to the cfm (cubic feet per minute) of the fan. Although it's not required by code, consider using insulated duct, because uninsulated ducts vented outdoors can sweat in the winter and cause water stains on the ceiling.

A large sheet of aluminum forms the back of this return-air setup. Drywall will enclose the front. Air will be drawn up through the opening at the bottom to a return-air trunk line above.

Here, two ducts were needed to deliver sufficient air to the furnace's return-air trunk line.

IN DETAIL

To cut PVC pipe, a hacksaw works nicely for pipe that is already in place. A miter saw does a great job when you can bring the pipe to it. You can de-bur the cut ends with a file.

TRADE SECRET

If your home is older and the stacks and vents are cast iron or galvanized metal, do yourself a favor and hire a pro to cut into them. It's just not fun.

Plumbing

Basements in many newer houses were built with the groundwork for basic plumbing services installed, including a bathroom sink drain and vent stack, drains for a toilet and tub-shower, and possibly some water hookups. If yours is such a house, or if you had a plumber install basic services as part of your remodel, it is relatively easy to do the next, "rough-in" stage of plumbing.

Drains

Drains remove waste water and sewage from sinks, tubs, toilets, and washing machines. All drains are also attached, somewhere in the system, to a vent that extends up through the roof of your house. The vent keeps air and water pressure in the system equal, preventing water from being siphoned out of sink and tub traps and toilet bowls. This keeps sewer gas out of your house.

Sinks. Bathroom sinks are most common in basement remodels. But the procedure for installation is the same for sinks in wet bars, kitchenettes, or elsewhere.

The sink will hook up to a 2-in. PVC pipe called the vent stack, which connects to the waste and vent systems. At this time, you need to add a T-joint that will connect the stack to the sink trap. Inserted into the stack about 16 in. to 19 in. above the floor, this "reducer T" provides a horizontal 1½-in. dia. connection positioned to accommodate the sink trap, as shown in the drawing on the facing page. (The drawing also shows what to do if the vent stack isn't near the sink location. If the sink is between 5 ft. and 8 ft. from the vent stack, use a 2-in. diameter drain extension.) Installation of the reducer T is shown in the photos. After installation, remember to close the open end of the stub with duct tape to keep sewer gas from escaping.

Toilet. The in-floor drain will already be in place, either from original construction or your retrofit. (See the drawing on the facing page.) You won't need to do anything more to it until you hook up the toilet, as described in Chapter 10.

Tub-shower. Plumbing a tub-shower involves preparing the existing drain line, positioning and fixing the tub-shower unit in place, and installing the drain kit and P-trap to the drain line. The drawing on the facing page shows all the connections. All the parts are PVC, so they're easy to cut and glue together.

In addition to the fiberglass tub-shower unit, you'll need a drain kit that includes the overflow drain, the tub drain, the "T" to tie them together, and the parts to fit them to the tub. You'll also need to buy a P-trap, which connects the drain kit to the 2-in. drain line in the floor, and some 1½-in. pipe and a 1½-in.-to-2 in. reducer to make the connections. All these parts can be purchased at home centers or hardware stores.

The 2-in. drain line is buried in the floor but not cemented over. Dig away the gravel to expose it, and remove the plastic "knockout" over the end of the pipe. Set the tub-shower in place, with its drain hole over the exposed line. (Insulate behind the unit before you set it; it's much easier than trying to shove insulation between the studs with a stick after the unit is nailed in.) Assemble the drain kit and P-trap without glue and hold the assembly in place. If the assembly doesn't fit comfortably in the hole, chip away concrete and remove gravel until it does.

When you're confident you can make the connections, level the tub-shower unit and nail through its flange across the back into every stud and on 12-in. centers down the sides. I use 2-in. galvanized roofing nails. Predrill the fiberglass and nail carefully so as not to chip the edge of the shower. If you're a novice with a hammer, use screws, but make sure they're galvanized or some other rust-resistant metal.

Sink Rough-In

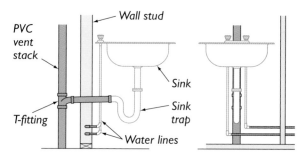

PVC vent stack

Wall stud

Sink

Sink trap

T-fitting

Water lines

Note: Ghosted fittings added at hookup.

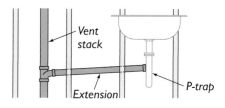

Vent stack

Extension

P-trap

If your sink is set away from the vent stack, connect it with a drain extension that drops toward the stack ¼ in. for each foot of run.

Toilet Rough-In

Wall stud

Bottom plate

Cold-water line

Position water line about 5 in. above the floor.

In-floor drain

Note: Ghosted fittings are installed at hookup.

Position water-line stub 8 to 12 in. to the side of the in-floor drain centerline.

To connect the sink to the drain and vent stack, cut out a section of the stack with a hacksaw (above). Clean up the cut edges with a file or rasp. Using the fittings appropriate to the type of pipe in your home, coat the mating surfaces with cleaner/prep solution and then adhesive (top right). Quickly slide the pieces together — the glue grabs fast. Insert (without glue now) a piece of **PVC** into the bathroom so the drywall can be fitted around it (right).

Tub-Shower Drain Hookup

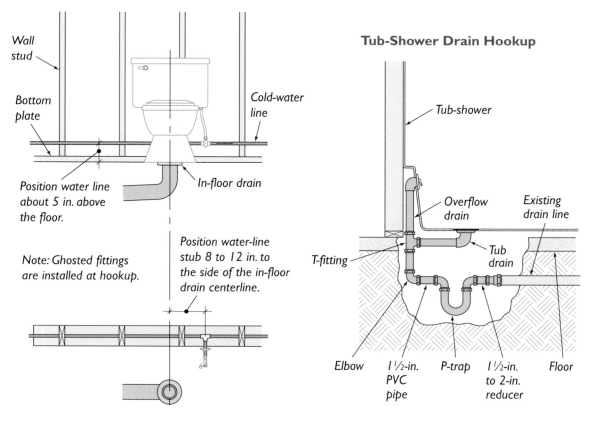

Tub-shower

Overflow drain

Existing drain line

T-fitting

Tub drain

Elbow

1 ½-in. PVC pipe

P-trap

1 ½-in. to 2-in. reducer

Floor

TRADE SECRET

When you've set the tub-shower in place, you need to protect it. You'll be in it and on it while drywalling, painting, and finishing the plumbing. At the very least put a good tarp over the tub and tape it in place. You can also use a covering, such as Scratch Protection®, which you paint on and peel off, or a tub liner, such as Pro Tecta® Tub Kit. Both products are available from Protective Products International.

IN DETAIL

If you need to run a water line parallel to a floor joist, code requires that you fix the pipe to the joist with plastic clips at least every 5 ft. This also helps prevent rattling pipes.

Washing Machine Hookup

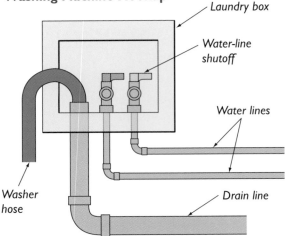

Laundry box

Water-line shutoff

Water lines

Washer hose

Drain line

Assemble and glue the drain kit and P-trap to the in-floor drain and tub-shower overflow. Working in back of the tub on your knees, and reaching into where you can't see, isn't easy; it challenges even the pros. But take heart. If you cut and dry-fit everything to make sure the pieces fit the space, and then glue them together, you should succeed. If you make mistakes, it's PVC; any mistakes you make while fitting are only costly if you don't redo.

Washing machine. A washer requires sources of hot and cold water and a drain, all of which may already exist in your basement or may need to be provided. Water-supply lines are relatively easy to run (see the facing page). But I recommend engaging a professional if you have to install a drain line. The easiest way to hook up a washer is to buy a "laundry box." As shown in the drawing above, this plastic compartment houses a connection for the drain and connections and shutoffs for the water lines.

Sump pump. Now is also the time to cut, fit, and install the PVC pipes that discharge the sump pump. Remember that codes require a sump pump to discharge outside the house, not into your house sewer system.

Plumbing Codes

These are the most common code considerations for tub, sink, and toilet. Check with your local codes department for other regulations, and for plumbing situations not covered here.

- **Tub-shower.** A tub is required to have an overflow drain, which is predrilled in the tub. A PVC drain kit, P-trap, and reducers will complete the hookup. The tub spout must be at least 6 in. above the tub rim. A tub-shower must have its own vent stack.

- **Toilet and sink.** There must be 15 in. of free space each side of the center of the toilet drain, for a total clear width of 30 in. A sink with a 1½-in. drain can be no more than 5 ft. from the vent stack; with a 2-in. drain the distance is 8 ft. If the toilet and sink don't share the same vent stack, check with the codes department.

- **Water-supply lines.** Any water line that runs through a stud closer than 1¼ in. to the edge of the stud must be covered with a nail-on metal protective strip.

- **Sump pump.** The line draining the pump must run to the outdoors where the water will end up in the ground or in a storm sewer. Sump pumps must not drain into the sanitary sewer system.

- **Handicap accessibility.** If you're planning on wheelchair accessibility, or wish to meet ADA requirements, check with your codes department for the required clearances and fixture positions.

- **Inspection.** It's your responsibility to call for an inspection before you cover up plumbing with insulation and drywall. If you forget, inspectors can require you to remove whatever is in the way of an inspection.

Running water lines to a tub-shower is more complicated than running them to a sink. Supply lines at bottom right serve the sink and stool, too.

Typical Tub-Shower Hookup

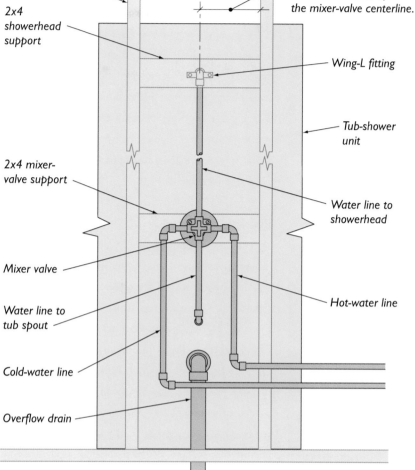

Stud

2x4 showerhead support

2x4 mixer-valve support

Mixer valve

Water line to tub spout

Cold-water line

Overflow drain

Position studs at least 8 in. on each side of the mixer-valve centerline.

Wing-L fitting

Tub-shower unit

Water line to showerhead

Hot-water line

Water-supply lines

In modern homes, water-supply lines are copper or, in an increasing number of communities, plastic. (See Plumbing Materials on p. 87.) Copper lines must be soldered together, a process called "sweating." The results are lovely to behold but require skill to achieve. Students in my classes who have made the effort to learn often enjoy sweating copper joints. If you're interested, the sidebar on p. 86 introduces the basics; if not, consider plastic (if codes allow), or subcontract the work to a pro.

For both copper and plastic systems, you'll need to tap into existing hot- and cold-water lines near the sink, tub-shower, or washer. Even if you're doing your own installation, I suggest having a plumber do this part. Have the plumber install shutoffs at the connections, which will make it much easier to install the new pipe.

The drawing above and those on p. 83 show water line connections for typical basement fixtures. Run new lines between wall studs from the existing service overhead down to the level of the fixtures. You'll usually need to run lines horizontally, too, through holes bored in the joists or studs. I run both lines below the drain line (where possible) and one water line at least 1 in. above the other. That way, the copper lines

SWEATING COPPER

A tubing cutter cuts copper neatly and quickly. A small one, shown here, can be used to cut existing pipe in place.

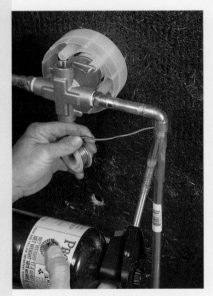

After cleaning and coating the mating surfaces with flux, assemble the joint and sweat it with solder heated by a propane torch. (The plastic fitting is a tub-shower mixer valve.)

Running copper water lines seems intimidating initially, but many in my classes find it both fun and rewarding. The most difficult task is tying into the existing lines, which I suggest you have a plumber do for you. Have the plumber install shutoffs at the points of connection. Code doesn't require them, but if you have shutoffs, you can work on the individual hookups without shutting off water to the rest of the house.

Sweating a Joint

You can cut copper pipe with a hacksaw, but a tubing cutter (shown in the photo above left) makes a neater job. Slip the jaw over the pipe and tighten the knurled knob. Roll the cutter around the tube, re-tighten the knob to press the cutting wheel tighter against the copper, and roll it around the pipe again. Repeat until the tube is cut through.

To prepare the pipe for soldering, clean at least 1/2 in. of the end of the pipe with emery cloth or a special steel brush made to slip over the end and burnish the surface. Clean the inside surface of the female end of the fitting with emery cloth.

Slip the pieces together to check the fit. Disassemble and make sure the joints are clean and dry. Solder will not adhere if the surfaces are wet or soiled. Brush flux on both the male and female ends and assemble the joint.

I use a small propane torch (available at most hardware stores) to sweat joints. Light the torch and adjust for an even blue flame. Heat the joint from one side only and touch the solder to the opposite side. When the parts are hot enough, the solder will melt and flow. Feed the solder wire into the joint until you see it flow around to the side where the flame is heating the pipe. If you want professional-looking joints, wipe quickly around

Tools and materials for sweating copper include (from top down) solder, tubing cutter, cleaning brush, flux, flux brush, and fittings.

the sealed joint with a rag to clean up the extra solder. Remember, the joint is hot, so be careful.

Sweating joints is as easy as that. But it's a good idea to practice on some scrap pieces until it *is* as easy as it sounds.

Making a Run

When you get the hang of it, you can prepare and assemble a whole run. Solder each joint in turn. Then open the shutoff valve and check for leaks. If you have some, shut the water off, drain the lines, and repair. You can repair some leaks by heating the joint to eliminate moisture, pushing some flux into the hole (when the pipe is cool), and melting solder into the leak. This takes some patience, because if you heat the flux too hot, it can burn and the solder won't take. If this doesn't work, melt the solder, remove the fitting, and install a new one. Don't try to re-use the old ones.

A quick tip if you're installing water lines to a tub-shower: Solder the threaded pipe fittings to the copper lines first, before you screw the couplings to the mixer valve. That way the heat of soldering won't damage the O rings in the valve.

won't be in each other's way when you install the 90-degree elbows that turn the lines out of the wall for hookups to sinks, showers, and so on.

To prevent pipes from puncture by drywall screws or nails, drill holes at least 1¼ in. back from the edge. A 1-in. hole dead center in a stud will be 1¼ in. away from both edges. But it's not worth taking time to measure to the center of each stud. If the wall is unfinished on the back side, it won't matter that the pipes run closer than 1¼ in. to the unfinished surface. If the wall will be finished on both sides, code requires that you nail a short metal protector strip on studs where pipe is closer than 1¼ in. from the edge.

In addition to water-line connections, you'll need a large-diameter, can-shaped drill bit called a hole saw (shown on p. 132) to cut a hole in your fiberglass tub-shower unit for the mixer valve. Size will depend on the valve you buy.

Wiring

Homeowners are often surprised to learn that they can legally wire their own basements. Basic wiring is not unduly complicated and it can be done safely.

That's not to say that electricity is not dangerous; it is. But in your basement you can install most of the electrical system without hooking anything up to the panel. None of it is hot, so it's safe. I encourage my students to hire an electrician to wire up the panel. This must be done right

+ SAFETY FIRST

The number one rule for working with electricity is to work with the power off. The second rule is to treat the wire as if it's hot, even if you know it's not. It's a good idea to wear gloves and rubber-soled shoes. If you do come across a hot wire, there'll be less chance of grounding it through your body.

Plumbing Materials

For basement remodeling, you just need to know about three materials for drain and water lines: PVC, copper, and CPVC or PEX. For drains, you'll need rigid polyvinyl chloride (PVC), a white plastic pipe. For water lines, you'll need copper tubing or, if your codes allow it, CPVC or PEX, the newer plastic water lines.

- **PVC.** For drains, you'll buy mostly schedule-40 PVC. Lighter-gauge plastics are used for P-traps and some drain lines, but schedule 40 is an industry standard for anything that goes in a wall. (Your codes department can tell you what kind of pipe to use for your specific applications.) Most drain runs require 2-in.-dia. pipe.

Measure the straight runs and buy a little extra. Buy T connections and elbows as needed. You'll need some primer to soften the PVC pipe and to remove the paraffin left over from the manufacturing process. Be sure to buy the PVC adhesive that is specified for plumbing applications.

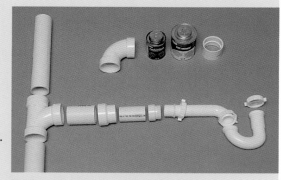

PVC drain lines use fittings like these.

- **Plastic water lines.** CPVC (chlorinated polyvinyl chloride) and PEX plastic piping are relatively new, and some communities, like mine, don't allow their use for water lines yet. Like PVC drains, plastic systems are much easier to install than traditional ones. CPVC systems, like PVC drains, are made of rigid pipe and various fittings all glued together. In the PEX system, barbed fittings join the pipe, Ts, elbows, and so on with the aid of a special tool—no torches or solder. The pipe flexes around corners and is easy to snake through studs and joists. Connected to a manifold, flexible PEX pipe can eliminate many fittings, allowing continuous runs from the manifold to a sink, shower, or other fixture. PEX may be more expensive than copper to buy, but a plumber friend of mine says he can install a PEX system in half the time it takes him to install a copper system.

- **Copper.** In most bathrooms the hot-water line services two fixtures (tub-shower and sink) so code allows the use of ½-in. pipe. The cold-water line serves three (tub-shower, sink, toilet), for which code requires ¾-in pipe. Buy Type L pipe, which is less expensive and also a bit easier to cut than Type M, made for commercial use. You'll need a variety of copper elbows and Ts, as well as caps to close the pipes until you install the fixtures. You'll also need solder and flux for making the joints. Flux cleans the copper before soldering and helps draw the hot liquid solder into the joint. Use lead-free solid-core solder. Your plumber or a knowledgeable hardware store salesperson can help you get what you need.

PRO TIP

When placing switch boxes, be aware of the way doors swing on your plan; you don't want a switch hidden behind an open door.

TRADE SECRET

A circuit's connection to the service panel does not have to come from the last box on the circuit. For instance, in the plan on the facing page, the outlet circuit in the bedroom runs under the service panel. It makes more sense to connect that circuit to an outlet right below the panel than to run wire all the way back from the last outlet. Because the outlets are wired parallel rather than in series, you can tie into the panel from anywhere on the circuit.

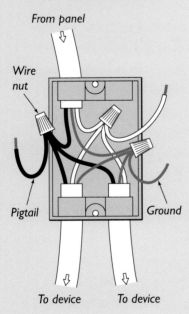

From panel

Wire nut

Pigtail   Ground

To device   To device

or you and your family could be at risk of fire or electrocution. The electrical inspector will make sure you don't make serious errors (and that you conform to code). But it's also a good idea to have a knowledgeable electrician check your work.

That said, there is really no reason for you to shy away from the grunt work of wiring: nailing up boxes, boring holes, pulling wire, even "making up" the outlets and switches. It will save you money and is immensely satisfying.

Almost all basement electrical work involves providing 110-volt service to lights, switches, and wall outlets. A laundry room will require a 220-volt outlet for the drier. Hot tubs and other special fittings may require special wiring. When you install the electrical system, it's also sensible to run wire for phones, TVs, and computer networking. See the sidebar on p. 92 for a discussion of electrical materials and fixtures.

Locating fixtures

When you planned your project, you figured out, more-or-less, the type, number, and position of electrical fixtures. To get started, use the plan you made then. The number of outlets, lights, and switches on your plan determined the cost of the electrical permit, but the plan isn't necessarily final. As long as the placement of your devices meets code, you can alter your plans, putting extra outlets where you've added an entertainment center, for example, or just wherever you think you'll need more plugs. Remember, the inspectors aren't there to harass you; they're there to keep your installation safe and in compliance.

The first step is to nail up boxes for every outlet, light, or switch. I walk around with my hammer and a magic marker and on each stud where I want an outlet, phone, TV, or computer connection, I draw a line at the height of my hammer handle and nail a box to the stud centered on the line. Simple. Some people check the

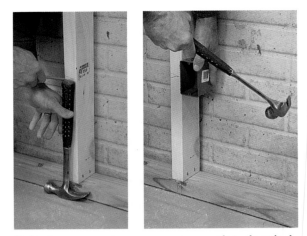

Nail a box every place you want an outlet, electrical fixture, and switch. A hammer handle-length is a convenient height for outlet boxes.

height of the outlets upstairs and duplicate that, but it's probably the height of the original electrician's hammer handle.

Switches are usually centered at 46 in. from the floor. Where necessary, switches and outlets must clear countertop and backsplash heights. Bathroom vanities are usually 34 in. high. Kitchen or bar counters are 36 in. high. Backsplashes are usually 4 in. high. Make sure you check the dimensions of the units you're buying.

You can place wall-mounted lights or other individual fixtures at any height you wish. Boxes for ceiling-light fixtures are mounted on the floor joists. Position those by measurement from your plan or by eye. If you want them in a row, measurement is best. Recessed-light fixtures and bathroom fans contain their own box, so nail the entire fixture in place now. Run a line for makeup or medicine-cabinet lights into the appropriate bathroom wall; you'll hook up the line to the built-in boxes in these fixtures later.

Circuits: Planning and wiring home runs

Next, decide how best to tie all those boxes into circuits that will connect to breakers in the main service panel. Electricians call these circuits home runs. Here, I'll call each outlet, light, or switch a device, another electrician's term.

Most circuits in a basement will be #14 wire, and code allows up to 10 devices that draw current on one #14 home run. Since switches don't draw current, they do not count when adding up the load on a circuit. For basement remodeling, it is simplest to run the lights off one home run and the outlets off another. Usually there will be several home runs, some for outlets, some for lights, and some separate ones for the bathroom. You may also want a dedicated run (only one device) for a refrigerator, freezer, wall heater, computer, or other appliance that you want to isolate from interference or load. When you lay out circuits, an electrical inspector can be an invaluable aid.

The wiring plan for our class basement is shown at right; a similar sketch will be a big help in planning your own home runs. On one #14 run, we ran all of the outlets for the bedroom, picked up a few outlets from one wall of the rec room, and included the light in the storage area and the bedroom. The rest of the rec room outlets made up another #14 home run, and the bathroom light and fan a third. A 12/2 (20 amp) dedicated run to the bathroom took care of code requirements for that room.

We used a lot of can lights in the rec room, so to meet code two separate home runs were needed to carry that load. One of the runs was switched in three different locations; it required a run of 14/3 wire between the switches.

Running wire

You have nailed up all the boxes, and you know which boxes need to tie together for home runs. Now you connect the dots.

Wire must pass through studs or joists between devices on each circuit and the panel. (To be precise, sheathed cable containing a bundle of insulated wires passes through the holes, but nearly

Electrical Codes

Here are some common electrical requirements for a typical basement remodel.

- **Outlets.** Codes require an outlet within 6 ft. of a doorway or opening in a wall and at least every 12 ft. around the perimeter of each room (except the bathroom). When you place outlets, measure the 12 ft. around and through corners, but not through a doorway. Codes also require that a 6-ft. cord running along a wall be able to reach an outlet from any point on the wall. An outlet is required on any wall longer than 2 ft., and in any hallway longer than 10 ft. There is no rule as to how high the outlet must be off the floor, but it can't be higher than 46 in. and still count for the 12-ft. rule.

- **Bathroom.** Codes require only one outlet in a bathroom, but it must be a GFCI (Ground Fault Circuit Interrupter) within 3 ft. of the sink and on a separate 12/2-wire home run to the panel. Lights and fan can tie into another circuit.

- **Circuits.** In general, you can service 10 devices (anything that draws current) on one 14-gauge circuit, and 12 devices on one 12-gauge circuit.

- **Wire.** 14-gauge wire must connect to a circuit breaker rated no more than 15 amps, and 12-gauge wire must run to a 20-amp or less breaker. Wires must be stapled to a stud within 8 in. of plastic boxes, and every 4 ft. along a run, unless the wire is running through studs. If a wire comes within 1 1/4 in. of the edge of a stud, you must nail a metal plate on the edge to protect the wire from puncture by a nail or a screw.

- **Smoke detector.** You're required to have a smoke detector in every bedroom and one at the bottom of the stairs. Some codes require them to be hard wired to the electrical system in specified existing rooms in the house if you remodel.

- **Inspection.** Get your electrical inspection before you drywall.

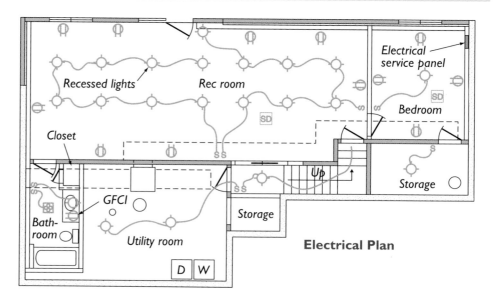

Recessed lights

Rec room

Electrical service panel

Bedroom

Closet

GFCI

Bathroom

Utility room

D W

Storage

Up

Storage

Electrical Plan

PRO TIP

Bore holes at least 1 1/2 in. from the bottom edge of a joist to avoid compromising its strength.

IN DETAIL

To do the electrical work described here, you'll need an electric-wire cutter with notches on the blade for stripping wire and a circuit tester. I have a tester that lights up when it is held near a live wire. It's handy for testing to see if a circuit is "hot," without unhooking or tapping into the wires. You'll also need an electric drill, and a 3/4-in. bit for drilling holes to run wire. I like to use a regular power drill rather than a cordless drill. Boring 3/4-in. holes in dozens of studs eats up a battery in no time. I like to use a screw-type auger bit, because it pulls through the wood with less effort than a spade bit.

You can run several lines of sheathed cable through a 1-in. hole to make the wiring tidier.

everyone refers to it at this stage as wire.) I bore 3/4-in.-dia. holes about a foot above boxes for wall outlets and switches. This allows the wire to be fastened to the stud within 8 in. of the box, as required by code. Holes between lights can be any distance from the fixtures. The 3/4-in. hole accommodates more than one wire if need be.

Bore holes for the wire about 1 ft. above outlet boxes.

Run wire between boxes on the same circuit through the holes in the studs.

Code requires the holes to be at least 1 1/4 in. back from the edge of the stud. A 3/4-in. hole bored in the center of the stud meets code; if you're off, you'll just need to nail protective plates on the studs. Never drill a hole closer than 1 1/2 in. from the bottom edge of a joist; doing so can compromise the joist's load-bearing capacity.

Note that cable TV wire and computer wire can be run together, but should be in a separate set of holes from the electrical service. The magnetic fields that accompany electrical runs can cause interference on some TV channels and in some computer wire. Phone lines can run in the same holes as electrical wire.

Now you're ready to run wire for the circuits. The procedure is the same for all circuits, whether they serve outlets, lights, or hard-wired fixtures.

Insert wire into the boxes through knockout holes. Make sure there's at least 6 in. of wire protruding from the box.

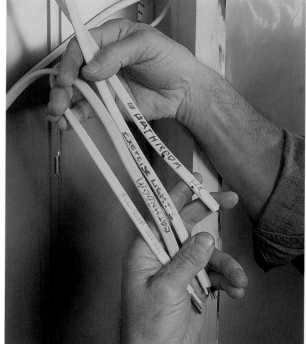

All home runs end at the service panel. Pull enough wire to extend below the panel.

With a magic marker, write the name of each circuit on its wire at the service panel.

Code requires wires be stapled tight to a stud within 8 in. of each box.

Lay the coil of wire on the floor near the last box on the circuit and pull the wire to the next box through the holes in the studs. Tap out a tab on the top of the second box (a screwdriver works well) and pull the wire through it. Cut the wire so at least 6 in. sticks out of the box.

Back at the first box, cut the wire from the coil, making sure you have enough to thread through the box with 6 in. protruding. The first two boxes are now connected. Do the same thing from the second box to the third, and on down the line. Then run the wire from the last box back to the panel. There, pull enough wire so that it hangs past the bottom of the panel.

For light circuits, it's best to wire the lights and switch together in each circuit; then pull the home run from the switch to the panel.

With a magic marker, write the name of the circuit on the panel-end of the wire, for example, "Rec room outlet." It's very important to do this. Otherwise, when your electrician comes to connect the panel, he or she won't have a clue what the wires are for.

Once all the wire is pulled, code requires that it be secured. Wires going into plastic boxes need to be stapled tight within 8 in. of the box. Wire running along the length of a joist or stud needs to be stapled tight every 4 lin. ft. I use staples made for electrical wire.

Circuit Basics

Electrical circuits are wired in one of two ways. In a parallel circuit, power flows continually through the circuit. Even if one device connected to the circuit malfunctions, the power will still flow to the other devices. In a series circuit, power flows from one device to the next. If a device malfunctions, it breaks the circuit and all devices downstream lose power.

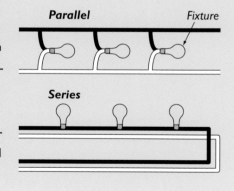

ELECTRICAL MATERIALS

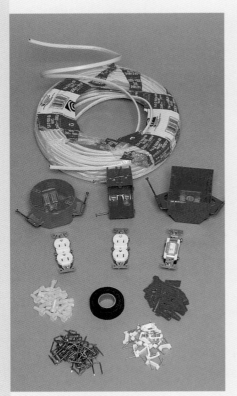

Basic electrical materials include (from top down): sheathed wire, boxes, outlets and switches, wire nuts, electrician's tape, and staples.

It's easy to be overwhelmed by the hundreds of electrical fittings and fixtures in a big home center or even in your local hardware store. Fortunately, for most basement remodels, electrical needs are simple.

Wire

Electrical wire is sold by its size (gauge) and the number of conductors in the plastic-coated bundle. You'll need only two, possibly three, types of bundled wire (often called Romex®, the name of a common brand). Most of your basement will need wire designated 14/2, which is a bundle of two 14-gauge shielded conductors (black and white), and an unshielded (bare) ground wire. By code, 14/2 wire will run on 15-amp circuits. If you're wiring a bathroom, you'll need the heavier-gauge 12/2. And you'll probably need some 14/3 wire (three conductors and one ground) for three-way switches or smoke detectors.

I figure about 20 ft. of 14/2 wire for each plastic box or light fixture, and I measure to determine amounts of other wire for specific items. Order more than you need; it's cheaper than driving for more. For our class basement, we had 42 boxes and light fixtures, and we bought 820 ft. of wire. We used 750 ft. You may also need cable TV line, computer lines and phone wire. Measure the runs and buy more than enough.

Boxes

Wires for outlets, switches, lights, and other fixtures must be housed in special boxes at the point of connection. Buy plastic boxes, not metal, which are for exposed or commercial wiring. Each box is stamped inside with its volume in cubic inches and the number of connectors of various types it will hold. In general, for single outlets and switches, use rectangular 18-cu.-in. boxes. Buy double or triple boxes for double or triple outlets and switches. If lots of wires will come together in a single box, simply buy a larger box.

Ceiling lights and smoke detectors are best attached to round plastic boxes. For a heavy ceiling fixture, buy a heavy-duty box built to carry the weight. To center a light between two joists, buy a plastic box mounted on an adjustable metal rod that nails up between the joists.

Count the number of outlets, switches, and fixtures on your plan, and buy two or three extra boxes; it's easy to miss one or two in the count. You can use 18-cu.-in. boxes for cable TV, phone, and computer locations, too.

Outlets and Switches

There are some really cheap outlets and switches out there. They're probably okay for very low-use areas, but I suggest you buy at least one grade up; the extra quality is worth a few cents more. You'll need 15-amp outlets for 14/2 circuits and 20-amp outlets for 12/2 circuits. The capacity is stamped on the outlet. Code requires that you install a GFCI outlet (Ground Fault Circuit Interrupter) in the bathroom for safety.

Most of your switches will be single pole, that is, they switch lights or outlets on and off from one place. To switch lights from more than one location, you'll need double pole switches (inexplicably called three-way switches) at both locations. If you are switching from more than two locations, each additional location needs a four-way switch. Buy switches rated for the amperage of the circuit.

If you want to install dimmer switches, buy higher quality ones. Because they absorb the power not going to the light, they get hot in use. The cheap ones burn out quickly. Check the power rating on the switch; it must be able to carry at least the assigned power load (total watts of the lights controlled), or it could overheat.

Recessed Lighting

Don't buy really cheap can lights (as they're called in the trade) that are not UL approved. If you're going to insulate the ceiling for sound-proofing, make sure the can lights are listed for insulated installations. Use the proper bulb size; most good can lights are thermally protected, which means the fixture shuts down if it gets too hot. Using the wrong-sized bulb will guarantee the fixture will shut off, cool down, turn on, heat up, shut down . . . which can be irritating.

Staples and Wire Nuts

Electricians use flattened U-shaped staples made specifically for holding electrical cable against wood. There are several types. You'll need at least a box of 100, possibly two boxes for larger remodels. Wire nuts are plastic connectors that you twist onto two or more wires to hold them together. They are color-coded to wire size and number of connections. You'll mostly need nuts for 2 to 5 wires of the 14-gauge size; they're usually yellow. You'll need at least 3 for each outlet and switch; a box of 100 should get you by. For multiple-wire connections, you will also need some nuts of the next larger size (usually red). Probably around 25 of those will do.

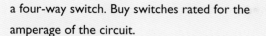

Making up a switch box

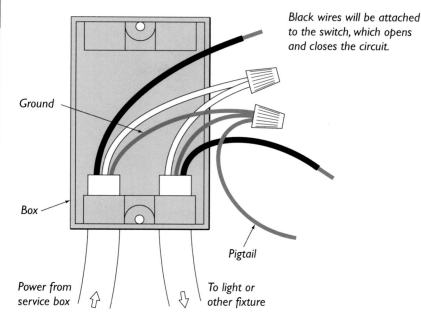

Black wires will be attached to the switch, which opens and closes the circuit.

Ground

Box

Pigtail

Power from service box

To light or other fixture

Switches. The simplest switching connection is shown in the drawing above. The switch can attach to the circuit at any point. The switch can itself be on a circuit with other devices (if the lights it controls don't overload that circuit). Or you can make a run from the switch back to the service panel.

Be sure to label all the cable in a switch box so that you know which wire is power, which is switch, and, for multiple boxes, which switch controls which light. (If there are multiple wires in an outlet box, label those, too.) If you forget to label before you insulate and drywall, it's a guessing game when it's time to make up those boxes.

Making up boxes

In the next step, you'll prepare the wires in a box for connection to an outlet, switch, light, or other appliance. Electricians call this making up a box. At its simplest, this involves joining the wires from the two cables in each box and adding short lengths of wire called pigtails, which will be hooked up to the device. (At this stage it is important to distinguish between the sheathed cable and the wires bundled inside it.)

TRADE SECRET

Note that all shielded TV cable is not alike. Some of the cheaper material is likely to pick up interference from your house wire or other stray electrical signals. You can usually buy the stuff the pros use from your local cable company, at about the same price as the local "good deal" and end up with a better deal.

IN DETAIL

Electricians assure me that three-way switches are really simple. And, for someone who works on them all the time, three-way switches *are* simple. My three-way track record, however, is a bit sketchy. I've had lights that would go on, but not go off, and ones that would go off, but not on. There are as many variations to switching and getting power as you have switches and numbers of lights. So if you have three-way switches, I strongly suggest getting some professional advice.

Slit the plastic sheathing of cables in the box to expose the wires inside (above). Bare ½ in. of the insulated wires, then twist a wire nut on the colored pairs from each cable and a pigtail (right).

Tuck the joined wires out of the way in the box, ready to attach to the outlet or switch later on.

Outlet boxes are wired in parallel. (See Circuit Basics on p. 91.) Here's how you do it: With a utility knife, strip off each cable's outer sheathing, leaving at least ¼ in. of sheathing inside the box. That will expose a black wire, a white wire, and a bare copper ground in each cable. Bare about ½ in. of the copper at the ends of the insulated wires. For pigtails, cut a piece of cable about 6 in. long from the spool or scrap, and strip out the separate wires. Bare about ½ in. of one end of the two insulated wires. (Sometimes I strip both ends of the pigtails now.)

Now bundle the three bare ground wires together (one from each cable in the box and the pigtail) and twist on a wire nut — tightly. Test the connection with a healthy pull on each wire; if one pulls out, redo the connection. Bundle and wire-nut the three white wires and then the black ones. You won't hook up the device until after you've drywalled and painted, so push the wires to the back of the box to get them out of the way. The last box on the run doesn't need pigtails, because the wire doesn't pass through to another box. Just strip back the cable sheathing and roll the wires back into the box.

Making up switches. In the simplest switch box, power comes to the switch and then goes to the light or outlet. The switch breaks or completes the circuit to turn the light off and on. To do this, switches are wired into the circuit in series rather than in parallel. To make up the switch box, wire-nut the grounds together with a pigtail, just as you would an outlet box. (See Making Up a Switch Box on p. 93.) Then, wire-nut the two whites together without a pigtail, which passes this part of the circuit through the box and on up to the light. For now, leave the black from the power and the black from the light free. Later, you'll connect them to the switch. When the switch is "on," power will flow through the black to the light, and back down through the white. When the switch is "off," the circuit is broken and the light goes off.

Making up lights. Like outlet boxes, lights are connected in parallel so that a defective bulb in one won't interrupt current to the others.

Making up a Box for an Outlet or Light

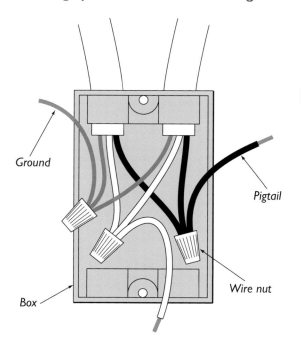

Ground

Box

Pigtail

Wire nut

Connecting a Single Light (or other fixture) to a Switch

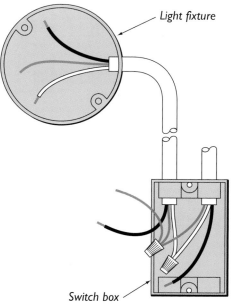

Light fixture

Switch box

Wiring a Light Circuit

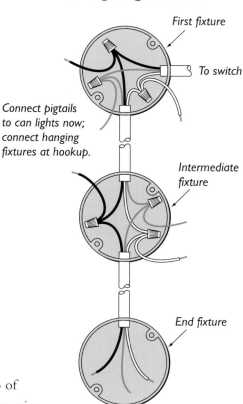

First fixture

To switch

Connect pigtails to can lights now; connect hanging fixtures at hookup.

Intermediate fixture

End fixture

Lights connected to boxes are made up as for outlets, and the fixtures are installed and connected later. (See Chapter 10.) For a single light, or the last one on a run, you simply leave the three wires in the box alone, to tie into the light when you mount it at finish. You've already fixed recessed can lights in place, so connect those to the circuit now. (See the photo on p. 74.) As the drawing shows (above right), power lines run in from the switch, and at each fixture you join the blacks, whites, and grounds together with pigtails. Then you connect the pigtails to the fixture.

Light to remodel by

Before you can drywall the basement ceiling, you need to remove all the old lights and wiring. That leaves you in a bind. Unless you have night vision scopes, you'll need more than natural light for finishing your basement. One option is to use auxiliary lighting, such as set-about job lights or old lamps. These lights work, but they can get in the way, and must be moved constantly.

Another option is to fire up one or two of your new lighting circuits (a good reason to wire your lights on separate circuits). If you're using can lights, all you have to do is screw in some bulbs and you have light. The cans are recessed and out of the way. If you're not using can lights, you can buy some inexpensive light sockets for bare bulbs (or use the old ones you took out of the ceiling) and connect them to the new lighting boxes. It's a bit of a pain to hang the ceiling rock around the old sockets, but it beats moving lights all the time.

Hooking up these lighting circuits requires connecting them to the panel. As for final hookup, this is a good spot to bring in a pro. If you hook up the lights now, remember as you insulate and hang rock that these lights and these switches are hot. You'll be fine if you tape around the sides of the switch with black electricians tape to cover the screw heads. This way the switch won't short out if it bumps into a ground wire or some wet mud when you're taping drywall.

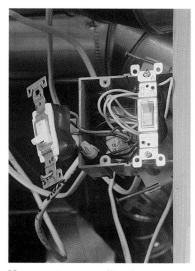

You can temporarily wire up a light circuit and switch to illuminate work in the basement. Note the tape wrapped around the switch to prevent shorts.

Walls and

CHAPTER SEVEN
Ceilings

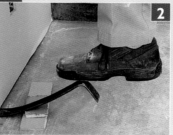

In this chapter we'll cover the satisfying work of making your new basement spaces look like rooms rather than wooden cages.

Before covering the walls, most basement remodelers add insulation. Placed on outside walls, insulation retains heat. Placed above ceilings, and sometimes in interior walls, it deadens sound. I'll show how to insulate with fiberglass batts, an easy, if itchy, task.

Prior to the invention of drywall, walls and ceilings were plastered, a skill well beyond most homeowners. But most folks can hang drywall or other panel materials on walls and even on ceilings, using the techniques that are covered here.

After the drywall is up, skimming joints and nail or screw heads with drywall "mud" creates flat, unbroken ceilings and walls. Finishing is not strenuous, but neither is it easy to do. If you don't want to serve this apprenticeship in your own basement, hire a pro for this part of the job. If you want to tackle it yourself, I've covered the basics in this chapter.

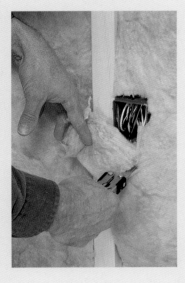
Insulation

In basements, insulation can help retain heat and deaden sound. In all climates, the natural insulating value of the soil around the basement helps maintain a constant, cool temperature. In cold-winter climates, you need to heat the rooms so they're warm enough to enjoy. Insulating the exterior walls helps retain the heat you add. Sound transmitted through floor joists can be annoying, and insulation can also help tone it down.

Thermal insulation

There are two homeowner-friendly methods of insulating basement walls. Fiberglass batts are best for the 2×4 framing method I prefer. They are very easy to install with just a utility knife and a stapler. When walls are furred out with 1×2 or 2×2 strips, extruded foam panels do the job.

Fiberglass insulation is commonly sold in widths that fit between standard stud spacings. Some batts are sold with a kraft paper on one side; this style is no longer code approved for basements. Buy the unfaced type.

Friction holds the batts in place between the studs, making installation fast and easy.

Insulation is rated by its ability to impede heat flow. This is called its R-value. The higher the R-value, the greater the insulation value. Fiberglass batts rated R-11, R-13, and R-15 are sold for 2×4 wall cavities. Buy the highest value you can find or afford.

Fiberglass batts are simple to install, but not fun. They shed tiny fibers that itch and are unhealthy to inhale. When you install fiberglass insulation, wear at least a mask and a long-sleeved shirt. A cotton hat and gloves also help. Rubber gloves are nice because you can feel your work through them and the fibers are easy to wash off.

Installing batts. I lay in all the full-sized, full-length batts first. Since basement walls are usually shorter than 96 in., you'll need to slice off the extra length, using the bottom wall plate as a backer for the utility knife. Cut the insulation around the electrical boxes; the insulation should be snug, without arching around the box. Around wires and pipe, I split the batt through its thickness and push half of it behind the wire or pipe.

Next, insulate between irregularly spaced studs. Each bale of insulation usually has two or more batts that are perforated lengthwise at various

Install full-length batts first.

widths and can be easily separated. Occasionally, you'll need to cut a batt to width. I lay a stud underneath and one on top to sandwich and compress the insulation for easier cutting. Using the same technique, cut short pieces to fit over and under windows and doors.

Stuff little pieces of insulation into odd nooks and crannies. I use the blade of my combination square to push strands of fiberglass into the space between door or window jambs and studs. Do this gently. If you force in too much insulation, you chance pushing the window or door out of true. Also, if you compress insulation too much, it loses its loft and thus its R-value.

Avoiding mold and mildew. Research compiled by the Building Science Consortium presents a new consensus on the best way to keep your basement warm while avoiding mold and mildew problems and unhealthy air quality. As a result, codes are changing around the country— check with local authorities to find out the status of your insulation codes.

Basement walls react to insulation according to the wall's position—above grade, less than three feet or so deep, or deeper. Because of this, the Building Science Consortium reports, the best practice is to insulate the *outside* of the concrete wall rather than the inside. Unfortunately, this is impractical for most cost-conscious remodelers.

Basement walls insulated with vapor barriers applied in the old approved manner have been found to be damp because of moisture trapped in the wall cavity that migrated in from the outside, or from air infiltration from the inside. It seems that air infiltration is an even greater problem than vapor migration, and there is additional moisture wicked up through the footings and the foundation itself.

It is better to omit the vapor barrier altogether. Just frame basement walls next to exterior walls as we describe in this chapter, but simply don't install a vapor barrier.

While this will comply with most codes and avoid the newly discovered problems, it doesn't improve your basement's insulating qualities. There is more you can do.

Rim-joist insulation. The rim-joist space, created where the ceiling joists rest on the outer walls, is a porous border for air infiltration and moisture penetration. The old practice of stuffing fiberglass into this space doesn't do much good. Hire a contractor to apply Icynene®, an open-celled spray foam insulation, also classified as an air barrier, inside the rim joist. It's difficult to apply this material yourself because the foam dries fast, but spray foam is superior to cutting solid foam to fit in these irregular hard-to-access areas.

Polystyrene foam panels. For a well-insulated basement, before you start framing exterior walls glue 2-in. extruded polystyrene foam insulation (XPS) to the inside surfaces of the basement's exterior walls. This material prevents

Split a batt through its thickness to insulate wiring or pipes.

To cut insulation, sandwich a batt between 2×4s to compress the fibers and guide the knife.

TRADE SECRET

Measuring drywall is not a fine art. If you cut it too tight, drywall will break when you try to fit it in. Give yourself a quarter-inch or so of room to play with. To ensure the best joint, butt together the factory ends (not the ends you cut) wherever possible.

IN DETAIL

Basement ceilings, with their pipes, tubes, vents, and ducts are difficult to insulate for sound with fiberglass batts. An alternative is to install drywall on resilient furring channel (RFC, commonly called Z channel). Screwed perpendicular to the joists, these strips of metal break the hard-line transmission of sound through the joists without losing much ceiling height.

Glue extruded polystyrene foam insulation (XPS) to basement walls before framing new walls. Here a jerry-rigged "press" holds the sheet tight to the wall while the glue dries.

Frame the new exterior walls against the foam panels, insulate between the studs and drywall. Do not add a plastic vapor barrier.

any warm room air from reaching the cooler concrete and condensing, thereby keeping moisture from collecting in the wall cavity to produce mold and mildew. Installation is easy. Apply a continuous bead of adhesive to the top edge, to prevent air movement from top to bottom, and spot glue the rest of it, to provide breathing room between the concrete wall and the foam.

XPS, which is usually blue or pink, is preferred over expanded polystyrene foam (EPS), which is usually white, similar to the foam used in beer coolers. XPS is more resistant to water penetration and has a higher R value per inch. The 2-in. XPS has an R value of 10. Adding 1-in. of foam between the conventionally framed studs of the new basement wall, increased the R value to 15. You could use fiberglass batt insulation between studs instead.

Where a vapor barrier still works. Walk-out basements often have full or half-height frame walls on the walk-out side. A vapor barrier is appropriate on these framed elements. Insulate between the studs and install a vapor barrier on the inside, beneath the drywall. Treat each half of a combination frame-and-concrete wall as is appropriate for each type of construction; the framed half with a vapor barrier, the concrete half without.

Sound insulation

I seldom install suspended ceilings in basements. But they are superior to drywall ceilings in one respect. A suspended ceiling has better sound-deadening qualities than a typical drywall ceiling. If you put fiberglass insulation on top of a suspended ceiling, you're on your way to building a sound studio. You can also install Z channel to dampen sound (see In Detail at left).

If you want to sound-insulate a bedroom or bathroom, fiberglass batts are easy and inexpensive to install. And they keep heat in these rooms, too. Plastic plumbing pipes are noisier than the old cast-iron lines; wrapping them in insulation isn't a bad idea. Insulating the mechanical-room wall can cut down on some noise, but combustion-air vents that penetrate the walls transmit sound, too.

Hanging Rock

The most common way to cover the walls and ceilings of your basement is with drywall, also called Sheetrock®, gypsum board, or just plain rock. (See Materials for Drywalling on p. 102 for more on drywall.) Most homeowners can hang their own rock. It's not complicated, it's just hard, heavy work.

After you've purchased the drywall and other materials, drywall the ceilings first, and then the walls. Several basic techniques—cutting sheets to size and cutting openings in them—are common to both tasks and are shown on pp. 105 and 107.

Ceilings

Drywalling a ceiling can be a daunting prospect to a novice. Hoisting one sheet of drywall over-head, let alone a dozen in a row, is nobody's idea of a good time. Simple, homemade 2×4 T-braces make the job easier, particularly if you're work-ing with a partner. Renting a commercial panel lift makes ceiling work even easier. Both methods are shown at right. If neither appeals to you, and you still want to do some of the drywalling your-self, have a contractor hang the ceiling.

I start drywalling ceilings in one corner and work in rows over and down the ceiling, stagger-ing the end-to-end joints. Always arrange the sheets with the long dimension perpendicular to the joists. Before you hang a sheet, check to see if the wall receiving the first row of sheets is straight. Pushing sheets tight against a curved wall will throw off the drywall joints. To check for curves, stretch a string from corner to corner. If the wall is concave, snap a chalkline on the joists 4 ft. out from each end of the wall, and lay the first row of drywall to that line. If the wall is convex, snap a chalkline 4 ft. from its innermost point.

Measure and cut the first sheet to length; make sure the joint falls in the center of a joist. Locate the factory end on the joint. To make fixing the

A panel lift makes hoisting even long ceiling sheets easy.

As you jack up the panel, you can maneuver the lift to position the panel precisely.

If you use T-braces to support a sheet of drywall on the ceiling, make the braces long enough to wedge the sheet between the floor and the joists.

MATERIALS FOR DRYWALLING

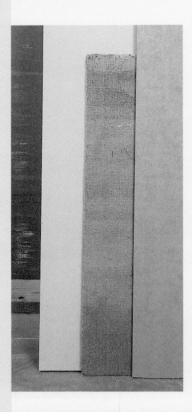

Drywall is made of gypsum (the same mineral used in plaster of Paris) sandwiched between two sheets of thick paper. It is commonly available in sheets $1/4$ in. to $5/8$ in. thick, 4 ft. wide, and 8 ft. to 16 ft. long. When two sheets adjoin, tapered edges along the length form a shallow hollow for taping and finishing. The ends of a sheet are full thickness, because they are usually cut to fit.

Use $1/2$-in. gray rock (the color of the backing paper), for walls and ceiling joists that are 16 in. on center (o.c.). For those 24 in. o.c., use $5/8$-in. rock. Around a tub-shower, you can use "green rock." Green rock is moisture resistant but not waterproof, and is not usually required by code. As a substrate for ceramic tile, use cement board, not drywall. Finally, code requires the use of fire-resistant drywall under stairs to protect the wooden stair stringers, risers, and treads.

What to Buy

The rule of thumb is to order the longest sheets that you can get into your basement. Long sheets minimize the number of joints you'll have to tape. But short sheets may be all you can get down the stairs. Check your access first, and then order specific lengths. Remember that an extra sheet or two won't cost much and will save travel time and frustration. When you're pricing drywall, ask if the supplier will deliver to your house or your basement. Drywall is heavy and awkward; having it delivered into your basement is often worth an extra charge.

Fasteners

You can hang drywall with screws or nails, and both are sometimes used in conjunction with glue. Figure 5 lb. of fasteners ($1 1/4$-in. drywall screws or $1 3/8$-in. galvanized nails) per 1,000 sq. ft. of drywall. I use Dritite® nails, which hold better than ring-shank nails. Even if you're using screws, you'll want some drywall nails for corner bead and to help hang sheets. For areas to be glued, buy a drywall glue such as PL 200®. Use a 1-qt. tube per three 8-ft. sheets of rock. (See Gluing Drywall on p. 106.)

Corner Bead

These metal or plastic strips protect drywall joints at outside corners and make finishing the corners easier. I prefer metal corner bead. If you want rounded corners, you can buy bull-nosed corner bead. For rounded openings, buy segmented corner bead, and for corners that aren't 90 degrees, buy flexible corner bead. Most inside corners are finished with tape and drywall compound. J-bead makes a neat inside-corner joint where a new wall butts against a finished wall or a concrete wall. Made of plastic or metal, it caps the raw drywall edge and

Materials and tools for drywalling your basement are available at most home centers. The top photo shows (left to right) gray rock, cement board, and green rock.

shows just a narrow strip of metal where it butts into the existing wall.

Drywall Compound

Commonly and accurately called "mud," this paste-like mixture of gypsum and water covers joints and nail and screw heads. When it dries, you can sand it to make a flat seamless wall. Buy about 140 lb. of mud per 1,000 sq. ft. of drywall. A 5 gal. bucket of mud weighs 62 lb.

Mud is sold in two grades, "all-purpose" and "topping." All-purpose is just that; you can use it for everything. Topping compound is a bit smoother and thinner; it works nicely for the final skim coat and for texturing ceilings. If you want to use both, order about two-thirds all-purpose compound and one-third topping. Order generously. Mud is not as expensive as driving for another bucket because you're short a couple of pints.

Standard drywall mud shrinks when it dries, and sometimes it takes a day or two for it to dry. For patching and filling holes, a better choice is Durabond Light® compound, a powder you mix with water. Durabond doesn't shrink when it dries, and it dries quickly. Buy the Durabond that comes in the blue bag, because it's sandable. Durabond in the green bag sets up as hard as cement.

Drywall Tape

This inexpensive paper, about 2 in. wide and sold in rolls, reinforces the drywall compound on edge-to-edge and end-to-end joints. Buy 500 ft. of tape for every 1,000 sq. ft. of rock. Paper tape has no adhesive. If you want a tape with a light adhesive, you can buy mesh tape. It works fine, but it's more expensive than paper, and I find it a little harder to work with than paper.

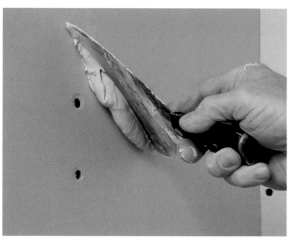

A single swipe of a 6-in. knife will cover pairs of drywall screws or nails.

sheet easier, measure and lightly pencil lines across the face at 16-in. centers.

Raise and secure the panel against the joists with T-braces or a panel lift. Check, and, if necessary, adjust the fit of the precut light or vent openings. Or tack the sheet in several places and cut the openings in place with a drywall router. (See p. 107.)

Whether you nail or screw, space fasteners about 8 in. o.c. across each end. On intermediate joists, nail each edge in the tapered area. Then add six fasteners along the joist. You can space these evenly (as on the ends). I use three sets of two fasteners, placing each pair about 2 in. apart and evenly spacing the pairs. Then, I can mud two at a time with one swipe of the blade.

With the first full sheet in place, start an adjacent row with a half-length piece. Staggered end joints are easier to hide with drywall tape and mud during finishing. I usually complete the first two rows simultaneously, then add remaining rows one at a time.

As you move across the ceiling, butt the sheets together nice and tight end-to-end and along the edges. But relax the fit against the walls. When you do the walls, you'll butt $\frac{1}{2}$-in.-thick rock against the ceiling and cover most gaps.

If the joists are properly spaced, you should be able to use full-length sheets for all but the ends

PRO TIP

For the best drywall joints, butt together the factory ends of sheets rather than the ends that you cut.

TRADE SECRET

Most professional drywallers fix drywall with screws, not nails, using a screw gun with a special nose adapter that disengages the drive when the screw is set to the proper depth. These guns are expensive. You can buy an attachment for a regular drill or cordless screw gun that works the same way.

I don't recommend that you use the clutch mechanism on most cordless screw guns to set drywall screws to the proper depth. The clutch works on a resistance principle rather than a depth-specific gauge, and the wood that you screw into will vary in its resistance. Some screws won't be set deep enough, and others will break the paper. Either condition causes problems when taping and finishing a wall.

Lift the top sheet against the ceiling and tack it in place with the nails you started for each stud.

When the sheet is tacked in place, cut out the opening. You can use a drywall router, as shown.

of each row. Sometimes, however, a piece may finish just short of or just beyond a joist. You can cut the sheet to fit. Or, nail a 2×4 to the side of the joist and fix the end of the sheet to it.

Walls

My students are sometimes surprised that pros hang drywall horizontally on walls rather than vertically. Combining horizontal joints and long sheets produces fewer joints than vertical sheets with floor-to-ceiling joints every 4 ft. And, because the long waist-high horizontal joint is illuminated less harshly than joints near the ceiling, it is less conspicuous.

Hang the top row of drywall first, then the lower row. In some rooms, a single sheet will span the entire wall. If you need to piece sheets together, make sure the joints fall on studs.

Pencil lines on 16-in. centers across the sheet. On a few of these lines, start some nails about 2 in. down from the upper edge of the sheet. Lift the sheet in place, tight to the ceiling and

corner (with a partner, if the sheet is large). Reach up and hammer in the nails you started. Then tack in a few more nails to secure the sheet. Now you can either finish screwing or nailing that sheet, or you can tack up a few more pieces, and then finish nailing them all at once. If you're using construction adhesive, it sets up fast, so finish nailing each sheet as you go.

You don't need to cut out for doors and windows before you hang the sheets. Just nail or screw the drywall right over the opening, and then cut out the opening. With a drywall router, you can cut up, across, and down, running the guide point against the opening's framing. If you use a drywall saw, cut up each side of the opening. For a window, cut across the top of the opening with a utility knife. The top photo on p. 106 shows how to cut out for a door.

When the top row is complete and you've cut door and window openings, install the bottom row. Stagger the end-to-end joints as you did for the ceiling. If yours is a typical basement, the walls

DRYWALL BASICS: CUTTING TO SIZE

Cutting drywall requires only a utility knife and a straightedge. You can cut freehand, but a 4-ft.-long aluminum T-square, available at most hardware stores and home centers, is a big help. Either way, I find it easier to cut drywall when the sheet is standing up, as shown at right.

You could leave the newly broken edge as it is. But you'll get much better joints if you straighten and smooth it with a Surform® plane, an inexpensive rasplike tool also available at hardware stores.

Occasionally, you'll need to cut a sheet along its length. The procedure is the same, but you'll need a longer straightedge to guide the knife. A straight 2×4 will work. Or you can use one of the techniques shown below.

Measure and mark the length on the face of the sheet. Then cut through the paper facing with a utility knife guided by a drywall T-square.

Break the gypsum core along the scored line. Then cut through the backing paper to free the waste.

Use a tape measure to simultaneously measure and guide a lengthwise cut. The top hand runs along the top of the sheet as a guide, the bottom holds the knife against the end of the tape.

A try square guides the knife at the correct distance from the sheet edge.

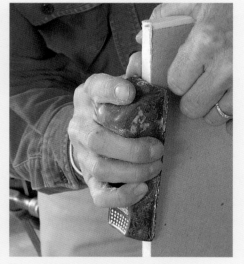

For tight-fitting joints, use a Surform plane to straighten and smooth newly broken drywall edges.

TRADE SECRET

When you're nailing drywall, make sure you "dimple" the surface: Drive the head of the nail below the surface of the drywall, leaving a depression. When you tape and finish, you'll fill the depression with compound and cover the fastener.

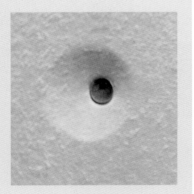

IN DETAIL

After you hang all of the drywall, it's time to get rid of the trash. Hang on to a couple of window or door cutouts to use as a staging area for mixing mud and for keeping some of the taping mess off the floor. Throw out the rest of the leftover pieces and sweep up before you start taping.

A drywall saw works well for cutting out door openings. After sawing up both jambs, score the backing paper across the header with a utility knife, and then break and cut the waste free from the front.

Use a flat bar and wooden fulcrum block to push a bottom sheet tight against the top row. Stagger butt joints of the bottom and top rows.

will be less than 8 ft. high, so you'll have to cut the bottom sheets less than full width. Measure and cut the sheets to finish about ½ in. above the floor. The gypsum is absorbent and will wick moisture if it contacts the concrete.

Hang bottom-row sheets like those on the top row. Start a few nails along the top edge, raise the sheet tight against the sheet above, and tack it in place. A flat bar and a fulcrum operated by your foot is a big help in getting the sheet tight to its neighbor. Hang the rest of the bottom row around the room. Finish nailing or screwing each sheet as you go (particularly if you're gluing), or tack a few nails on each sheet. Then finish nailing them all at once. Cut out for openings as for the top sheets.

Gluing Drywall

The fewer nails or screws you use to fix drywall to walls, the fewer you have to cover with drywall compound, and the fewer nail pops you'll have to fix in the months after the wall is finished and painted. (Nail pops are nail or screw heads that work their way above the surface of the drywall as time passes.)

To reduce the number of nails or screws, use construction adhesive when you're hanging drywall. Put a bead of glue down each stud and hoist the sheet into place. Nail along the edges of the rock as for a nonglued sheet, but use just enough fasteners in the center of the sheet to ensure the sheet is tight to the studs. The adhesive works better than nails, as you'll discover if you ever have to remove a sheet that's glued on.

DRYWALL BASICS: CUTTING OPENINGS FOR FIXTURES

There are two techniques for cutting openings in drywall for ceiling and wall fixtures (outlets, switches, and light boxes) and vents. You can measure and cut the openings, and then hang the sheets. Or, with a special drywall router, you can measure and mark the openings, tack the sheets in place, rout the openings, and finish nailing the sheet.

To precut, measure and mark accurately on the face of the sheet. Draw the outline of the box or vent on the sheet. Then cut the opening. A simple drywall saw works for rectangular openings. Round openings for recessed lights can be cut with a trammel cutter. Allow a 1/8-in. clearance on each side of the fixture. Lift the sheet into place, and check the fit of the openings to the boxes. If they don't fit without forcing, take the sheet down and adjust them. Remember, if you have gaps, you can easily repair them later with tape and drywall compound.

A drywall router features a thin side-cutting bit with a blunt guide tip. You just plunge the bit through the drywall, ease it over to contact the edge of the outlet box or vent, slip the tip over to the outside of the box, and follow it around. With a drywall router, you need only mark a box or vent by indicating a point that falls somewhere inside its outline. Fasten the sheet in place with a few screws or nails, zip out the openings, and finish nailing or screwing the sheet.

Sounds easy, and it is, but it takes a bit of practice. Move the cutter around the box in the opposite direction of the bit's rotation, so the force of the cutting holds the guide tip against the box. Otherwise, the bit rotation will tend to pull you off the box and wandering out into the unmarked gray expanse. And don't forget to mark those center points. After the sheet is up, it's tough to rediscover exactly where you installed boxes and vents.

To cut openings for boxes and vents, measure carefully and mark the outline (left). Cut rectangular openings with a drywall saw (above).

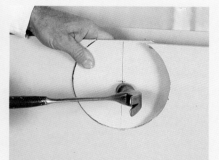

To cut a circular opening, set a trammel cutter at the radius. Pivoting around the center, score both sides of the sheet (above left). Then tap with a hammer to break the gypsum core and remove the waste (above right).

A drywall router cuts openings after the sheet is tacked in place. A guide tip on the cutter bears on the fixture, ensuring an accurate alignment. If you use a drywall router, wear safety glasses and earplugs to protect against dust and the high-pitched whine of the cutter.

PRO TIP

Drag the edge of a drywall knife across the sheet face. If you don't hear the blade hit a nail or screw, the fasteners are set deep enough.

TRADE SECRET

When you first open the 5 gal. bucket of drywall mud, stir it up. Over time, in storage, the mud tends to dry out a bit, at least on top. You can buy what looks like a large potato masher for stirring it up. A mixing attachment is also available for use in a 1/2-in. or larger drill. Or you can mix it up with a stick. Just mix it to a smooth consistency.

IN DETAIL

When you install corner bead on a soffit where a side, end, and bottom meet, cut back the nailing flange at an angle so the flanges don't overlap. Lapped flanges are too thick and the mud won't cover them.

Wrapped Drywall Window

The simplest way to finish a window is to "wrap" the drywall back to the window over the exposed studs, sill, and header. No jamb extensions, no trim, just a drywall corner and back to the window. The window jamb is usually 3/4 in. thick, so the 1/2-in. drywall wrap will butt to the window and allow a nice, 1/4-in. "reveal" of the window jamb.

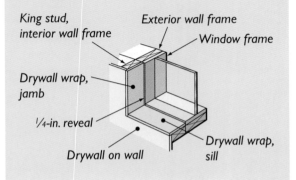

King stud, interior wall frame
Exterior wall frame
Window frame
Drywall wrap, jamb
1/4-in. reveal
Drywall on wall
Drywall wrap, sill

Drywalling soffits. Hang rock on soffits just as you do for ceilings (the underside of the soffit) and walls (the sides and ends). Avoid the temptation to use up lots of little drywall offcuts, and use the longest pieces you can. The money you spend on a few extra full-length sheets is worth the time and irritation you'll save by not having to tape and finish dozens of joints.

Corner bead

Every outside corner needs a metal or plastic corner bead, which makes finishing easier and protects the corner from damage. Installing corner bead is a simple process. Put it over the corner and nail through predrilled holes into the adjoining sheets. Use nails, not screws, to install bead; the heads don't protrude so far. Nail through all of the smaller holes, which are spaced about every 6 in. The larger holes are for mud to squish through to grip the bead.

Metal (or plastic) corner bead protects outside corners from damage and makes finishing easier.

Properly installed corner bead shows a gap between the spine edge and the drywall.

There is a trick to this simple task. To understand what it is, cut off a short piece of bead and lay it over a corner. With the edge of a 6-in. drywall knife, span from the spine of the bead to the flat drywall surface. The knife should bridge over the bead's nailing flange by about 1/16 in., then lie fairly flat on the wall. If you push harder on the bead, it will flatten out, and the knife will hit the nailing flange before it hits the wall. This is not good. When you lay on drywall compound, the flange will show through. On the other hand, if you pull the spine of the corner bead out too far, the corner will stray appreciably from 90 degrees, which makes fitting the wall's base trim more difficult.

So, the trick is to nail on the corner bead so that it allows mud to fill in and conceal the flange without the spine sticking out so far that it looks like the prow of a ship.

Finishing Rock

As I said at the beginning of the chapter, taping drywall and troweling on mud isn't easy to do well. Unfortunately, a poor wall or ceiling finish can stand out like a sore thumb. But, with practice, you can produce handsome walls and ceilings using the techniques covered here. So, start climbing your learning curve in the least trafficked areas of your basement.

Drywall is usually finished in three stages, each involving a new coat of mud. The first coat fills joints and covers nail and screw heads. This stage includes the application of a 2-in.-wide paper tape to reinforce the butt and edge joints between sheets. The second coat feathers out the butt joints (vertical end-to-end joints), fills in the flats (edge-to-edge horizontal joints), and feathers out the corners. "Feathering" a joint means blending it in with the surrounding flat surface. The third coat is the skim coat, and it gives the wall a smooth finish. Before you begin the finishing process, repair any drywall damage as described in the sidebar on p. 111.

First coat and taping

I tape butt joints first, then the flats, then the wall-to-ceiling joints, and finally the inside and outside corners. Starting with the butt joints ensures that the ends of the tape on those joints will be covered by the ceiling-corner tape and the tape in the flats.

Tools for Drywall Finishing

To spread and level mud, I use a 6-in. drywall knife (a dull, not sharp, blade) most, but it's handy to have several widths. I recommend a 12-in. blade for final finishing. A 4-in. blade is useful for setting tape in corners, and a 1-in. blade is good for tight spots. A corner trowel simplifies setting tape in corners, but it takes a while to master. There are lots of wonderful and expensive finishing tools, all of which take time to learn. You really don't need any of them unless you're going into the business.

A drywall pan is useful for holding mud and cleaning knives as you tape. I prefer a metal rather than a plastic pan. Some plastic pans have a little metal edge for cleaning blades. I find this edge just one more place for mud to dry and flake into the clean mud I'm trying to finish with.

I use 120-grit sandpaper and sanding screen to smooth cured mud; rectangular sponge abrasive blocks also do a nice job. A pad that holds the sandpaper and a pole sander for reaching the upper wall and the ceiling are a big help.

You don't need many tools for drywall finishing. A 6-in. knife and a drywall pan are shown here.

As I tape along the walls and ceilings, I swipe mud on all the nail and screw heads. To check that all the heads are below the drywall surface, I run the edge of a 4-in. or 6-in. knife across the wall or ceiling and listen for the telltale ping of metal on metal. Set the nail or screw where you hear it.

PRO TIP

Drywall finishing is messy. Wear old clothes and shoes and keep the dog out of the basement.

TRADE SECRET

Professional drywallers are in and out of a basement in about five days, ceiling textured and walls finished. You'll be there a lot longer. But the truth is, even if you do a poor job of mudding initially, you will catch on. And mistakes you make early on are repairable later. Start in the closets and under the stairs, not on the show wall of your rec room.

IN DETAIL

Drywall mud is dark when you lay it on, and it lightens as it dries. If you rush on to a second coat before the first one is dry, you'll ruin the first coat. Once mud starts drying it loses its plasticity, and any messing with it pulls off chunks and flakes. So, do yourself a favor and wait until there are no dark spots before starting on the next coat.

Butt joints and flats. These are taped more-or-less the same way. The photos below show a butt joint.

1. Use a 6-in. knife to cut daubs of mud from the pan and trowel them 4 in. to 5 in. across the joint all along its length. Lightly smooth the mud with the trowel.

2. Lay a piece of paper joint tape over the joint, press it in lightly to hold it in place, and cut it off at the end of the joint.

3. For vertical joints, start in the middle of the length of the joint. Pull a 6-in. knife along the joint, pushing the paper into the mud to squeeze out excess. Hold the paper in place if necessary. Don't force all the mud out, or there will be nothing to adhere the tape to the wall, and the tape will bubble. Continue to the ceiling. Go back to the middle and smooth the paper into the mud toward the floor. Clean off ridges of excess mud alongside the tape, smooth from the middle one more time, and leave it.

For most people, the toughest part of this stage is knowing when to stop. It seems so sensible just to touch it up here or smooth it down a bit more there. You can do that, but you'll spend most of your first day on that joint. Leave it. Go on to the next one.

The whole idea of finishing drywall is to eliminate as much sanding as possible. There's no reason to trowel on 5 gal. of mud and sand off three. So mud-in the tape economically. Don't be miserly, or the tape will have dry spots underneath and bubble. Part of the art of drywall finishing is getting a feel for the right amount of mud.

After the butt joints have dried, tape the flats. The procedure is the same as for butt joints; just work from the middle to each corner. It's easier to do the flats after the butt joints are dry because you won't run the risk of pulling up the tape in wet mud as you cross the butt-joint intersection. If you're in a hurry, it is possible to slide over the wet joint without damage. But you need to do so

1 Lay daubs of mud across the joint. Smooth the mud with a 6-in. trowel.

2 Stretch paper joint tape across the mudded joint.

3

Trowel along the joint to push the paper into the mud.

carefully and be prepared to do some fussing at the intersections.

First-coating inside corners. The technique for taping inside-corner joints (ceiling-to-wall and wall-to-wall) is similar to that for butt joints and flats, but it is complicated by the angle.

1. Lay daubs of mud into the corner all along the length of the joint. Extend the mud about 3 in. onto each adjoining surface. Smooth it out with a 4-in. or 6-in. knife.

2. Unroll a piece of tape the length of the joint (or more; don't be short). Crease the tape along the little ridge running down the center of the tape. Using your fingers, push the tape into the joint, smoothing it onto the drywall surfaces with your fingers as you go. If it's too long, cut or tear it off to fit. It can be ½ in. or so short.

3. Starting in the middle of the joint's length, gently push the tape into the corner with a 4-in. or 6-in. knife, and trowel along one side of the tape, forcing out excess mud as you go. Work that

Making Drywall Repairs

No matter how careful you are when hanging drywall, you'll cause some tears, digs, and dings. Standard drywall mud shrinks when it dries, and it dries slowly, especially if it's thick. For patching and filling holes, a better choice is Durabond Light compound, which doesn't shrink and dries in as little as 20 minutes. (See Materials for Drywalling on p. 102). Durabond is a dry powder. Mix it thoroughly with water to produce a smooth thick paste that will hang in the holes without sagging.

Examine the ceiling and walls and repair these defects:

- Wherever the gypsum is broken (look for wrinkles in the paper), cut the paper and pull out the broken pieces and fill.
- Fill between joints that exceed about ⅛ in.
- Fill wherever you miscut around a fixture or plug and you know the face plate won't cover.
- Repair where paper is torn along an edge or end. (Loose paper makes difficulties when troweling on drywall mud.) Cut off the paper with a sharp utility knife and fill.

Many repairs can be done with a swipe of a 4-in. knife. For deep holes, buy mesh drywall patches and mud them in. For large holes, cut out the section of drywall from stud center to stud center, fit in a piece, and then tape and mud it in like a butt joint.

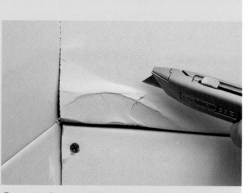

Cut out damaged drywall.

Remove the broken gypsum and fill with Durabond.

Smooth it well. Durabond dries harder than joint compound; it's not easy to sand.

TRADE SECRET

To keep unused mud from crusting over when left more than a few days, smooth out the surface and pour on about a half-inch of water. The drywall stays fresh, and you just pour the water off and remix the mud before you use it again.

IN DETAIL

If you're in the middle of mudding, using your tools and your pan every day, just wipe them down with a rough brush and leave them in a 5-gal. bucket full of water. That way they won't crust over and are ready to go with the wipe of a rag. Leave the brush in the water too; it's handy there.

1 Start taping an inside corner joint by daubing on mud and smoothing it into the joint.

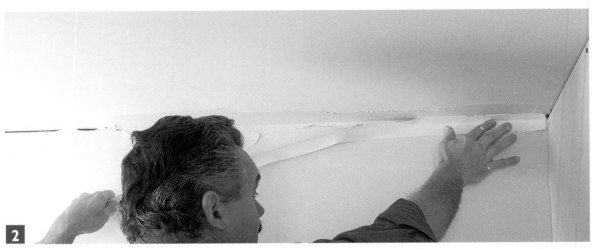

2 Crease the drywall tape lengthwise along its embossed ridge. Then gently bed the tape into the mud with your fingers. Do this along the entire length of the joint.

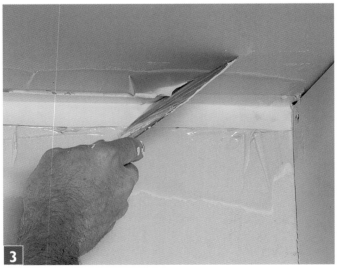

3 With a knife, work one half of the tape at a time down the entire length of the joint, pushing the tape into the corner and squeezing out excess mud.

4 Tape wall-to-wall corners after ceiling-to-wall joints have been taped and dried.

side to the end, and then from the middle to the other end on the same side. Remember not to force all the mud out and starve the joint. Then, trowel the other half of the tape, from the middle to each end. Clean up the excess mud forced out on both surfaces. If need be, smooth each side again the full length.

4. To avoid frustration, let the upper corner of the ceiling-to-wall joints dry before you tape the vertical wall-to-wall corners.

First-coating outside corners. Instead of tape, outside corners have corner bead. You've installed that already, so now all you do is lay on and trowel the mud.

Daub mud on the corner bead from top to bottom. Rest the edge of the knife on the bead and the wall, and run the knife up or down one side of one corner and then the other. Swipe off ridges of excess mud. Then leave the joint alone. It doesn't need pampering.

Applying the second coat

The second coat fills in low spots and covers defects in the first coat, and it begins to feather the mudded surfaces into the adjacent drywall. I proceed along the wall in the same order as for the first coat: butt joints, flats, inside corners, and then outside corners.

I don't sand between the first and second coats. At this stage, sanding takes time, creates more mess, and does very little you can't do with a drywall knife. Skim over the dry first coat with a 6-in. knife, knocking off ridges and stray lumps of mud. Do this thoroughly; these areas will cause problems otherwise. Of course, if you're really unhappy with a first-coat area, you may want to sand it back. If you sand, block off any return-air ducts in the basement, or shut off the furnace fan while sanding and until the dust settles. This keeps the dust downstairs.

Daub mud along the length of an outside corner, then trowel down, resting the blade on the edge bead and the wall (left). Finish one side of the corner (right), then do the other.

Start with the butt joints. To feather the joint, use a 12-in.-wide blade and trowel the mud down one side of the joint and then the other. (See the photos on p. 114.) You will probably have to load up and lay on mud more than once to get an even coat top to bottom. The result will be a newly mudded surface that is centered on the joint and up to 24 in. wide. When you have an even coat on both sides of the joint, make one more pull up (or down) each side. Put more pressure on the outside of the blade to feather the mud from a slight ridge in the center of the joint to nothing on the joint's edges. Then leave it alone. Again, resist the temptation to "just touch it up a little" here and there.

Finish all the butt joints, and this time let them dry before you move to the flats and upper corners. It takes a very experienced hand to lay second-coat mud right next to fresh second-coat mud. Do it the easy way; let it dry.

Before second-coating, remove ridges and blobs of dried mud with a 6-in. blade.

TRADE SECRET

Taping and finishing around fixtures can be frustrating. If gaps are large, build up the mud in layers rather than trying to fill the gaps all at once.

Because of the tapered edges of the drywall, flats have a slight recess in the center of the joint. A single 12-in.-wide second coat will cover sufficiently. Lay in the mud from the ends of the joint to the center. Then finish off with one pull of the 12-in.-wide blade from end to end. Then leave the flats to dry.

Second-coat the wall-to-ceiling joints next. (Because these joints intersect only an occasional ceiling flat, you can start on them while the flats are drying.) With a 6-in. blade, lay mud along the wall half of the joint first, finishing it with one steady pull along the whole wall. Again, exert pressure on the outside of the blade to feather the coat from the joint out. Let that half dry; then do the same to the ceiling half.

The technique for second-coating the inside and outside corner joints is the same as for wall-to-ceiling joints, except you work vertically. While you're waiting for the first halves of the wall-to-ceiling joints to dry, do the first halves of the vertical corners. Then return to the dry wall-to-ceiling joints and do the second halves.

Second-coat nail and screw heads as you go.

Final, or skim, coat

Before the final coat, go over the dry second coat with a 6-in. blade and scrape off any lumps, bumps, ridges, or slop. Again, if you have troublesome areas, you can sand them now; but a full-fledged sanding is premature.

The final coat skims the surface, forcing mud into any imperfections in the joints and feathering any ridges out onto the flat of the drywall. Use topping compound or slightly thinned all-purpose joint compound. I use a 12-in. blade for butt joints and flats and a 6-in. to 8-in. blade for corners and nail heads. This layer dries much faster than the first two coats because it is very thin. You don't really have to wait long to move from joint to joint or corner to corner.

To second-coat butt joints, apply mud to both sides of the joint with a 12-in. knife, then make a final pull down each side, feathering the outside edges.

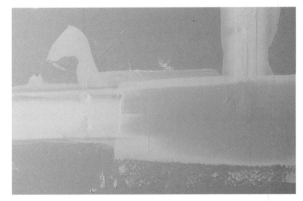

For flats, a 12-in.-wide second coat is enough. On this flat, the wet second coat on the right contrasts with the narrower, dry first coat at left.

Second-coat wall-to-ceiling joints one side at a time with a 6-in. knife. Let the first side dry before doing the second.

Some areas, like the sides of these soffits, will be completely covered by the skim coat.

The final, or skim, coat completes the process of feathering mud out from the joints to produce a (nearly) flat smooth surface.

TRADE SECRET

Before sanding, seal off the basement from the rest of the house. Turn off the furnace blower or cover the basement return-air ducts.

After sanding, when the air clears and the dust settles, you'll want to get rid of the dust that covers everything. Because it's so fine, drywall dust is hard to sweep. I suck it up with a workshop vacuum lined with a drywall filter. Available for most models, the filter captures most of the dust instead of just recirculating it.

Sanding

When the skim coat is thoroughly dry, it's time to sand. Ideally, you sand only to produce a smooth surface for painting; your trowel work has already made the surface flat. Ideally. But unless you quickly get the hang of applying mud, you may need to sand away a lot of drywall compound to achieve a flat surface.

Before sanding anything, seal off the basement from the rest of the house as best you can. Shut

A sandpaper block (right) holds a half-sheet of sandpaper. A lightweight abrasive block will work, too.

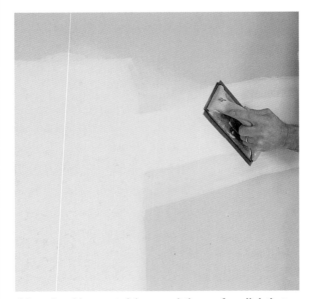

After the skim coat dries, sand the surface lightly to smooth it for painting.

off the furnace blower, or tape plastic over any basement return-air grills. Lay a damp towel at the base of the stairs to catch dust before it can escape to the upper levels. If you have windows or doors to the outside in your basement, open some of them, and use a fan to expel the white cloud and to draw in fresh air.

Wear a mask. Buy the paper masks with two rubber straps instead of one; they cost a little more, but the two straps hug the mask to your face better.

When you sand, sand lightly. You're trying to minimize the unavoidable humps over joints, not create a dead flat surface. You'll quickly see how easy it is to eliminate those small ridges that drove you crazy when you were spreading mud, and how difficult it is to eliminate the small crevices you hardly noticed. Try not to sand into the tape or fuzz the drywall paper. If you do either, don't worry. Circle them with a pencil and move on.

After you've sanded everything once, pick up your trowel and mud and skim the places you fuzzed and the crevices that didn't disappear. Let those areas dry and sand them lightly.

Ceiling texture

Why texture the ceiling; why not go with smooth? Because it's difficult to produce a nice smooth surface. Light rakes across the ceiling at an unforgiving angle, revealing any imperfections. Pros usually skim the entire ceiling surface to make sure it's flat, but even then, some flaws show up. Most homeowners (and pros) texture; it not only covers up taping and finishing sins, but it also gives some character to the ceiling.

To texture a ceiling, you roll on topping compound (thin drywall mud), and then texture the surface with a "stomp" brush. Achieving a light hand-textured look is not rocket science, but it takes some practice. Try texturing some pieces of rock left over from door or window cutouts.

For a textured ceiling, start by rolling on an even coat of topping compound with a long-napped roller (far left). "Stomp" the entire surface with a stomp brush to create a stippled surface. Rotate the brush between stomps to avoid making a noticeable pattern.

When you're ready to try it for real, do a closet first. Textured well, a ceiling doesn't need paint.

Use a long-napped paint roller on a pole to roll the mud on. The compound should be the consistency of thick paint. Be sure to cover the drywall completely and evenly. If you miss spots, the gray drywall shows through; thin spots will also stand out. Next, "stomp" the ceiling with a stomping brush on a pole. Stomp the brush into the wet mud over the entire area, rotating the brush between stomps to avoid making a pattern, which will catch the eye. You'll need to work fast or you'll be texturing dry mud. Enlist a helper: One person can texture while the other rolls.

Cleanup. Texturing, like taping and mudding, is very messy. If you've ever been in a farmyard, you can imagine what your floor looks like now, though the color and the aroma are different. Easiest thing to do is let the floor dry, and scrape it off with an old blade or a flat hoe-like scraper.

Let the mud and topping compound dry on the floor. Then scrape it off.

Finish

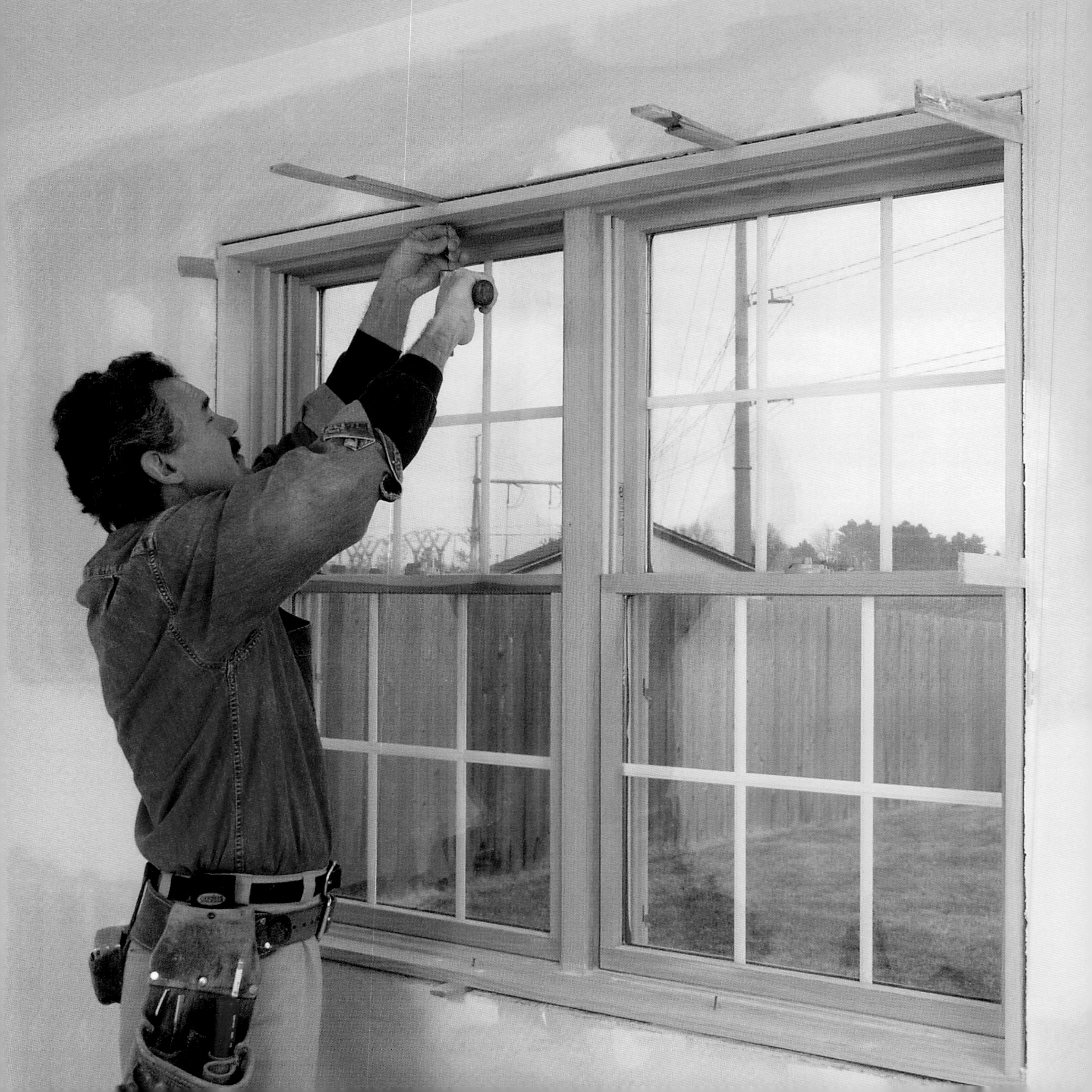

CHAPTER EIGHT
Carpentry

This is my favorite part of a remodel. Trim carpentry requires patience, a good eye, some problem-solving skills, and yes, some additional tools. The result is the satisfying sight of your trimmed-out rooms, with their doors and cabinets installed, the casing and baseboard making handsome frames around openings and floors.

Here, I'll cover setting prehung doors, fitting jamb extensions, installing door and window casing, and running baseboard. In the process, I'll explain how to miter and cope joints, and I'll discuss setting cabinets and installing built-in shelving.

With these basics, you can trim most or all of your basement. And, I hope, you'll experience the satisfaction that comes from creating a particularly nice fit on a particularly recalcitrant piece of trim.

IN DETAIL

When setting a door jamb, professional trim carpenters use a 6-ft. level that gives an accurate read the whole length of the jamb. If you plumb jambs with a 2-ft. or 4-ft. level, it may read a bow in the jamb, rather than true plumb. To get an accurate read with a shorter level, tape it to a very straight 2×4 cut 6 ft. 6 in. long (standard doors are 6 ft. 8 in.).

TRADE SECRET

When hand nailing through a jamb and shims, the pounding can move the jamb. Don't worry. Just drive the shims in or out to adjust the plumb or reset the gaps. Nails driven with a trim gun go in so fast that the jamb barely moves.

Shimming

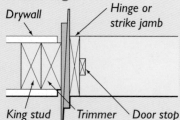

Use pairs of shims to plumb jambs. Slide a shim in from both sides of the opening to keep the jamb at right angles to the plane of the door.

Setting Doors

Like most jobs, trim carpentry goes best when things are done in a certain order. I install doors first. Then, if needed, I extend window or door jambs. Door and window casings come next, followed by setting cabinets (bathroom vanity, kitchenette, or bar) and installing baseboard. Shelving and door hardware complete most trim jobs. If you need them, add chair rail, half-wall caps, stair rail, crown molding, and other special trim last.

I highly recommend buying prehung doors. (See Choosing a Passage Door on p. 122 for more information.) Prehung doors are easiest for novices (and pros) to install, particularly if you do the installation methodically. The process is straightforward. Set the door and jamb into the rough opening. Placing shims between the jamb and the frame 2×4s as necessary, level the head jamb, plumb the hinge jamb, and then plumb the strike jamb. As you go, make sure that the gap between the door and the jambs remains even all around. The drawing and photos at right show the steps.

Before installation, clean up the rough opening. Cut any drywall that sticks into the opening even with the trimmers. Drive in nail heads that aren't flush with the faces of the trimmers; they can get in the way of the jamb or shims.

When you unpack a prehung door, pull the plug out of the hole that is bored in the edge of the door for the striker. The plug is hard to remove after the door is set. Some manufacturers screw through the jamb into the edge of the door for shipping; remove that screw.

The opening, like the jamb, has a hinge side, a striker side, and a head. Check the hinge side of the opening with a level for plumb. If it's dead on, you can nail the hinge jamb directly to the trimmer on that side. Chances are, however, that it will be at least a little out of plumb and the jamb will require shimming. In the description

Leveling and Plumbing a Door Jamb

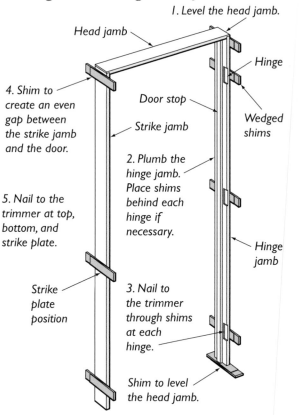

Add shims as necessary to level and plumb the head and the hinge jamb. Use shims to create an even gap between the door and the strike jamb.

that follows, I'll cover how to work on an opening that is out of plumb.

Set the door and jamb in the rough opening. Make sure the handing is correct: Is this really the way you want the door to swing? Start by shimming both ends of the head jamb so it is tight in the opening. Now check the head jamb with a level and shim under one or both vertical jambs, if necessary, to level it. Make sure that the edges of the head jamb are in the same plane as the drywall. Then nail the hinge jamb through the top shims to the trimmer. (Don't nail the strike jamb yet.) Use 8d finish nails if you're hand nailing. With a pneumatic trim nailer, use 2½-in. nails. Now, and as you proceed, just drive one nail at each fixing point; you'll add more when the jamb is completely set.

Shim the head jamb tight in the rough opening.

Check the head jamb for level.

Push shims between the ends of the vertical jambs and the floor to level the head jamb.

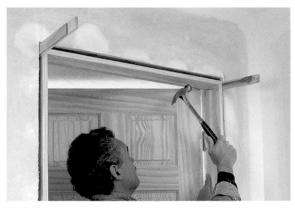

Nail the top end of the hinge jamb through the wedges and into the trimmer.

Cutting a Door Down to Size

Some lumberyards will cut doors to length for a fee. Here's how you do it yourself.

Most of the procedure is the same for hollow-core, solid-core, and solid-wood prehung doors. Pull the hinge pins and remove the door from the frame. Mark and cut the jambs to the height of the rough opening minus $1/2$ in. clearance for flooring. To maintain the proper clearance for the door, cut the same amount off the bottom of the door that you cut off the jambs. Measure from the top of the door and square a line across the door at the mark. Clamp a straightedge on the line across one face. (A level makes a good straightedge.) With a sharp utility knife, carefully cut along the straightedge several times, deepening the cut with each pass. Guided by a try square, knife down both edges of the door from the line scored across the face. Scoring prevents chipping the face veneer of hollow- or solid-core doors or the vertical grain of solid-wood stiles when you cut with a portable circular saw or jig saw. You only need to score the face that the saw base bears upon. Because the saw teeth come up through it, the bottom face won't chip out.

Clamp the door to sawhorses and carefully cut about $1/32$ in. away from the scribe line. Take your time. As you near the end of the cut, make sure to support

Glue a filler piece into the cavity at the bottom of a of a cut-down hollow-core door.

the waste piece or it will break away before you finish the cut and leave a ragged end on the door. (If you pop out a chip or two of veneer during the cut, save the pieces and glue them back.) For solid-core and solid-wood doors, just clean up the edge of the fresh cut on both faces and edges with a file and you're done.

If you cut more than an inch or two off a hollow-core door, you'll have removed the bottom wood filler and exposed the door cavity, which you'll need to refill. You can cut a new filler from $3/4$-in. stock, or you can remove the ply faces and splinters from the piece you've just cut off and reuse it. With a chisel, cut the cardboard spacers inside the door core back about $1 1/2$ in. Check and adjust the fit of the new or reused filler. If you push it in too far, set a drywall screw part way into the edge and pull the piece out by the head of the screw. When it slides in smoothly, spread glue inside the core, slide in the filler, and clamp evenly across the door faces. When the glue has cured (overnight is safe) clean up the edges with a file.

CHOOSING A PASSAGE DOOR

Interior passage doors are hollow-core, solid-core, or solid-wood construction. All are usually 1 3/8 in. thick and 6 ft. 8 in. tall. There are several standard widths: 2 ft., 2 ft. 6 in., 2 ft. 8 in., and 3 ft. (called "two-O," "two-six," "two-eight," and "three-O").

- **Hollow-core.** Most common are hollow-core doors. They're inexpensive, lightweight, and dimensionally stable—they don't expand or contract with changes in humidity, and they won't, therefore, jam in an opening. As the name implies, they are hollow, consisting of a frame, 1 in. or wider of fir or pine, sandwiched between thin plywood faces. Cardboard spacers fill the gaps inside. Hollow-core doors come with flat faces, commonly with oak, birch or lauan surface veneers; or with pressed-wood faces made to look like those of a solid-wood paneled door.

- **Solid-core.** Closely resembling their hollow-core cousins, solid-core doors have a particleboard core. They're heavy and more unwieldy to hang. But they

deaden sound better than hollow-core doors, which is a plus for a bedroom or mechanical room, and they're more durable.

- **Solid-wood.** These doors consist of solid-wood horizontal rails and vertical stiles enclosing solid-wood or veneered panels. Solid-wood doors can be beautiful, but they're more expensive and tend to expand or contract with seasonal humidity changes.

- **Prehung doors.** Regardless of the style you choose, I recommend that you buy doors prehung. That means the jamb is assembled, the door is hung in it with hinges routed into the door and jamb, the door stop is nailed in place, and the holes are bored in the door for the handset and striker. Having these fiddly tasks done for you is well worth the extra cost.

- **Door handing.** When you order a prehung door, you need to specify its "handing," that is, the way it will swing. An easy way to determine handing is to stand in the door opening with your back to the side the hinges will be mounted on. If you want the door to swing out in the direction of your right arm, order a right-hand door; if you want it to swing left, order a left-hand door. A caution: Don't assume the person you order doors from understands handing; make sure you both agree on how handing is determined.

- **Door hardware.** Buy knobs, latchsets, and strike plates when you buy the door, to ensure that they're compatible. Unless you need a secure area in your basement, all you'll need are privacy and passage latchsets. A privacy set allows you to lock the door from one side, while a passage set has no locking mechanism. In most basements, people use privacy locks on the bathroom and sometimes the bedrooms. Otherwise, passage latchsets work just fine. Don't buy the least expensive latchsets. After only a few months of use, the knobs will feel loose, and the striker mechanisms will feel sloppy.

Door Types

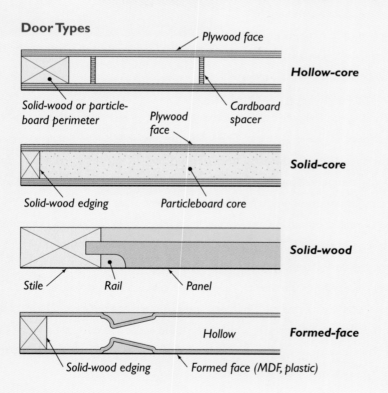

Hollow-core
- Plywood face
- Solid-wood or particleboard perimeter
- Cardboard spacer

Solid-core
- Plywood face
- Solid-wood edging
- Particleboard core

Solid-wood
- Stile
- Rail
- Panel

Formed-face
- Solid-wood edging
- Hollow
- Formed face (MDF, plastic)

Plumb the hinge jamb, shimming between it and the trimmer as needed.

Examine the gap between the door and the jamb. Make it uniform along the length of the jamb by adjusting the shims.

Shim behind the strike jamb at the position of the strike plate and near the jamb's bottom end. Adjust shims to make the door-to-jamb gap uniform.

Placing shims behind the hinges as necessary, plumb the hinge jamb. If the top of the jamb is too close to the trimmer to allow plumbing, you can drive in the shims that wedge the head jamb in place to move the hinge jamb out a bit. Check that the head jamb remains level. When the hinge jamb is plumb and its edge is in the same plane as the drywall, nail at each hinge through the shims into the trimmer. I place the nail even with the center of the hinge.

Standing in the room into which the door swings, close the door. Examine the gap between the door and the head and hinge jambs. If the gap isn't uniform, drive the shims in or out as necessary to make it uniform.

Open the door and check that the edges of the strike jamb are in the same plane as the drywall. Then nail through the strike jamb and the shims

that hold the head jamb in place. Shut the door and shim behind the strike jamb a couple of inches up from the bottom end of the jamb and behind the strike plate. Adjust the shims until the gap between strike jamb and door is uniform. Nail through the jamb and shims at the strike plate and at the bottom of the jamb.

There may be one more task to do before you nail through the shims behind the strike plate. If the walls are plumb and the door hangs in the opening correctly, the closed door should touch the door stop evenly all along the strike jamb. But sometimes a door is warped, or sometimes the walls aren't plumb. Then the door will hit only the top or bottom of the stop. Rather than rebuild the walls or buy a new door, you can adjust the jambs to achieve a better door-to-stop fit. (If the door is warped beyond the industry standard of

BUYING TRIM

Common Trim Profiles

Baseboard and casings shown are usually between $\frac{3}{8}$ in. and $\frac{5}{8}$ in. thick and from $2\frac{1}{4}$ to 3 in. wide. If you ask for colonial or ranch trim, you're likely to get some variation of the profiles identified here. The other profiles are also common, but may be called by several names.

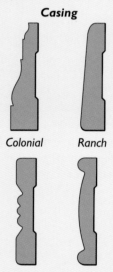

Casing

Colonial   Ranch

Other common casings

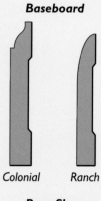

Baseboard

Colonial   Ranch

Base Shoe

Basement trim includes doors, casing (narrow pieces that frame door and window openings), and baseboard (pieces that protect and embellish the bottom few inches to a foot of wall). Because cabinets and shelves are installed at the same time, I include them with trim. Some basements also require jamb extensions to complete the window trim. Here are tips on figuring what and how much trim you need.

- **Doors.** Start your trim-materials list with passage doors. List the doors you need, their size, and handing. To set prehung jambs and doors in their openings, figure a bundle of shims for every six doors. I like cedar shims (made from cedar roofing shingles) better than pine or fir; they're easier to cut off, and they tend to have a longer, slimmer taper.

- **Casing.** Some lumberyards will figure the door casing for you; just give them the door sizes. If you have to figure your own, be sure to take into account the corner treatment when determining length. For a door cased in $2\frac{1}{4}$-in.-wide trim mitered at the corners, you'd order four 7-ft. pieces of casing and two pieces at least 6 in. longer than the door width. (Assuming you're trimming the door front and back.) These lengths are sufficient to miter the top corners without too much waste. Figure casing for windows in the same manner.

- **Baseboard.** I measure around the perimeters of all the rooms I need to trim. I measure right through the doorways, which usually provides enough for waste. You can order the total number of lineal feet, say 240 lin. ft., and let the lumberyard send out various lengths. Or you can order specific lengths. If I have some 16-ft. walls,

and I don't want to splice the runs, I ask that the specific number of 16-ft. lengths I need be included in the lineal-foot total.

- **Sizes.** Casing and baseboard trim are sold in full 1-ft. increments. Order pieces a foot or so longer than needed to allow for splits and defects at the ends. Make sure pieces of the same profile are the same thickness. Cutter profiles vary from mill to mill and batch to batch, so try to buy material from the same mill run. Trim is also sold pre-packaged, cut to length, and mitered. If you don't have a miter saw, this might be a good option. But I don't recommend it. I once bought two packages for a job, examining the wood entombed in layers of shrink wrap as best I could before buying. On the job, I discovered the two packages varied dramatically in thickness.

- **Jamb extensions.** If you need to extend window or door jambs (see Extending Jambs on p. 126), you'll need to make the extensions yourself. I buy clear white pine and pay a premium for it. I don't want knots in the jamb extensions, and the extensions don't require much wood. Measure the depth from the face of the drywall to the door or window jamb and order the next largest width of $\frac{3}{4}$-in. stock available. For example, if the depth is 3 in., you'll need a 1×4 ($3\frac{1}{2}$ in. wide). Or order wider stock and rip the pieces to width yourself. The depth around the window or door may not be uniform; use the widest measurement when ordering.

- **Shelving.** There are a wide variety of shelving styles and systems. The simplest is to rest shelves on 1×2 cleats nailed to walls or, if the shelves don't butt into walls, to mount brackets on metal strips. You can buy poplar or primed 1×2 particleboard for cleats. For shelving, you can buy raw particleboard, or particleboard prefinished with a melamine coating. If the shelf needs to support more weight than a pile of light sweaters, use plywood or solid-pine shelving—particleboard sags easily. Vinyl-coated wire shelving systems are neat and easy to install, and they allow more air circulation.

- **Cabinets.** Widely available and inexpensive, bathroom vanities come in standard sizes (18 in. or 21 in. deep and 30 in. high) and a variety of styles and wood species, finished or unfinished. The range of tops, sinks, and hardware is equally large. If you don't see what you want at a store, you can order a size or style you want from a custom cabinet shop. Like vanities, kitchenette and bar cabinets come in a wide range of styles, features, and prices. Base units are a standard 24 in. deep and 34½ in. tall (for 36-in. height with countertop). Wall-hung units are 12 in. deep and vary in height and width.

- **Fasteners.** For jambs, casing, and baseboard, you'll need 4d, 6d, and 8d finish nails. (Casing nails, which have larger heads, are for outdoor work.) A pound of each size nail will install a lot of trim. If you're using a pneumatic nailer, you'll need 1-in., 1½-in., and 2½-in. collated nails. Kits containing a compressor, nail gun, and air hose are remarkably inexpensive and many are more than adequate for homeowner use. Buy a pint of carpenter's glue for assembling trim miters. To fix cabinets to walls, buy #10 or #12 wood screws 2½ in. or 3 in. long.

When the jambs are adjusted and nailed in place, cut off the protruding shims. Score along one face with a utility knife; the shim usually breaks off cleanly (left). Then set all nails.

¼ in. along its length, your supplier should replace it on warranty.)

Using a scrap block to protect the wood, you can drive the top or bottom of the hinge or strike jamb horizontally, in or out of the opening, to even out how the door touches the stop. If you make small adjustments to all four corners rather than bigger adjustments to one or two, the edges of the jambs should protrude only slightly past the drywall in some areas, and hang shy of the drywall face in others. Small protrusions are easier to cover with casing than are large ones.

After all that pounding, you might need to re-adjust the door-to-jamb gap here and there. Then nail through the jamb and shims behind the strike plate. Before you complete the nailing, examine the gaps a final time. Shim and nail where needed to close wide spots. Then drive two more nails at each hinge, one above and one below the hinge. I also drive another nail at the top, bottom, and strike plate on the strike jamb. You can set all of the nail heads below the surface now, or do so as you go along. Finally, cut off the shims flush with the drywall. I score them with a utility knife and break them off, or cut them with a small saw.

IN DETAIL

The gap between jamb and door on most prehung doors varies from top to sides and side to side. Usually the gap is less along the hinge side, and the gap on the top differs from the one on either side. When you're installing a prehung door, just try to make each gap consistent. Don't worry about making them the same size all around the door.

TRADE SECRET

When I hang a solid-core door or a solid-wood door, I replace one of the screws on the top hinge with a 2¼-in. screw, which is long enough to bite into the stud. A heavy door tends to sag away from the jamb over the years, and this long top screw helps hold it in place. I use one of those gold-colored deck screws. The head is about the same size as the hinge screw and the color is very similar. Be careful just to snug it up, because if the screw bites into the stud, it will tend to move the jamb around.

Extending Jambs

Windows and doors installed in exterior walls are often narrower than the thickness of the wall, leaving part of the rough opening and the edge of the drywall exposed. If you've also added a frame wall beside the exterior wall, there will be even more rough wood exposed. Cover this area with a wooden jamb extension or drywall. Now is a good time to add jamb extensions. The process is similar for windows and doors.

A window jamb extension is just a four-sided wooden frame butted against the existing jamb. Extensions look better and are much easier to make if you do not try to fit the inside face of the extension exactly flush with the inside face of the existing jamb. I make the extension frame so it reveals at least ⅛ in. of the edge of the jamb.

I make extensions from ¾-in. clear pine (unless the jamb being extended is a different wood that is to be clear finished). Cheaper wood won't look as good or work as easily. Extensions are usually narrow. I can rip the four strips from

The finished jamb extension.

two 1×6s. If you don't have a table saw, ask a cabinet shop to cut pieces to size for you.

The inside dimensions of the frame should measure ¼ in. longer than the inside dimensions of the window jamb, providing a ⅛-in. reveal all around. Cut a 1×6 to length for the side strips and one for the top and bottom strips. Add 1¾ in. to the inside dimension for the top and bottom strips (¼ in. for the reveals and 1½ in. for the butt joint formed with the sides).

To determine the width of the extension strips, carefully measure the distance from the edge of the window jamb to the plane of the drywall face at all four corners of the opening. (Before you measure, make sure the drywall is nailed tight to the trimmers, header, and sill all the way around the opening.) Rip the extension strips to the largest measurement. Then nail the corners of the frame together. If you're using a nail gun, take care to keep your hands clear of an errant shot.

Jamb Extension

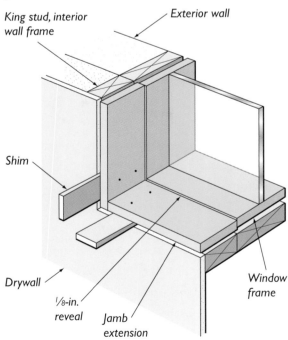

King stud, interior wall frame

Exterior wall

Shim

Drywall

⅛-in. reveal

Jamb extension

Window frame

A wooden jamb extension covers the drywall and rough opening inside a basement window. Measure from jamb to drywall face at each corner to determine the extension's width.

You can rip the top, bottom, and sides to width from 1×6 pine. When ripping narrow stock on a table saw, use a push stick to finish the cut, rather than pushing your fingers between the blade and fence.

To provide a reveal between jamb and extension, make the extension ¼ in. larger than the inside dimensions of the jamb.

Nail the extension frame together with 8d finish nails.

TRADE SECRET

If you've nailed and pounded the drywall and still can't get the trim around a door to lay flat, all is not lost. You can cut the drywall back and set the trim in the recess. First, tack the piece in place. Wherever it doesn't lay flat, cut along the outside edge through the drywall paper. Remove the casing. Where you've cut, use an old chisel or scraper to peel off the paper and as much gypsum as required for the trim to lay reasonably flat. When the trim is stained and the wall painted, no one but you will be able to tell what you had to do to make everything fit.

IN DETAIL

Some people prefer to finish trim before installing it. This works well if you don't have to plane or sand the trim joints flush after installation. Otherwise you'll have a lot of touchup staining or painting to do. Check how well the trim fits on the drywall before deciding to prefinish it.

Use shims to align the extension frame and jamb so there is a uniform reveal at the corners.

After the corners have been nailed in place, shim as needed to make the reveal uniform all round the jamb. Nail through the shims; then trim them off.

If necessary, plane the extension flush with the drywall surface.

Set the frame in the opening. Shim each corner, side and top if necessary, to align the reveal. Nail through the shims at the corners into the rough-opening studs. Then space shims along the top, bottom, and sides to set a consistent reveal, and nail through those shims. If the jamb extension is narrower than 2 in., you can nail through the face of the extension into the window jamb to draw the surfaces tight. (Don't do this on a vinyl window.) But be careful. It's easy for a nail to go astray and poke out of the face of the jamb. Set all the nails below the wood surface.

If the jamb extension protrudes past the face of the drywall more than $1/16$ in. at any point, it will cause problems when you trim the window. Plane the extension flush with the drywall using a block plane.

Installing Casing

Casing, the decorative trim that frames door and window openings, can be done in a variety of styles, as discussed on the facing page. I'll cover the style almost all my students and clients choose, "picture-frame" casing.

Whatever style you choose, before you start installing casing, check all the openings to see if the drywall is flush with the jamb. Seldom (well, almost never) are all openings perfect.

If the jamb extends a little beyond the drywall, the misalignment doesn't usually cause installation problems and will generally be hidden by the casing. Drywall that extends past the jamb, however, often causes problems and should be fixed, if possible. It may not be nailed tightly to the studs or header, so first try persuading it with some drywall nails. If the drywall is tight to the studs, try the "Neanderthal" solution: Pound the drywall down with your hammer, not straying farther out onto the rock than the width of your casing. It's simple, fast, and it usually works.

Casing: Mitered Corners

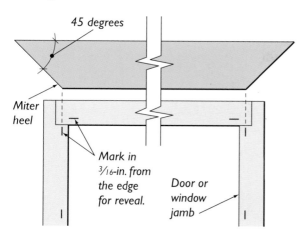

Picture-frame casing

Casing, like extension jambs, looks best and is easiest to install when it is set slightly back from the face of the jamb it abuts. The first installation step, then, is to mark on the edge of the jambs 3/16 in. in from the inside face of the jamb. Make these marks at all corners, at the bottom of door jambs, and midway on vertical door jambs and long window runs.

Casing a window. Install the head casing first. Along the head jamb, measure between the marks on the side jambs. Cut a piece of casing to that measurement between the "heels" of the 45-degree miters on each end, as shown in the drawing above. (A miter saw makes this task easier.) Position the piece of casing on the head jamb, making sure the miter heels are aligned with the marks on the jamb and the reveal is correct. Tack it with a 4d or 6d finish nail in the center of the jamb and about 1 in. back from the miter. For now, tack only into the jamb, not into the wall.

Side casings come next. Measure and cut them to length, a miter at each end, as you did for the top casing. Hold the side casing in place against the reveal marks and check the fit of the miter with the top casing. If the side casing doesn't fit snugly all along the cut, use a sharp block plane or

Casing Styles

The trim around doors and windows is called casing. Where you install jambs and run trim around an opening, you have a cased opening instead of a drywalled opening. Every style of architecture has its characteristic casing. All the treatments here are simple, but they can look quite different depending on the moldings used.

- **Picture frame.** The most common contemporary style. All the corners are mitered, so the trim visually turns the corners and carries on around the frame.
- **Corner blocks.** A modification of an old style. The casing butts into square blocks at the corners. On windows, it is often used with a stool and apron. Door jamb casings can rest on a plinth block, abutting the baseboard.
- **Butt joint.** Here, flat jamb casings simply butt into a flat head casing. The effect is simple, but aligning the joint, and keeping it aligned, can be a problem. You can glue and pin it with smaller finish nails, as shown in the photo at right.
- **Stool and apron.** Used for windows. In this style the side pieces rest on a stool, a flat projection of the jamb extension below the window. The apron is the trim piece beneath the stool. The trim at the top and sides may be mitered, butted, or blocked.

A picture-frame joint in oak.

Oak casing with corner blocks.

A butt-joint casing in pine.

A stool-and-apron window treatment.

PRO TIP

To produce a tight miter, you can under-cut the joint by removing more material along the back of the mitered surface than along the front.

TRADE SECRET

When hand nailing into hardwood, predrill the nail holes, or you'll usually split the wood. (A pneumatic pin nailer usually won't split it.) The easiest way to do this and to get the correct size hole, is to use a nail as a bit. Snip off the head of one of the finish nails you're using and chuck the headless nail into a drill. Nails aren't hardened like drill bits, so they bend rather easily. But it's simple enough to snip the head off another nail to make a new bit.

IN DETAIL

If you're installing linoleum flooring, cut the door casing a little more than the flooring's thickness short of the concrete floor. When you install the flooring, slipping it under the trim is much simpler than cutting it to fit the trim profile, and it gives a nicer finish.

Adjust the fit of miters with a rasp (shown) or a sharp block plane.

Nail through the top of the joint to tighten the fit. Drill a pilot hole to prevent the wood from splitting. Note the exposed edge of the jamb, or "reveal."

After nailing the top miter, nail the casing into the jamb and wall.

a rasp to adjust the miter on the side piece to fit. Check that the misaligned miter isn't the result of projecting drywall. If it is, fix the drywall and then the joint.

When the miters fit, spread some carpenter's glue on the joint. Press the mitered surfaces together and nail through the side casing into the jamb about 1 in. down from the joint and again about 8 in. below the first nail. Then pin the joint together with a 4d finishing nail driven from the

edge of the side casing into the head casing. To avoid splitting the wood, first bore a pilot hole. (See the Trade Secret at left.) If the joint needs to be tightened further, you can drill and drive in another 4d finish nail from the top. Now, nail the rest of the casing to the jamb, about every 12 in. or so. Then nail through the casing into the wall with 8d finish nails every couple of feet. Be careful around the joints; driving an 8d nail too close to the miter may open the joint.

The bottom casing is tricky. Fitting a piece between two miters usually requires fine-tuning at least one, if not both, of the miters. Be patient. Leave the bottom foot or so of the two side casings unnailed until you get a reasonable dry-fit on the bottom miters. Next, nail one side casing solid and put the bottom piece, with both ends glued, in place. Then nail the corner on the solid side, and finish with the last corner, where you can adjust the position of both pieces for a final fit.

Door casing. The process is the same for casing doors, except that there is no bottom piece. Start with the head-jamb casing, then add the side-jamb casings. For the side casings, measure from the floor to the base of the miter on each side. Cut each trim piece about $1/16$ in. shy of that measurement. Where some type of floor covering will cover the bottom of the casing, there's no need to work hard to make a snug fit to the floor. If the finished floor is concrete, stopping the casing short of it keeps moisture from wicking up from the concrete and into the wood.

Setting Cabinets

The most common basement cabinet is a bathroom vanity. Kitchenettes, laundry rooms, rec rooms, and offices also feature base cabinets or upper, hanging, cabinets. There are a wide range of styles, and cabinets may be store-bought or custom-made. Basic installation techniques, which I'll cover here, are the same for most cabinets. But consult with your supplier before you make your purchase to determine exactly what will be required for the cabinets you buy.

Installing base cabinets

These should be installed before you install baseboard trim. Bathroom vanities and kitchen or wet-bar cabinets must accommodate plumbing for sinks. Measure where the drain and the water

Trim Materials

Popular as it is, oak is not the only wood available for trim. I've trimmed jobs with poplar, pine, fir, cherry, red gum, alder, redwood, cedar, birch, walnut, mahogany, and maple. Here's some information about these other possibilities.

- **Poplar.** If I'm painting woodwork, my first choice is poplar. It's reasonably hard and smooth, takes paint well without telegraphing grain through the finish, and, relative to other species, it's inexpensive. Widely available in several styles, it's easy to work with.

- **Preprimed pine.** Some trim carpenters say this is the best trim for painting, but it's too soft for my taste. Made of short lengths of pine finger-jointed end-to-end, it isn't suitable for clear finishes. But it is knot-free and doesn't warp or twist. And it's already primed.

- **Pine and fir.** Clear-finished, these softwoods work well for a casual or a "country" look. They do not stain well and they dent easily.

- **Redwood and cedar.** Though beautiful to behold, redwood is expensive and very soft, so it doesn't wear well. Cedar is also very soft, and tends to be lighter than redwood in color.

Both of these species are generally available in $3/4$-in. stock but not usually in shaped casing.

- **Birch.** This light-colored hardwood wears very well. It was used extensively in the 1950s, then fell out of vogue, and now seems back in favor. You can usually find it in $3/4$-in. stock and in molded casing and base.

- **Maple.** Soft maple, which is actually quite hard, and rock maple, which is very hard, are light woods that take paint well, but it's a shame to cover them up. They work well with sharp tools and are usually available in $3/4$-in. stock. Some stores carry molded casing and base in maple.

- **Plastic.** If you're on a tight budget and don't want to paint the trim, plastic trim is a viable option. There's no room for error with the joints, but you can hide errors with colored putty. Moldings come in 8-ft. lengths; lots of joints to fit (and errors to putty) if you're running plastic baseboard.

- **Primed Particleboard.** Available in many styles, this inexpensive trim is a good option for painted trim.

| Cedar | Pine | Poplar | Birch | Maple | Oak |

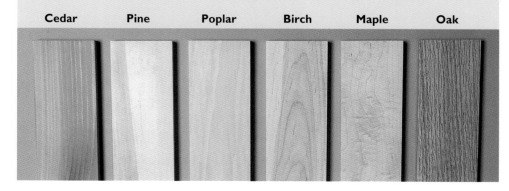

IN DETAIL

A hole saw is useful for cutting holes for large diameter pipe in cabinets, in shower surrounds, or in walls. It consists of a metal cylinder, one edge of which has been ground to form sawteeth. A central twist drill centers the hole and keeps the sawteeth on track.

Begin setting a bathroom vanity by boring a hole for the sink-drain connection with a hole saw and an electric drill.

lines penetrate the wall, and mark those locations on the back of the cabinet. (Some vanities have no back.) I like to use a hole saw, which is a can-shaped drill bit, to drill the drain-line hole. Make the hole about $1/4$ in. larger than the diameter of the drain line. A 1-in. auger or spade bit works well for the water lines. To prevent splintering the back of the cabinet, drill from the back face until the point of the bit pokes through on the inside, then finish the hole from the inside.

Set the cabinet in place and check the fit of the pipes and drain. Cabinet backs are usually thin, so you can enlarge an opening with a rasp, if need be. A trim ring around the drain or water pipes can cover an irregular opening if it concerns you.

All cabinets must be level front-to-back and side-to-side. Check with a level and shim beneath the cabinet sides as necessary. If the cabinet isn't tight to the wall, shim between the wall and the cabinet's back rail, placing the shims on studs.

Set the cabinet in place and level it with shims.

Shim any gaps between the cabinet back and the stud locations. Then screw the cabinet to the wall.

Before fixing the cabinet in place, check the fit of the sides and the face frame against their respective walls (if any). The face frames and back edges of some cabinets project slightly beyond the cabinet body, allowing you to scribe the cabinet to the wall for a close fit. Otherwise, you can use caulk after installation to fill in a narrow gap, or add a trim strip to cover a wide one.

Reposition the cabinet and shims if necessary and fix the cabinet to the wall. I drive 2½-in. screws through the back or back rail into the studs. The shims at the back prevent the cabinet from being thrown out of level when the screws are tightened.

I install countertops at the end of a basement remodel, when the walls have been painted and the floors laid. This makes painting easier and avoids possibilities for damage to the countertop from tools inadvertently tossed onto a convenient surface. See Chapter 10, p. 163, for countertop installation techniques.

Hanging upper cabinets

A friend or family member to help lift and steady the cabinet and a cordless drill with a screwdriver bit are invaluable aids for setting an upper cabinet. Start by lightly penciling a level line on the wall at the height of the bottom of the cabinet. Then pencil a plumb line on the wall to position one of the cabinet's ends.

Find and mark the studs in the wall behind the cabinet. Measure from the plumb line to the center of each stud. Remove the cabinet doors, and locate the center marks for the studs on the rail at the top of the cabinet back. Drill a clearance hole for a 2½-in. screw at each mark, and then insert a screw in each hole.

If you don't have a helper to hold the cabinet while you position and fix it to the wall, make a support. Cut a couple of 2×4s to the height of the level line on the wall. Nail them to a crosspiece or

To hang an upper cabinet, rest it on a 2×4 support while screwing it to the wall studs.

two (for stability) and set the support against the wall. Lift the cabinet onto the support. Align it with the level line and plumb line, and drive one of the screws that you inserted into the top rail. Double-check the level and plumb. Then drive home the rest of the screws. Most cabinet backs have a bottom rail underneath the cabinet. Drive screws through it into the studs, too. If the wall isn't flat, shim behind the rail to keep the screw pressure from distorting the cabinet face and door.

Upper cabinets may have extended sides and face frames for scribing. If yours does, scribe it to the wall, then screw it in place.

PRO TIP

Before nailing base-board (or other trim) in place, erase pencil marks. They'll show through stain, and sometimes even through paint.

IN DETAIL

Finding studs by tapping on the wall with a hammer and listening for the difference in pitch is, to say the least, frustrating. Metal-detecting electronic stud finders aren't much better. But, fortunately, a new generation of electronic stud finders are almost infallible. The new models are density meters. First, you place the meter on the wall and press a button to calibrate it. Then, just slide it along the wall. It measures variations in density, alerting you to the exact position of each stud. Expensive models can locate wires, metal studs, and conduit, but you really don't need all that power. A simple stud finder will cost about $15 to $20 and will work just fine.

Installing Baseboard

Like casing, baseboard (or "base") comes in a range of styles and materials. The only real challenge when installing base is fitting corners; the rest is just accurate measuring. With few exceptions, I install all baseboard using mitered joints on outside corners and coped joints on inside corners. (See Cutting Mitered and Coped Joints on p. 136.)

I also position baseboard about ⅜ in. above the concrete floor, which keeps moisture from wicking up into it and avoids having to fit it to uneven floor surfaces. Carpeting or other types of flooring is installed after the baseboard, and any gaps between flooring materials and the base can be covered with base shoe.

Before starting on the base, check the drywall you'll be installing it against. With a putty knife, scrape off globs or ridges of drywall compound at corners and along the length of the runs. It's a good idea to sweep or vacuum the floor—you'll be crawling on your hands and knees around the perimeter of every room.

Now find and mark the location of studs along all the walls to be trimmed with base. If you marked the locations on the floor before you hung drywall, great. If not, an inexpensive density-reading stud finder works very well. (See In Detail at left).

Installation

To get the hang of running baseboard, it's a good idea to start in a closet or a small room. First, cut a dozen or more ⅜-in.-thick shims and set them along the length of the wall. They'll be used to raise the base above the floor. Because the drywall doesn't extend all the way to the concrete, I also cut a couple dozen spacers to fill the ½-in. gap between the base and the exposed wall plate. The spacers prevent the base from twisting into the gap during nailing. Make sure you put spacers

at the inside corners, otherwise it's difficult to get a tight-fitting miter.

Pros often measure an entire room, cut all the pieces, including copes and miters, and install them one after the other. If you're a beginner, I suggest you measure, cut, and fit each piece as you go, at least to start. I work around the room from my left to my right (as I face the wall) because I find it easier to cut coped joints on the right-hand pieces in a corner. See what works for you.

So, for a small room (or a closet), with one doorway and all inside corners, installation proceeds from the door casing to the wall, then from that wall to the next wall, and on around to the casing on the other side of the door, as shown in the drawing on the facing page.

Measure and cut both ends of the first piece square, to fit snugly between casing and wall. (Use this measurement and fitting to "calibrate your eye," so you read the tape to produce snug fits.)

The next piece will be coped on its left end to fit over the first piece in the corner, and square cut on the right to butt against the next wall. The next two pieces are cut, coped, and fit in the same way. The final piece, which fits between the door casing and the wall, finishes the room or closet. I nail base near its top and bottom edges at every stud. To prevent hardwoods from splitting if you're hand nailing, bore pilot holes first; then carefully set the nail heads below the wood's surface.

If a wall is longer than your longest piece of baseboard, you'll need to fit two pieces together. Rather than butting two ends together, I use a scarf joint, in which the ends are cut at 22½ degrees and glued. The slight overlap allows the top piece to slide over the bottom, putting pressure on the joint to hold it together with minimum gap.

Baseboard Installation: Coped Joints

Green shading indicates the coped end, which is installed over its mating piece. Here, you'd install the baseboard in a clockwise direction, starting to the left of the door as you enter the room.

Baseboard

Casing Door

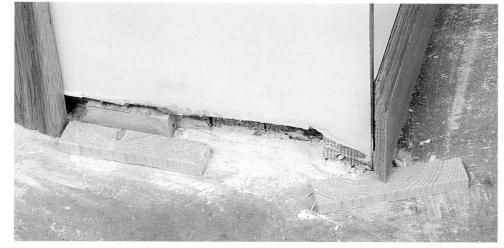

Shims ³⁄₈ in. thick hold the baseboard above the floor. A ¹⁄₂-in.-thick spacer fills the gap between the baseboard and the exposed wall framing.

Nail the top and bottom of the trim. Bore pilot holes to avoid splitting hardwood trim. Wipe off the glue before it hardens.

For long walls, join two pieces of trim with a scarf joint. Cut and nail one piece in place. Then fit the other to it.

Baseboard looks best with mitered outside corners and coped inside corners.

CUTTING MITERED AND COPED JOINTS

Where baseboard meets at a corner, the best-looking joint for almost all trim is a miter or its cousin, a coped joint. When accurately cut and fitted, both joints give the impression that the baseboard, with its molded profile, has been neatly bent around the corner.

Mitering an Outside Corner

This simple joint, made by cutting mating pieces at 45-degree angles, is used for outside corners.

Start by cutting the two pieces so that each runs past the corner about 1 in. Using the corner as a guide, mark the position of the miter on each piece. Extend the mark across the top edge of the trim and cut a 45-degree angle on that mark. Cut the opposite miter on a scrap piece of baseboard and hold it against the other piece at the corner to check the fit.

When the first piece fits, set it on the 3/8-in. shims and nail it in place. To ensure that the joint

Use the corner as a guide for marking the position of the miters for an outside corner.

A miter saw cuts clean, accurate miters quickly. If you don't own one, borrow or rent one for installing trim.

Check the miter on the first piece against a piece of mitered scrap.

Spread glue on the mitered surfaces and nail at the top and base of the trim.

will be correctly positioned, I hold the mitered scrap against the joint while nailing.

Next, fit the second piece to the first. You can adjust the miter with a block plane or rasp. Spread glue on the mitered ends, nail the piece to the wall, and then nail through the joint with a small finish nail to ensure a tight fit. Use a piece of sandpaper to ease the sharp edge slightly.

Coping an Inside Corner

Miter joints at inside corners are difficult to fit and prone to opening up over time. A coped joint looks like a miter, but one piece of trim is square cut and butts into the corner. The end of the other is cut with a coping saw to the profile of the first piece and butted against it.

Cut and fit the square-cut piece first. Then cut the piece to be coped to the length of its wall. I cut baseboard with coped joints a bit long, so each cope presses into the mating piece for a snug fit.

Cut a 45-degree angle on the end to be coped. The heel of the miter should fall on the front face. Following the profile formed by the intersection of the miter and the face of the piece, cut away the mitered wood. Darken the profile line with a pencil to make it easier to see. I cut along the straight section of the profile with a miter saw, but a fine-toothed handsaw works well, too. Cut along the molded profile with a coping saw. The coped end should fit seamlessly over the face of its mate in the corner. If it doesn't, you can rework the profile with flat and round rasps.

Coped joints take some practice to master, but they are worth the effort and very satisfying to make. Try out the technique on a piece of scrap wood before tackling the real thing.

For a coped joint, miter the end. Outline the profile with a pencil.

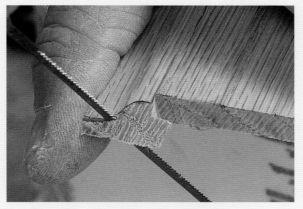

Cut away the mitered material. Cut the straight section with a miter saw or handsaw. Cut the molded profile with a coping saw.

The coped end fits over the mating piece to give the impression of a mitered joint.

IN DETAIL

Precut particleboard shelves, melamine coated or unfinished, are easy to install. But they also sag under even a moderate load. If your shelves are going to support more than towels and linen and are more than 30 in. long, consider making them of ¾-in. plywood or solid wood. Regardless of material, it's a good idea to support any heavy-load bearing shelf over 30 in. long with intermediate brackets.

TRADE SECRET

If you're installing linoleum flooring, cut the door casing a little more than the flooring's thickness short of the concrete floor. When you install the flooring, slipping it under the trim is much simpler than cutting it to fit the trim profile, and it gives a nicer finish.

Fitting Closets

Closets range from a simple hole-in-the-wall space to an entire room. Most people like to keep things simple in a basement, so that's what I'll outline here.

The easiest way to make shelves is to nail cleats to the side and back walls and rest the shelves on them. You can buy primed 1×2 particleboard for shelving cleats, or use solid poplar. Many stores sell shelving in precut widths and lengths (which you'll usually need to trim to fit). These are available as unfinished particleboard, or particleboard prefinished with a melamine coating. You can also buy larger sheets and cut your own shelves, or have them cut for you.

Rubber-wrapped wire shelving systems are widely available, easy to install, attractive, and allow more air circulation. The systems include shelves and the clips and brackets that support them. They can be installed with little more than a drill, hammer, screwdriver, and hacksaw.

Bathroom linen closet

Common in many basements, this closet is usually about 2 ft. deep and 2 ft. to 2½ ft. wide. I usually set the lowest shelf about 2 ft. off the floor, so larger items can fit underneath. The next shelf is set about 16 in. up from that, and 12 in. separate the rest. Pencil in level lines at those heights on the side and back walls and nail 1×2 cleats positioned on the lines. Of course, you can space shelves however you want them. If you can't get your level into the space, measure down from the ceiling to position the shelves; the ceiling is more likely to be level than the basement floor.

Bedroom clothes closet

For a standard clothes closet behind bifold doors, I usually install a row of shelf cleats at 64 in. above

Shelves in an open niche are handy in a bathroom.

Wire shelving is versatile and simple to install.

Trimming a Half-Wall

The top surface of a half-wall needs a covering. Some people drywall the top, but drywall is soft and easily damaged, so most people use a wood cap.

Shown here is the simplest way to cap a half-wall. The cap projects over the face of the wall, and the joint between the drywall and the cap is covered by a trim piece. When you order the cap piece, make sure it is wide enough to cover the half-wall and the trim piece. I add twice the width of the trim because I like caps to extend past the trim at least by the thickness of the trim.

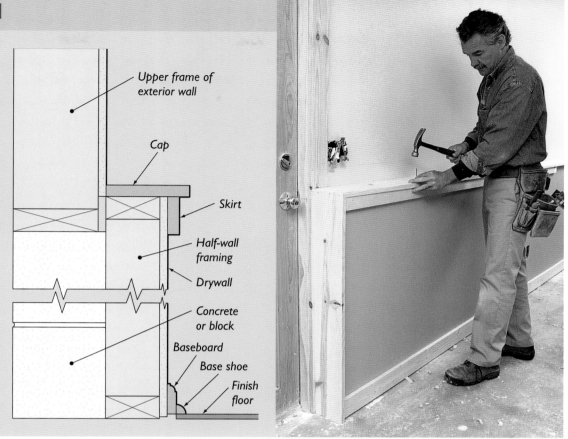

Upper frame of exterior wall

Cap

Skirt

Half-wall framing

Drywall

Concrete or block

Baseboard

Base shoe

Finish floor

Don't forget about the space beneath the stairway.

the floor and a second row at 76 in. I use a 16-in. shelf on the bottom and a 12-in. shelf on the top. To support the shelves along their length, you can add a metal shelf bracket about every 32 in. along the back wall. Use 1×4 cleats for the lower shelf to provide support for clothes-pole sockets. An intermediate bracket with a pole hook can help keep the pole from sagging.

Under-stair closet

The space underneath a stairway is ideal for a closet (and not much else). This area is deeper than other closets and, therefore, useful for storage of boxes and other large items. A clothes pole at the front makes use of the taller end of the slanting space. If you're short of drawer space, there's enough room for a built-in chest of drawers under the stairs, too.

Paint, Stain, and

Floors

Painting and staining walls and trim and installing floor coverings put the final "face" on your basement. Yes, there are still sinks to hook up and knobs to install. But when you're finished with the painting and flooring, you deserve a little celebration.

Most readers of this book will, I imagine, have done some painting or staining. If you have, you'll appreciate that although these tasks are not difficult, they do require attention to detail and a steady hand. I can't impart steadiness in this chapter, but I can help you with the details.

Fewer readers, however, will have installed flooring, a more difficult do-it-yourself task. Here, I'll discuss the common basement flooring materials—carpet, linoleum, tile, and wood—and how they're installed, so you can make an informed decision on whether to tackle the job yourself or to hire a pro.

IN DETAIL

Different woods absorb stain differently. In general, hard-woods, such as oak, mahogany, maple, and birch, stain more evenly than softwoods, such as spruce, pine and fir, which can look blotchy. To obtain a more even stain on these (or any wood), use a pre-stain sealer, also called wood conditioner. Paint manufacturers offer a range of sealers. Less expensive, but equally effective for both water and solvent-based stains, is a seal coat of shellac. After sealing, apply stain as directed on the can.

Finishing the Trim

Adding sheen to unfinished trim and color to unpainted walls will bring your basement vividly to life. I usually stain, enamel, or clear-finish the woodwork first, and then paint the walls. But you can have equal success if you paint before finishing the trim. The main advantage to finishing the trim first is that you don't have to protect painted walls while you stain or enamel the trim. You can just paint over any stain or enamel that gets slopped on the walls.

Most of the basements I work on have stained or natural wood trim protected by a clear fin-ish, so I'll outline those finishing procedures here. (See Choosing Stain and Clear Finish on p. 145.) If you want to paint your woodwork with enamel, the process is much the same as for staining. If you've decided to finish the trim before installing it (see In Detail on p. 128), lay the pieces on sawhorses and apply the finishing materials as described in this chapter.

Preparation

A wood finish can never be better than the prepa-ration that underlies it. Closely check glued joints. Stain won't penetrate glue, so slice off beads of glue with a sharp chisel or knife and sand any glue smears (where you wiped wet glue off a joint).

Brush stain on the trim and then wipe off the excess with a rag to the desired depth of color.

Most trim will benefit from sanding before the finish is applied. If you didn't sand the trim before installing it, now is the time (see Sanding on the facing page). After you've sanded, wipe the dust off the woodwork, and sweep and vacuum where you'll be staining and finishing. Then, if your rag or brush touches the floor, you won't pick up dirt and dust to spread throughout the finish. For the same reason, use a vacuum with a wide nozzle to suck up the drywall dust left on the walls.

Doors and jambs count as trim and are finished now, too. Remove latchsets, hinges, strike plates, and other hardware from doors and jambs. Mark the hardware locations with a piece of masking tape and a numbering system. The hardware should be interchangeable, but I've found it best to re-install in the original locations if possible. For staining and finishing, I find it easiest to lay doors and other large, flat surfaces on a pair of sawhorses or on some 2×4s on the floor. To pro-tect door faces, rest them on old towels or rags.

Applying stain

I prefer to brush on stain and wipe it off with a rag. You can also apply the stain with a rag or a throw-away foam brush. Wipe stain off with smooth, long strokes in the direction of the grain, eliminating streaks and lap marks.

A stain will be darker or lighter depending on how much you put on and how long you let it sit before wiping it off. Experiment on scrap pieces of trim to get the color you want. Don't let the stain dry before wiping it off. If you want a darker color, apply several coats of stain.

For doors, wipe or brush on strips of stain the full length of the door and work your way across the face, overlapping the long runs. Wipe off in the same pattern, pulling the rag the full length of the door without stopping. When you've finished a face, stand the door up against a wall to dry, making contact with only one corner of the door. Examine the stained face; if you find lap marks or fingerprints, blend them in with your stain rag.

Applying clear finish

Once the stain is dry, brush on the first coat of clear finish. (Spray outfits can be rented, but unless you've done some spraying before, stick with brushes and rollers.) Applying a clear finish isn't all that different from painting. Coat the surfaces completely, and then, with long strokes, touching just the tip of the brush, flow the finish out evenly. Several thin coats are better than a thick coat, which may sag and run. Watch for runs at the top, bottom, and around the panels of doors, or wherever your brush tends to flop over the edge and unload a glob of finish. Brush out the runs before they have a chance to dry.

Two coats of finish provide much better coverage and protection than one. After the finish has dried for as long as is recommended on the can, run your hand over the surface. It will feel a bit rough. Although you don't have to do so, sanding lightly to remove the roughness before applying the second coat will produce a better finish. Use a fine-grade sanding sponge, 220-grit sandpaper, or

Over dry stain, brush on a clear finish to protect and enhance.

Lightly sand between coats of clear finish to remove dust stuck in the first coat.

Sanding

Doors and trim are often sold "ready to finish" or primed for painting. If you're applying stain or clear finish, the machine planing or sanding marks left on these pieces will show in the finish. A little additional sanding can make a noticeable difference in how your woodwork looks. You can do this sanding before or after you install trim. If you do it before you trim, remember to go over the installed trim to remove any tears or dings resulting from nailing.

Sand with the grain, so the scratches from the sandpaper grit blend in with the grain. For coarse-grained woods like oak, 100-grit paper followed by 120-grit will produce a nice surface. For close-grained woods, like maple, birch, or poplar, use 150-grit paper after the 120-grit. If there are still visible marks, move to 180 or even 220. Sand each piece with each grit so the pieces will absorb stain similarly. If you sand after installation, or you're touching up then, take care not to sand across the grain where pieces join together.

Narrow pieces are most easily sanded with paper backed by a flat block or a block shaped to match the molding profile. You can buy sanding blocks, including ones easily shaped to a profile, at home centers and hardware stores. Wide surfaces on doors or cabinets can also be sanded by hand. If you have many such surfaces, consider a random-orbit sander. Inexpensive (about $70) and easy to hold in one hand, these sanders do fast, accurate work on surfaces wider than 4 in. or 5 in.

To sand trim, shape a block of wood to conform to molding details and use it to back the sandpaper.

PRO TIP

It's easier to stain and finish base-shoe molding with the rest of the trim rather than after installing the flooring and shoe.

IN DETAIL

When you select a paint roller, try this simple test. Make a circle with your thumb and forefinger around the roller and pull down its length quickly several times. If you create a haze of fine strands, try another roller. The loose strands won't stop coming off; they'll just be painted onto your wall.

TRADE SECRET

If the joint between the trim and the wall is uneven, paint can bleed. To prevent that, spray the tape-to-wall joint with clear lacquer or polyurethane, and then paint. (You can buy these finishes in aerosol cans; make sure the finish is dry before you paint over it.) The lacquer seals the gaps that paint could seep through. When you pull off the tape, you'll have a clean paint line.

If you want a clean line between two colors on the same wall, paint the first color through the demarcation line. Let it dry. Then tape on top of the first color to reestablish the line and repaint over the edge. When that is dry, paint the second color and let it dry. Pull off the tape.

After the first coat of clear finish, fill nail holes with a color-matched putty.

some fine steel wool. Sand just enough to remove the roughness without, if possible, sanding through the finish.

Filling holes. After the first coat of finish has dried and been sanded, I fill nail holes, splits, and any small imperfections with color-matched wood putty. If need be, you can mix colors to match your stain; you can also use different colors for woods with lots of color variation, so the filled areas are less visible. Filling holes between the first and second coats of finish has the advantage of maintaining an even sheen over the puttied and surrounding surfaces. Make sure to fill in the holes evenly, and wipe off the excess so that the holes don't become bumps under the final coat.

Wipe or vacuum to remove dust. Then apply a second coat in the same way you did the first. If you sanded between coats, this coat will go on smoothly and should require no final sanding.

Painting

After the woodwork is stained and finished or painted, you're ready to paint the walls. (See A Paint Primer on p. 146 for tips on purchasing paint.) Actually, you're ready to caulk and tape in preparation for paint; sometimes it seems this prep work takes longer than the actual painting.

Paintable caulking compound makes gaps between trim and wall disappear.

Caulking. There are always places where the trim hasn't pulled tight to the wall. I fill them with caulk, paint over the caulk, and the gap disappears. Buy paintable caulk (avoid silicone caulks), and an inexpensive caulk gun. Cut a small hole in the caulk-tube tip, and gently squeeze out the caulk as you move the tip along the trim-and-wall joint. Smooth the caulk into the joint with your finger, and wipe off any excess with a rag. (I wet my finger, which produces a smoother caulk surface.) Let the caulk dry thoroughly and then tape up to, but not over, the caulk.

Taping. Shielding trim with tape and paper protects the finish you just applied from paint spatters and makes a cleaner line between the painted and stained surfaces. If you have a steady hand and a good eye, you can paint without taping off. Drips that hit the finished trim can be removed with a damp rag if still fresh, or later with a latex paint remover like Goof-Off®.

Pros tape off using strips of gummed or taped paper. (See In Detail on p. 146.) You can buy gummed paper in widths from 2 in. to 12 in.

Protect trim during wall painting with adhesive-backed paper.

Only one edge is covered with adhesive, so the tape is easy to roll out onto the trim. The adhesive won't pull off the finish. But because it isn't tenacious, it needs to be smoothed out very firmly to fully adhere. I stick it on the edge of the trim, and then crease it around the face.

Brush and roll. With a paint brush, start by "cutting in" the prime coat. Begin at the trim and brush out at least 2 in. onto the wall or ceiling. Do the same at the inside corners, brushing out onto both sides of the wall 2 in. or more. This way you don't have to try to control a roller in difficult spots. (On a textured ceiling, the drywall mud provides a finish that requires no paint.) Novices often assume you need to use a 2-in. or narrower brush to cut in. I prefer a 4 in. brush, which holds more paint and, I feel, more easily maintains a straight line where the paint meets the trim. If you're uncomfortable brushing, try a painting pad with small wheels that stand the pad off the trim or adjacent surface about $\frac{1}{16}$ in. It works remarkably well.

Once the trim, ceiling, and corners are cut in, you're ready to roll. Pour primer into the roller tray up to, but not over, the corrugated slope. Work the roller from the deep depression in the tray up onto the slope to cover the nap entirely

Choosing Stain and Clear Finish

Stain enhances the appearance of wood. Clear finish also enhances, but its main job is protection. Water-based penetrating stains and clear finishes (varnishes and polyurethanes) are now widely available alternatives to traditional oil-based materials. Water-based materials produce fewer toxic fumes, and the equipment is cleaned with soap and water. For most basement finishing work, I recommend water-based products. These and other finishing materials for trim are discussed here. Sanding sealer, wood filler, or primer, all of which are useful for furniture, are unnecessary for finishing new basement trim.

Stains

- **Color.** Stains come in a wide range of stock colors. If you can't find what you want, some stores will mix a stain to match a sample.
- **Type.** Several types of stains are available. Penetrating stains soak into the wood. Wiping stains tend to be more viscous, both penetrating and sitting on the surface, rather like a translucent paint. The more color you want, the more you leave on. Gel stains are more viscous still. Use them when you want a lot of color and don't want to build it up with many coats of wiping stain.

Clear Finishes

- **Polyurethane.** The simple answer to the question of finish is two coats of polyurethane. A type of varnish, it provides a hard, clear, durable finish. It brushes on easily and dries to the touch in as little as 30 minutes (depending on the brand) so it tends to pick up less dust than varnish.
- **Varnish.** Producing a hard, durable finish, varnish can take hours to dry and therefore is susceptible to any dust floating around. Nevertheless, it's my second choice, after polyurethane.
- **Shellac.** Offering less protection than other finishes, shellac is inexpensive and dries in minutes, which can be an advantage, but it can also produce lap marks. Amber shellac produces a rich golden tone.
- **Compatibility.** Not all stains and finishes like each other. Make sure the ones you choose are compatible. Read labels and ask paint-store staff about potential problems.
- **Sheen.** Clear finishes range from flat, to satin, to semi-gloss, to gloss, or some variation of this progression. Personal taste determines how shiny you want your trim. Gloss finishes tend to be a little less forgiving in application and in their compatibility with other finishes. A reduced-gloss finish is just a gloss finish with a dulling compound added in suspension; make sure you gently stir this finish from time to time during application to keep it mixed.

TRADE SECRET

If your walls require more than one can of the same color of paint, mix the contents of the cans together as you paint. Work through half of can one, then pour in half of can two, and so on. The machines that paint stores use to measure out color additives aren't perfect. If you mix as you go, the color on the wall will be uniform, even if the color varies from can to can.

IN DETAIL

All masking tape is not alike. The ubiquitous beige tape tends to pull off the finish when you remove it. "Low-tack" painter's masking tape (sold at paint stores and home centers) costs a little more, but it pulls off more easily, so it's better for fresh finishes.

Roll on an even primer coat to seal the surface of the wall. To avoid drips, don't overload the roller with too much primer.

Begin top-coating by cutting in around baseboards, ceiling, corners, and trim. A 4-in. brush works well for cutting in.

Work from corner to corner when rolling. A roller-frame extension makes this work a lot easier.

with paint. Roll back and forth a few times on the corrugated slope to work the paint into the nap; you don't want the roller dripping with paint, just saturated.

I like to start at a corner and work my way across the wall. After unloading the roller on an area, roll lightly from the unpainted area back into the freshly painted wall, to blend in the paint and minimize roller lines. Reload and roll again, starting in the adjacent unpainted area.

Try to get an even coverage of primer. If you use tinted primer, you may need only one top coat. When I finish a coat on a wall, I like to look at it from several angles to see how well it's covered. That way, if I want to re-roll part of it, the paint is still wet and it's easy to blend it in. If you re-roll, start in the area you want to touch up, and roll out onto the surrounding wall to unload the roller and blend in the paint.

Follow drying-time directions on the paint can. Then top-coat. The procedure is the same—cut-in and roll. Some colors are notoriously difficult to cover in less than two or three coats.

A Paint Primer

Most readers will have gone through the ordeal of choosing paint. What type, what color, what gloss, how much? A knowledgeable paint-store employee can help make choices. I'm not a paint expert, but here are some tips based on my experiences with basement remodels.

- **Paint type.** Use latex. The cleanup is easy, it's low-odor and non-toxic. If you're painting your trim, use a latex enamel.

- **Color.** Before you commit to a color, buy a quart and put it on the wall. That's the only way you'll know what it's going to look like in your room. Buying an extra quart or two is worth getting the color you really want.

- **Primer.** Don't skip the primer—it's worth the time and money. Primer makes the top coat cover the different surfaces of drywall and drywall compound uniformly, and it provides better adhesion for the top coats than painting them directly onto the wall.

Examine the wall closely under good light to make sure you've achieved the coverage you want.

When the final coat of paint is dry, pull off the protective tape and paper. Because the paint might bridge onto the tape and tear off in spots, it's sometimes helpful first to cut along the tape line with a sharp utility knife.

Cleanup. This job is much easier with water-based latex paints than oil-based paints. Use a pail of water and a tub or sink. I clean up brushes and rollers thoroughly at the end of a day's painting. Work your fingers into the strands of the brush, cleaning out the paint all the way up to the metal piece that holds the bristles. I use a drop of dishwashing soap and lather it up for a final cleaning. Make sure to rinse all the soap out. Dry the bristles by spinning the brush between the palms of your hands, or by slapping the bristles against the heel of your hand. Smooth the bristles and store the brush in its cover to reshape it.

Follow the same procedure with rollers. If you can, work the paint out of the nap under running water until the water runs clear.

Pour the paint from the roller tray back into the can, using a brush to clean out the excess, and rinse out the pan. Some paint will dry and build up in the pan, but if you leave too much in there, it will come off in the fresh paint the next day and leave bits and pieces on the wall when you paint.

Floor Coverings

Nothing brings a newly remodeled basement room together like finishing the floor. The most popular flooring materials for basements are familiar ones: carpet, linoleum, and ceramic tile. Prefinished, easily installed wooden floors are a more recent alternative. (See Wood Floors on p. 149.) Homeowners can install all of these surfaces, but many of the students in my classes choose professional installation. I'll discuss how

Tools for Stain, Finish, and Paint

Tools for decorating your basement walls and trim are basic and relatively inexpensive. Chances are you'll have some of them in your house already.

- **Rags.** Whether you brush on or wipe on stain, you'll need rags to wipe it off. You can make rags of old cotton clothing (washed clean). Or you can buy inexpensive boxes of rags at a paint store.

- **Rubber gloves.** Stain colors hands as well as wood, so I usually wear rubber gloves when I use it. If you're not a tidy painter, you may also want gloves when you brush and roll. Cheap latex surgical gloves sold at paint stores tear easily. Buy heavier duty. Dishwashing gloves sold at the grocery store work well.

- **Brushes.** The quality of any brushed finish, whether shellac, polyurethane, or paint, is highly dependent on the quality of the brush. A $2 throwaway brush produces a throwaway finish. I use Purdy® brushes and spend $20 to $30 each for them. The bristles are fine and soft, and they spread the finish evenly and smoothly, leaving no brush marks. The results are worth the cost, even for just one basement, but they'll last for years if you take care of them.

- **Rollers.** A dizzying array of rollers and whiz-bang gadgets are sold for rolling on paint. There are foam rollers, sheepskin rollers, and rollers of varying width and nap thickness. Here are my recommendations for basic rolling:

  1. A 9-in. rolling frame. Buy one with a threaded handle so you can screw in a short extension to roll walls or a longer extension to roll ceilings. A push-broom handle often has the same threads; or you can buy an adjustable metal extension. A 3-in. or 4-in. roller and frame can be helpful in narrower spaces.

  2. Several good-quality 9-in. rollers with 3/8-in. nap. If you want to paint over ceiling texture, use a roller with a 1/2-in. or longer nap.

  3. A large roller pan. Metal or plastic work equally well. If you don't want to clean the pan after every session, use inexpensive disposable plastic pan liners.

Professionals sometimes scoff at them, but cutting-in gadgets can be a big help to an amateur painter. The one shown here is a pad mounted on a plastic frame. Two small wheels on the frame ride against the ceiling, making a neat edge.

PRO **TIP**

Stretched carpet laid on a pad is difficult to install, and the tools needed can cost almost as much to rent as having the job done professionally.

TRADE SECRET

Kneeling on concrete to install flooring can be painful. Kneepads make a big difference. They don't have to be expensive. I've had good luck with the padded elastic knee protectors volleyball players use.

IN DETAIL

The simplest solution to basement flooring is to use the existing concrete. But concrete tends to feel cold, and it has an industrial look to it. And no matter how much you sweep, it still maintains a fine haze of dust. The next simplest solution is to paint or stain the concrete, which will seal the surface and let you coordinate colors or decorate it with designs. Make sure to buy good quality paint or stain, formulated for use on concrete floors.

each is installed so that you can make an informed decision about doing it yourself. There are myriad colors and styles available in each flooring material. I won't even try to make recommendations, other than to say that if you buy the cheapest, you usually get what you pay for.

Carpet

There are four ways to carpet a basement. First, you can buy loose carpets or rugs, up to room size, and lay them on the floor, no fitting or fixing required. And if you get water in the basement, you just roll the carpet up and take it outside to clean and dry it.

Fitted carpets, cut to size and fixed to the floor, are the second option. Low-pile "action-back" carpet can be laid with no backing pad. The third option, carpet laid on a separate pad, is more expensive and more difficult to install. The fourth is carpet attached to interlocking squares of plywood or synthetic backing. These carpet "tiles" are supported slightly above the floor on plastic "feet" to reduce moisture.

Low-pile action-back carpet. Often seen in offices, this carpet can rest directly on the concrete floor. A synthetic backing ("action back") has replaced jute, which is more prone to problems with mold, mildew, and rotting in damp environments. Installation is easy. The carpet is either glued to the floor with mastic or fixed with double-sided tape along its edges and seams. Mastic fixes the carpet securely. Taped carpet is best used in rooms that don't get much rambunctious use, which breaks tape joints. If you have moisture problems in your basement, taped carpet can be rolled back and dried out fairly easily.

To fit carpet into a room that is smaller than the piece of carpet, I lay the piece tight against two adjacent walls in the room. Then, with a utility knife, I cut it to fit along the other two walls. To get a good fit, push a 4-in. scraper into

To install a carpet with mastic or double-sided tape, first push the carpet into a corner against two walls.

To cut carpet to fit, push a 4-in scraper into the joint between the baseboard and carpet and run a utility knife against the scraper.

the intersection of the floor and wall (or baseboard) and cut along the top edge of the scraper, as shown in the photo above. Move the scraper along the wall as you cut.

At doorways, cut from the corner of the jamb at an angle away from the opening so the carpet is wider than the opening. Then push the piece against the base of the jamb with the 4-in. scraper and cut tight to the jamb.

Cut the carpet in the doorway so the break is under the door. That way, if you transition to another carpet or another type of flooring, the break is invisible under the door when it's closed. Cut along a metal straightedge to produce an edge that will fit into a metal threshold transition piece, or make a tidy seam with the carpet in the next room.

When the carpet is cut to fit, pull back a corner to expose the floor along two adjacent walls. Apply tape or mastic close to the wall and smooth the carpet back in place. Do the same for the other two walls.

Rooms larger than the width of the carpet require seams, which require some skill to do well. Practice on some scrap to decide if you want to tackle seaming yourself. If you do, try to locate the seam in an inconspicuous, low-traffic area. Don't butt factory-cut edges together—the joint will be obvious. Instead, overlap the two pieces by a few inches and cut both at once with a sharp utility knife running along a sturdy straightedge. (A 4-ft. drywall square works well.) Align the pieces so the weave runs the same direction in both. Pros join seams with hot-melt glue and cloth tape, and they can make them virtually unnoticeable. This is harder to accomplish with just mastic or double-stick tape.

Carpet and pad. If you're going to install a more expensive carpet and a pad stretched to a tack strip around the room perimeter, I strongly suggest buying the installation with the carpet. A room 15 ft. by 30 ft. requires 50 sq. yd. of carpet. At $20 per yard with pad, the carpet is $1,000. Installation at $4 to $5 per yard adds just $200 to $300. For that extra money, you'll get a couple of installers and all their experience and equipment.

Carpet "tiles." Interlocking tiles covered with carpet are a very good solution for basements that have moisture problems. Manufacturers of some of these systems allow only professional installation and are fairly pricey.

When the carpet is trimmed to size, pull it back and apply mastic or double-sided tape (shown here) around the perimeter. Then push the carpet onto the adhesive. Tuck the carpet edges under the baseboard with a wide-blade scraper.

Wood Floors

Wood flooring used to be an invitation to disaster in a basement. Concrete holds and passes moisture, and moisture is anathema to wood. But newer laminate and composite floor systems with tough factory finishes seem to have solved the moisture problem. And ingenious interlocking construction makes them one of the easiest floors to install.

Composite wood floors often consist of thin strips of wood laminated to plywood or particleboard backing, which reduces or eliminates movement with seasonal changes in humidity. Some have

This composite floor rests on a thin foam pad and snaps together.

the look of a wood-strip floor. Others offer parquet and bordered patterns. The flooring is laid on a thin foam pad and isn't attached to the underlying concrete floor. Most systems require no fasteners at all; they simply snap together.

PRO TIP

Unroll linoleum a day or two before installation to let it flatten out. Put the concave face down, and the linoleum's own weight will help flatten it.

IN DETAIL

Notched trowels for spreading adhesive come in a wide variety of notch sizes. Be sure to use the size recommended by the manufacturer of your flooring.

Resilient flooring

Durable and easy to clean, linoleum and vinyl floorings are ideal for areas like bathrooms and laundries. They come in large sheets or smaller, precut squares, both of which can be laid by a patient homeowner. I'm old enough to think of these materials as "linoleum," which is less of a mouthful than "resilient floorings," so I'll call them linoleum here.

I usually install linoleum in large sheets because it is less time-consuming than laying a lot of individual squares. (Often called "tiles," these should not be confused with ceramic tile.) And there are far fewer joints to pop loose over time. If you choose tiles, you can use techniques similar to those described for ceramic tile later in the chapter. Linoleum is thin and telegraphs irregularities

Vinyl vs. Linoleum

It's easy to be confused about resilient floor coverings, the trade term for linoleum and vinyl. Linoleum is the original resilient floor covering, patented in England in 1863 by Frederick Walton. It was manufactured from linseed oil, pine resin, and wood flour on a jute backing. Congoleum®, an asphalt-based floor-covering made with asphalt from the Belgian Congo, followed. And in the 1950s, Congoleum-Nairn introduced a 12-ft.-wide sheet flooring made of vinyl (polyvinyl chloride).

So, for the remodeler, what is the difference between vinyl and linoleum? Most vinyl flooring has a pattern printed on the surface protected by a vinyl or urethane layer. That is why vinyl floors are no-wax. In linoleum, the color goes all the way through the sheet to the backing. This makes it possible to buff out small scratches and dings. Without a protective layer, linoleum requires floor polish from time to time. Each type requires a different adhesive—make sure to consult with your supplier.

Patching Concrete Floors

Resilient flooring and ceramic tiles need to be laid on a flat surface. Irregularities will telegraph through linoleum and vinyl, which may wear badly or crack in those spots. Tile will rock on an uneven surface during installation and will itself make an uneven surface once it is installed.

Badly irregular floors may require a complete resurfacing, as discussed on p. 10. If the cracks and unevenness are less severe ($3/16$ in. or less), you can use leveling compound, available at home centers and hardware stores. Mix the dry powder with water to the consistency of peanut butter and trowel it over the crack. Gently feather the compound out from the cracks. The farther you feather out from the crack, the less noticeable it will be. For linoleum, feathering out a foot or so is fine. You may need to extend farther for ceramic tiles to make sure they don't rock when you lay them. Just test the result with a tile. The compound dries fast, so it's easy to check and fill in, if need be.

Linoleum and vinyl floors come in wide sheets or individual tiles. Some tiles, like the square at top left, have adhesive backs and can be pressed directly onto the floor.

in the floor. If yours is an older home, you may need to repair some areas of the floor, as described in the sidebar on the facing page.

Before starting, unroll the linoleum and leave it for a day or two to take the curl out of it. You'll be have a much easier time getting the edges to lie down flat during installation.

Cutting to fit. The most challenging part of laying linoleum is cutting it to fit. You can rough-cut the sheet over size, then lay it on the floor, and cut it to fit with a utility knife. I prefer to make a paper template, which I can adjust until it's just right, and then cut the linoleum to the template.

I make templates with builder's paper, a heavy brown paper like kraft paper. Instead of trying to cut one large piece, I cut and tape pieces together until the assembled template fits the space snugly. Butt the factory edges of the paper against the tub or shower or any other area where there will be no base shoe added later to cover gaps. Where there will be base shoe, try to fit the template within ⅛ in. of the baseboard, which will leave a little room for final fitting of the linoleum.

Lay the linoleum sheet on a flat, clean, and hard surface (a freshly swept concrete floor) and tape the template in place on the top surface of the linoleum. Position any patterns as you want them. Then, with a fresh blade in your utility knife, cut the linoleum along the outline of the template. Use a sturdy straightedge (a drywall T-square, for example) to guide straight cuts.

Remove the template from the linoleum and clean any particles off the back. Sweep and vacuum the concrete floor on which you're installing the sheet, making sure all the drywall droppings are scraped clean. Then lay the linoleum in place and check the fit. Make sure it's tight wherever there won't be base shoe. Where you will have base shoe, the linoleum should extend at least ⅛ in. beneath it, which gives you a little room to fudge the piece a bit.

Gluing in place. Once the fit is satisfactory, fold the linoleum halfway back on itself to expose half the floor. (Don't crease the sheet.) Trowel on the adhesive with a notched trowel of the size recommended on the adhesive container. Pour some adhesive on the floor and pull the trowel though it firmly, leaving parallel lines of adhesive,

To install a sheet floor of linoleum or vinyl, start by piecing together a pattern made of heavy kraft paper.

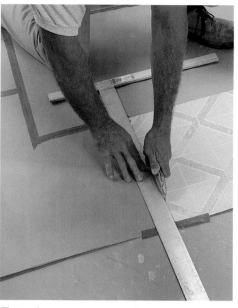

Tape the pattern to the flooring and carefully cut along its outline.

Fit the sheet, fold it back, and spread mastic on the floor with a corrugated trowel.

IN DETAIL

A linoleum roller is awkward and heavy, but it is the best way to smooth out the linoleum and ensure uniform adhesion. Fortunately, you can often borrow one from your linoleum supplier or rent one at a home center. They range from 25 lb. to 100 lb. Get the heaviest one you can manage.

TRADE SECRET

The easiest way to lay tile around door trim is to cut off the casing just above the height of the tile. Sliding the tile under the casing hides the joint. If you didn't cut the casing to accommodate tile during trim installation, you can cut it off now. Use an ordinary handsaw, resting the blade on a tile while you cut. You may need to flex the blade a bit to do it.

Roll the flooring into place on the mastic. Press it down first by hand, and then with a heavy linoleum roller.

like windrows of hay, criss-crossing the entire area. Too little adhesive compromises the bond; too much and you'll be chasing bubbles of adhesive as you try to smooth the linoleum flat. Unfold the sheet onto the adhesive and pat it in place. Then fold back the other half, trowel adhesive for it, and unfold the sheet again.

With the entire sheet patted in place, you're ready to flatten and adhere the linoleum with a heavy roller. (See In Detail.) Work from the center to the outside edges. That will push any air bubbles or excess adhesive to the edges, where you can clean it up with a damp rag.

It's best to stay off the linoleum for a day (or whatever is recommended by the adhesive manufacturer) after it is laid. Certainly don't move in washers, dryers, or refrigerators until then. They can squish grooves in the adhesive that will telegraph through the linoleum and become permanent. Adding base shoe will finish the job.

Ceramic tile

Even more durable than linoleum, and just as easy to clean, ceramic tile is increasingly used in basements. Tiles aren't cheap, but you can save money if you lay them yourself. You'll need to purchase or rent some equipment, and you'll need a methodical, patient approach. I'll run through the process for a simple floor. Borders, patterns, tiles of different sizes, and so on complicate matters; you might want to consider hiring a pro if you use them.

A concrete basement floor is a perfect substrate for ceramic tile: hard, flat, and strong. Irregularities in the floor surface can complicate installation and may need patching (see Patching Concrete Floors on p. 150).

Laying out the grid. Start by cleaning the floor thoroughly; dust impairs adhesion. Arrange tiles on a fairly large area of the floor to see how they fit the space and what size gaps you'll need between pieces. If you're using accent pieces or making a border, this "dry" layout is essential.

When you're satisfied with the arrangement, pick up all the tile except one near the center of the room. Use that one as a starting point for chalking a grid on the floor. Measure to the tile from the longest straight wall, transfer that measure to both ends of the wall, and snap a chalkline between the marks. Do the same for the longest wall adjacent to the first. Check that the two lines are perpendicular by using the 3-4-5 method described on p. 54. Adjust the lines if necessary—if the layout lines aren't square to each other the grout gaps will become increasingly smaller or larger as you lay the tile.

By measurement or marking from a tile, position and snap chalklines to construct a tile-width grid over the entire floor, working from the first two intersecting lines. Don't forget to include the grout spacing when you establish these lines.

Setting tile. With the tile positions established, you can start laying tiles anywhere on the floor. I suggest that you first lay all the uncut pieces (called field tile). Then rent a tile saw to cut all the special pieces. That way, you won't be paying rent on a saw to sit idle while you install all the field tile.

I lay tiles in squares of four at a time, always starting in the same corner of each square, as shown in the drawing below. Because most tiles

Lay out a section of tile on the floor to check the fit.

Leave a center tile in place and measure to it from adjacent walls. Transfer the measurements to both ends of the walls. Then snap chalklines between the marks.

Laying Ceramic Tile

Snap layout gridlines in chalk on the floor.

	B2	B1	A2	A1
	B4	B3	A4	A3
			C2	C1
			C4	C3

Lay sets of 4 tiles in the numbered sequence to ensure rows will be aligned.

Measure from the first snapped lines to establish a grid for your tiles. Then snap chalklines to mark the grid on the floor.

IN DETAIL

You can cut ceramic tile with a scoring tile cutter or a wet saw, either of which are commonly available for rent. The scoring cutter works like a glass cutter. A sharp point scores the tile. You then break away the waste on the score line. A wet saw cuts through the thickness of the tile, the blade cooled by a stream of water. The saw allows more complicated and delicate cuts. If you are installing a lot of tile (more than for a small bathroom), rent a wet saw.

Using a notched trowel, apply thinset to each of four squares in the grid.

Carefully align the tiles with the chalked grid and push them into place on the thinset.

aren't exactly uniform in size, following this sequence ensures that the rows will be straight, though the width of the grout joint may vary slightly between tiles within a square.

Start by troweling thinset adhesive within the four squares so you can still see the grid lines. Thinset, like linoleum mastic, must be applied with a notched trowel that conforms to the manufacturer's specifications. This ensures that the bond won't be starved or that excess adhesive won't squeeze into the gaps between tiles where it will have to be removed before grouting. Set each tile in turn, pressing it into the thinset. Continue laying all the field tile in the same manner. Next, cut and lay the partial pieces. Mark the cuts by measurement or with a template and cut with a scoring tile cutter or a wet saw (see In Detail at left).

Grouting tile. After the thinset has cured for the recommended time, you're ready to grout. Mix the grout according to the manufacturer's

specifications. With a rubber squeegee, spread grout on about 10 sq. ft. of tile, forcing it into the gaps. Pull the squeegee diagonally across the tile, pushing down hard. Make several passes to ensure all the gaps are filled. Then make a lighter diagonal pass to remove excess material.

Tool the joints with a rounded implement. This forces the grout to fill the gaps and produces an attractive joint. I use the handle of a drywall saw, as shown in the photo on the facing page. When the grout dries to a dull haze on the tile faces, wipe away the haze with a dry rag, being careful not to pull grout out of the joints.

Follow the recommendations for curing time for the grout. Installers I know recommend lightly misting the finished floor with water each day for about three days to help the grout cure properly. Some tile and grout require a seal coat after installation. Check with your supplier.

Adhesives for Flooring

Resilient flooring and ceramic tile are glued to a basement's concrete floor with special adhesives. Vinyl and linoleum sheets and tiles are usually laid using a ready-mixed glue called mastic. Traditionally, ceramic tile was bedded in thick mortar, a process requiring a mason's skills. Today, homeowners can lay their own tile using a cement called thinset. (Ceramic wall tiles are sometimes attached with mastic.) Grout, a cement-based paste, fills the joints between the ceramic tiles.

There are a great many varieties and brands of these adhesives. Fortunately, there's a simple way to determine which you should use. When you buy vinyl, linoleum, ceramic tile, or whatever you choose, ask the suppliers about adhesive. They warranty the flooring and will have specifications about what adhesives can and cannot be used. If they don't supply the adhesive, have them write down its name and the store where it can be purchased. When you buy the adhesive, read the manufacturer's recommendations for proper installation, the proper trowel-notch size, and so on, because the manufacturer must also warranty its product.

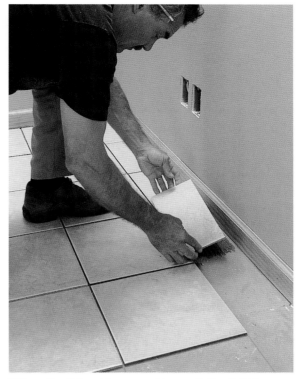

When the thinset has cured beneath the full tiles, cut and set partial tiles wherever needed.

Tool fresh grout to make a neat, solid joint. The rounded handle of a drywall saw does the job here.

Spread grout with a squeegee to fill the joints between tiles.

When the grout residue hazes over, wipe it off the surface of the tiles.

Finishing

CHAPTER TEN

Up

You might be surprised to learn that this, the last phase, is the most difficult of the whole remodeling project. Just a few things to finish up, just inches from the finish line. But the easy chair beckons, the golf course tempts, and other long-deferred projects, not to mention your family, are clamoring for attention.

Hang in there. There are a lot of final tasks—running base shoe, setting bath fixtures, hanging light fixtures, connecting switches and outlets, fixing vent covers, and installing door hardware—but each one is simple. And each completion brings an immediate reward. After hooking up the sink, you can wash your hands without traipsing upstairs, and you can dry them on the towel hanging on the newly installed towel rack. It's a great feeling.

Room by room, you're coming to closure on a successful project. You can schedule your coming-out-of-the-basement party now. Send a special invitation to those folks who doubted you could do it.

1 Running Base Shoe, p. 158

2 Final Plumbing, p. 158

3 Finishing Electricals, p. 163

4 HVAC, p. 165

5 Door Hardware, p. 166

TRADE SECRET

If you're splitting base shoe with finish nails, you can predrill the shoe, chucking a headless nail in the drill as a bit. Or you can use another old carpenter's trick. Just snip the points off the nails. Instead of wedging the wood fibers apart like a sharp point does, the blunt end crushes the fibers as it is driven in, avoiding a split.

IN DETAIL

Buying the parts needed to finish tub-shower, toilet, and sink installations can be trying. Many, if not all, of these items are sold separately: The showerhead extension is separate from the showerhead, which is separate from the tub spout, which is separate from the mixer, and so on. If possible, buy all these parts from the same place at the same time, so you can coordinate styles. And so you have only one place to go to exchange items that don't fit.

Running Base Shoe

After installing flooring, there's often a gap between the edge of the linoleum, ceramic tile, or carpet and the baseboard. Now's the time to nail on narrow strips of wood, called base shoe (or just "shoe") to cover these gaps. Base shoe comes in a variety of profiles. Common are quarter-round and a rectangular cross section with a slightly rounded top edge.

Compared to the trim work you've already done, installing shoe is easy. Cope inside corner joints as described for baseboard on p. 137. Measure just a bit long and the pieces will snap tightly in place with a mitered look. Miter outside corners as described on p. 136. Cut a couple of

Base shoe covers gaps between floor and baseboard. Cope inside corners (top), miter outside corners and return exposed ends with a mitered cap (above).

scrap pieces to get the exact angle setting. Nail the shoe to the baseboard with 6d finishing nails (or 18-gauge nails in a pneumatic brad nailer). Countersink the heads and fill with color-matched putty.

Where a length of shoe overlaps a door casing, I like to cut the end at 45 degrees. If you've prestained and finished the shoe, just dab some stain on the cut end. Where a piece of shoe stops short of butting into something, I finish the end by "returning" the shoe with a mitered cap.

Final Plumbing

You've already roughed in the drain and water supply lines for the sinks, tub-shower, and toilet. Now that the bathroom floor is finished, you can set the toilet. Sinks and tub-shower can be hooked up earlier in the job, but it's often more efficient to do them all at once.

Tub-shower hookup. The showerhead, mixer, and tub spout attach to fittings installed at rough-in. For the showerhead, remove the temporary pipe protruding into the shower and replace it with the extension of brass or chrome that you bought for your showerhead. Slip the trim ring over the extension to conceal the hole in the drywall and screw on the showerhead.

Installing a tub-shower mixer can be a little more involved, but shouldn't be a problem if you follow the instructions in the package. The spout is easy. There are usually several fittings that lock or twist on in addition to the spout, which twists on hand tight.

Setting the toilet. Installing a new toilet is much easier than fixing an old one—no leaks to track down and no corroded bolts to struggle with. Unless you've replumbed your drain lines to accommodate a wall-hung bowl, your toilet will consist of a floor-mounted bowl and a tank. Tank and bowl can be separate or one piece.

Screw on the new extension and then attach the showerhead. The rag protects the chrome finish.

Install the shower mixer, usually two or three pieces, over the mixer valve installed during plumbing work.

For a tub spout, fix the extension-sleeve to the copper stub in the wall. Then twist on the spout.

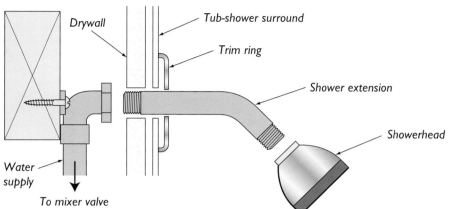

Typical Showerhead Hookup

Drywall · Tub-shower surround · Trim ring · Shower extension · Showerhead · Water supply · To mixer valve

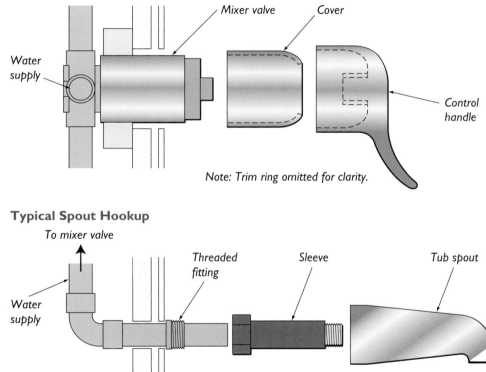

Typical Mixer-Valve Hookup

Mixer valve · Cover · Water supply · Control handle

Note: Trim ring omitted for clarity.

Typical Spout Hookup

To mixer valve · Threaded fitting · Sleeve · Tub spout · Water supply

Begin by cutting the PVC toilet-drain pipe embedded in the floor flush with the surface of the concrete, as shown on p. 156. (The pipe may have been cut flush when the house was built.) I use a reciprocating saw or an old handsaw that I don't mind dulling on the concrete. Then glue a PVC flange to the pipe. Make sure to align the flange as shown in the Trade Secret on p. 160.

Slide the bolts that hold the bowl in place into the slots. A beeswax or synthetic ring seals the base of the bowl to the flange and prevents sewer gas from leaking back into your house. Turn the bowl upside-down and squish the ring over the flared hole underneath.

Turn the bowl right-side-up and set it down over the two bolts, the flange, and the drain pipe.

PRO TIP

Do not overtighten the nuts that fix the toilet to the floor. Ceramics are brittle and easily cracked.

TRADE SECRET

When you set the PVC flange on the in-floor toilet drain, position the slots carefully. Make sure they are oriented so that you can locate the bolts parallel to the wall behind the toilet, as shown in the drawing below.

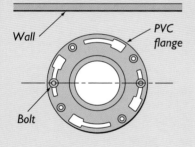

Position the flange slots so the bolts can be parallel to the wall.

Wall

PVC flange

Bolt

After the flange is glued in place, slide the bowl bolts into the slots.

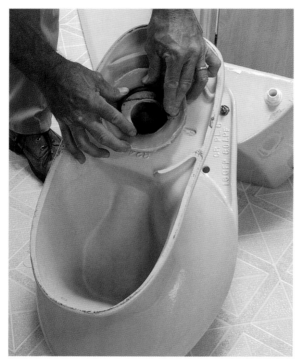

Press the beeswax ring onto the flared hole on the bottom of the bowl.

Setting a Toilet

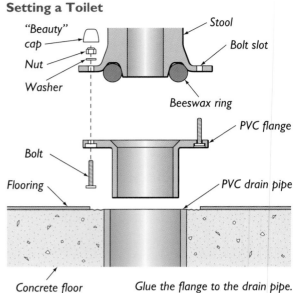

"Beauty" cap

Stool

Nut

Bolt slot

Washer

Beeswax ring

Bolt

PVC flange

Flooring

PVC drain pipe

Concrete floor

Glue the flange to the drain pipe.

Water Hookup for Toilet

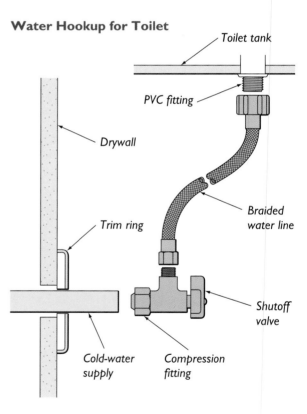

Toilet tank

PVC fitting

Drywall

Braided water line

Trim ring

Shutoff valve

Cold-water supply

Compression fitting

Twist it slightly to further compress the beeswax, and seat the toilet to the floor. Screw the nuts onto the bolts. Don't crank them down—too much pressure may break the porcelain base. "Beauty caps" hide the nuts. Most caps snap onto a special washer supplied with the nuts. If yours don't, use a little silicon caulk to hold them in place. If you have a separate tank, seat its rubber seal on the opening on top of the bowl, and bolt it in place.

Once the bowl and tank are seated, hook up the water supply. First, turn off the water line that runs to the bathroom. If there's a cap soldered or

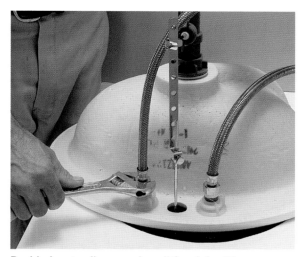

Braided water lines work well for sinks. It's easy to install the faucet set, tail piece, and water lines before installing the sink in the countertop.

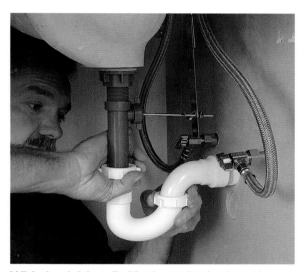

With the sink installed in the vanity, hook up the water lines. Connect the tail piece and drain line with a P-trap and extension cut to length.

Sink Hookup

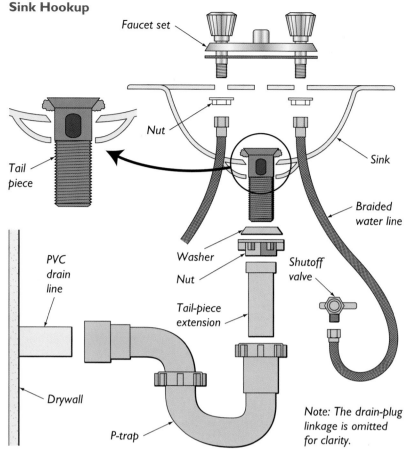

Faucet set

Nut

Sink

Tail piece

Braided water line

Washer

Nut

PVC drain line

Shutoff valve

Tail-piece extension

Drywall

P-trap

Note: The drain-plug linkage is omitted for clarity.

glued onto the copper or plastic water-line stub protruding from the wall, cut it off. Then slip a shutoff valve onto the stub and tighten its compression fitting.

Most toilets sold today come with the flushing mechanism already installed inside the tank. If yours doesn't, just follow the directions included with the flush mechanism you buy.

To connect the tank to the shutoff valve, I prefer ⅜-in. braided metal water-supply lines. They're a little more expensive but a lot easier to

work with than solid metal. They come in various lengths. Measure from the tank connection to the shutoff. Buy a braided line long enough to make a somewhat slack, not taut, connection. Tighten the compression fittings on the braided line to the tank and shutoff valve.

Installing a sink. In bathrooms, sinks are usually fitted into a vanity or mounted on a pedestal. Vanity sinks commonly come in several varieties. "Self-rimming" sinks have a flange that rests on top of the counter. "Undermount" sinks butt up against the bottom of the countertop, which extends over the edges of the sink. Pre-formed sink-countertops are molded as a single unit.

Plumbing requirements are similar for all types of sinks; the differences pertain to mounting the sink in the countertop. To install a simple self-rimming sink, first, fit the countertop to the wall and fix it to the vanity as described in the sidebar

IN DETAIL

Safety is as important in a basement as elsewhere in the house. A smoke detector (shown below) is required in every basement bedroom and at the bottom of a stairway. Many codes also require smoke detectors to be hard-wired into the electrical system. You should also seriously consider installing carbon monoxide (CO) detectors to avoid poisoning by this odorless gas. Because the furnace is in the basement, a CO detector makes sense there.

on the facing page. Then install the sink, faucets, and shutoffs.

Installing the faucet set. Two types of faucet sets are common. A one-handle set mounts a single control on the faucet. A two-handle set has separate hot and cold handles and a spout. Sinks come with holes bored for one style or the other. Make sure your faucet set and sink match when you buy them.

Turn the sink on edge or upside-down and slip the faucet assembly into the holes from the top side. To seal the joint between the sink and the faucet base plate, you may need to install a gasket that comes with the assembly or use plumber's putty. Next, press plumber's putty on the tail piece and slip it through the drain hole in the sink bottom. Tighten its retainer nut. Thread on the retainer nuts and the water-supply lines. (I like braided-metal supply lines for sinks.)

Hooking up. Set the sink in the countertop cutout so the sink flange overlaps equally on all sides. Install shutoffs to the stubbed water lines as for the toilet. Hook up the water supply lines to the shutoffs. Install the P-trap and connectors to the drain line. You'll need to cut a connector to length; use a hacksaw for metal and a hacksaw or miter saw for plastic. The drain parts are connected by compression fittings that squeeze a washer between the joints. Use a pipe wrench to

An E-Z Ancor (left) screws into drywall and is very difficult to pull out. A toggle bolt (right) has a spring-loaded, winged nut that spreads inside the wall.

tighten metal fittings. Hand tight is usually fine for plastic. Run water into the sink and tighten any leaky compression fittings.

Run a bead of caulk around the sink between it and the counter. (Most sink packaging includes a small tube of caulk.) With a damp finger, wipe around the edge to push the caulk into the joint and to remove excess.

Installing bathroom accessories

Towel bars, toilet-paper dispenser, robe hooks, wall mirrors, and the like are easy to install. There is no set height or spacing for any of these; put them where you want them. All these accessories, except some mirrors, should be attached to a wall with screws. If you can position at least one screw in a stud, great. Use drywall anchors elsewhere.

A small wall-mounted bathroom mirror can be fixed with screwed mirror mounts and push-fit plastic drywall anchors. For larger, heavier mirrors, I use mastic as well. Mastic for mirrors is a black adhesive that you squeeze onto the mirror with a caulking gun. Run a bead of mastic onto the wall or mirror back and press the mirror in place. I use at least four mirror-mount fasteners fixed to press-fit drywall anchors to hold the mirror in place while the mastic cures. I leave them in place as added insurance. If you're installing grab bars, just screw them to the wood backing you framed into the wall earlier.

Hanging a medicine cabinet. Install a wall-mounted medicine cabinet as you would other wall-hung cabinets. (See Hanging upper cabinets on p. 133.) The job is much easier if someone can help you hold the cabinet during installation. Ideally, all the mounting screws go into studs. If that's not possible (and it frequently isn't) you should be able to screw the cabinet to at least one stud. For the other attachments, use E-Z Ancors® or hollow-wall toggle bolts, as shown in the photo at left.

If your medicine cabinet includes lights, now is the time to hook them up to the loose wire you ran into the bathroom wall cavity for just this purpose. Remove the knockout plate in the fixture and pull the wire through it as you fix the cabinet in place. Then make the connections as described below. If you forgot to expose the bathroom lighting wire when hanging the drywall, take heart. Because the whole area behind the medicine cabinet will be covered, you can poke a hole in the drywall big enough to find the wire.

Finishing Electricals

After deciding when to connect the circuits to the panel, there isn't a necessary order to finishing the electricals, but it makes sense to install the lights first so you can see what you're doing as you complete the rest of the hook ups.

Connecting the panel. My recommendation for hooking up circuits in the electric-service panel is to hire an electrician. That will get you a double check on your wiring (counting the electrical inspector) and keep you away from some very hot wires. Be sure to label the new circuits for future reference.

The panel may be connected before or after you finish the lights, switches, and outlets. If you do so before, you can check the circuits as you go. Make sure, of course, to turn the circuits off when you're working on them. Otherwise, hook everything up, then connect the panel, and check all your work.

Hooking up lights. You've already wired the recessed lights when you installed the fixtures (see Making up lights on p. 94). Now all you need to do is install the interior light baffle, the trim ring, and the bulb.

Hanging light fixtures and ceiling-mounted lights need to be hooked up at their boxes. Simply wire-nut the fixture's black, white, and ground wires to the corresponding ones in the ceiling box. Test the wire nuts for a tight connection, push the excess wire into the box, and attach the light-fixture base to the box with the screws provided. Screw in a bulb, install the globe, and you're done.

Installing a Countertop

Countertops for bathrooms and wet bars (or the few kitchens installed in basements) come in a range of materials that include durable synthetics, such as Formica® and Corian®, and striking natural materials, such as marble, granite, and wood. Some are formed with a backsplash; others have separate backsplashes or no backsplash, allowing you to tile or otherwise provide your own.

When you buy a sink top, have the supplier cut it to size (if necessary) and cut the hole for the sink. If you don't buy the sink from the same place, make sure the hole is cut using the template supplied for the sink. (If you have a jigsaw, you can make your own sink cutout.) Countertops typically overhang the cabinet body 1 in. at the front (1/4 in. past the 3/4-in.-thick door) and 1/2 in. on the ends. Tops for corner cabinets are sold with the end that abuts the wall unfinished, so you can scribe the end to fit tightly against the wall.

Even if you had the top cut to size, you'll probably have to deal with some gaps between the top and one or two walls. Small gaps can be filled with caulk or covered by a backsplash. If a gap is too big to fill with caulk, you can cut and fit the top tightly to the wall. Hold a pencil upright against the wall and scribe a line along the length of the top, as shown at right. Cut to the line and the top should fit snugly. I grind away the waste with a belt sander and a coarse belt. A coarse wood rasp works, too, as long as you push it away from the top surface to avoid chipping the edges. Remember, you'll run a bead of caulk along the joint to prevent water penetration, so the fit needn't be perfect.

When the top fits satisfactorily, you can fix it to the cabinet by using an adhesive caulk or by driving screws up through the cabinet top or rails into the countertop. Make sure the screws aren't long enough to poke through the top.

IN DETAIL

Contrary to popular belief, the new compact fluorescent bulbs do not have to have a harsh, commercial glare. The color of light is determined by the temperature at which the bulb operates, in degrees Kelvin (K). The bulb packaging should give the K value of the bulb, from 2700 - 3000 K (warm), to 3500K (neutral) to 4100K (cool) to 5000K (daylight).

Photographers are well aware of the temperature difference in lighting, but it's somewhat new to the general public. Warm light should be used in areas where you plan to entertain or relax, because skin tones look better. Neutral light is a balance of warm and cool tones, and it's best for task lighting in kitchens or in the office. Cool lights are ideal for utility rooms or task areas like garages or hobby rooms.

Additionally, remember when you're buying fluorescent bulbs, they emit more light per watt than incandescent ones. A 13-watt fluorescent bulb gives off approximately the same light as a 60-watt incandescent.

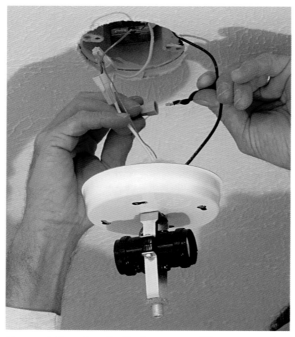

Connect the wires in the box to a ceiling-mounted fixture and attach the fixture to the box.

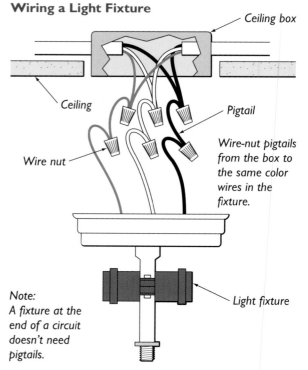

Wiring a Light Fixture

Ceiling box

Ceiling

Pigtail

Wire nut

Wire-nut pigtails from the box to the same color wires in the fixture.

Light fixture

Note: A fixture at the end of a circuit doesn't need pigtails.

Connecting switches. Single switches require only the connection of the wires in the box (two black wires and the pigtailed ground) to the switch. On the back of the switch is a slot that shows how much insulation to remove from the black wires (if you haven't already stripped them). Most switches now have push connectors that trap the end of the wire, so all you need to do is strip off the insulation and push each wire into a hole in the switch. It beats having to bend the wire around a screw and tighten it down.

When the wires are connected, fire up the circuit and flip the switch to check your work. Turn the circuit off, check that the connections are tight, push the excess wire into the box, and screw the switch onto the box with the screws provided. Screw on the cover plate and you have light.

Three-way switches are more complicated. You can finish them yourself following manufacturers directions. Or get some help with them (and other specialty devices) when your electrician hooks up the service panel.

Outlets. These are as simple as switches to finish. Strip back the insulation on the pigtailed black and white wires, using the slot on the back of the outlets to gauge the length. Push the black wire into one side of the plug and the white into the other, and screw the ground wire onto the ground terminal.

Wire up an entire circuit of outlets. Then flip the breaker on and check each plug with a circuit tester. (See In Detail on p. 40.) When all the outlets work, switch off the circuit, push the excess wire into the boxes, and screw on the cover plates. Flip on the circuit breaker and test the outlets in the circuit one more time, just to make sure.

Bath fan. During mechanical installation, you will have installed the bath-fan shell or housing. For most bath fans, you now need to wire-nut the black, white, and ground to their counterparts in the fan housing's electrical compartment. (You may need to remove the fan motor to do so.) Then plug the fan motor into the internal receptacle in the electrical compartment. Screw the face plate in place to finish the job.

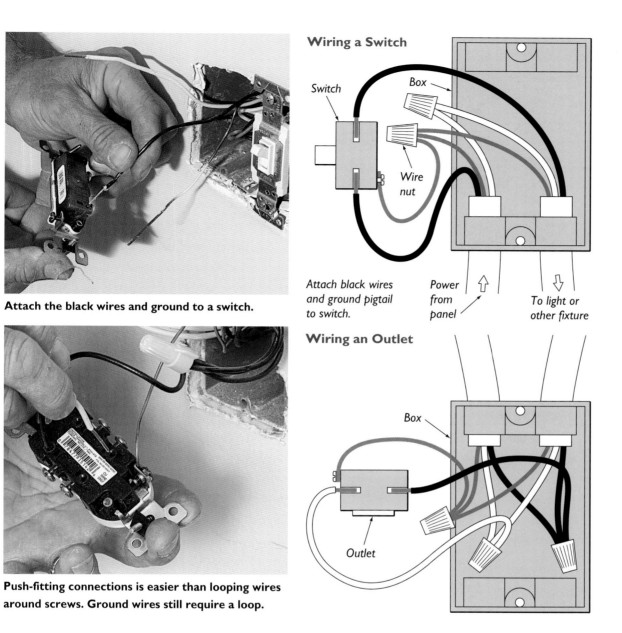

Attach the black wires and ground to a switch.

Push-fitting connections is easier than looping wires around screws. Ground wires still require a loop.

Wiring a Switch

Switch

Box

Wire nut

Attach black wires and ground pigtail to switch.

Power from panel

To light or other fixture

Wiring an Outlet

Box

Outlet

HVAC

This is the simplest mechanical system to finish. All you have to do is install the vent covers for the supply, return air, and combustion air. For wall-mounted vents, covers should come with screws long enough to penetrate the studs bracketing the opening. Covers for ceiling vents screw into the metal flange around the opening. Drill pilot holes through the flange for the screws, using the vent cover as a template. (The screws supplied usually aren't self-tapping. They'll slip around some on the metal if you try to drive them in directly.)

When you install vent covers, make sure they're oriented correctly. Covers mounted above eye-level should direct air up, so the vanes should slope up. Covers below eye level should direct air down, so the vanes should slope down. When covers are correctly installed, the vanes will obscure vision into the opening.

If you want to paint vent covers to match your walls, first treat the factory paint with a de-glosser or lightly sand with 220-grit or finer sandpaper. Either treatment increases adhesion of the new paint to the factory paint. Spray paint gives the

TRADE SECRET

When screwing the strike plate into its recess in a door's strike jamb, it's easy to misdrill a pilot hole. In order to drill a new hole, you'll need to plug the old one. I make a plug with a sliver of wood that is slightly larger than the diameter of the hole. It need be only roughly round. Dab some glue on the plug and drive it into the hole. Cut the plug flush with the face of the recess. Then reposition the plate and drill a new pilot hole.

best finish. I also like to spray paint the visible area inside the return-air ducts with flat black or the wall color. Be sure to shut off the furnace fan when you're spraying, and for a time after, so the fumes remain localized rather than dispersed around the house.

Door Hardware

Doorknobs, striker assemblies, and strike plates finish door installation; all these parts are sometimes collectively referred to as a latchset. Prehung doors eliminate most of the difficulty of installing door hardware. The door is already recessed for the striker assembly and bored for the knobs. A recess may also be routed in the strike jamb to house the strike plate.

Install the striker assembly first, then the doorknob assembly, and finally the strike plate. Follow the instructions included with the hardware and it should all go together smoothly. I recommend predrilling pilot holes for the screws

To install door hardware, start with the striker assembly. The one shown here is a cylinder you drive into a predrilled hole. Thread the knob hardware through the striker assembly and fix the two sides together with the screws provided.

that fix the strike plate to the jamb and the striker to the edge of the door. (Some strikers are just cylinders driven into the door; they don't need screws.) Drilling pilot holes lessens the chance of splitting out the door or the jamb, and the screws will hold and seat better.

If the door rattles when you close it, the strike plate is too far away from the door stop. If it doesn't latch at all, or pops open because the striker doesn't fully engage the strike plate, the plate is too close to the door stop. Many strike plates have a small tongue that sticks down into the jamb. For minor adjustments, you can remove the strike plate and bend the tongue as needed. If that doesn't work, reposition the plate.

Final Touches

A lot has happened in the basement since you finished trimming, painting, and staining. Inevitably, there is some scuffed paint or some gouges in the drywall. Fill these gouges or dings with drywall compound. When it's dry, sand flush and repaint. Remember to use primer, even on a small repair. Otherwise, the top coat will look different from the surrounding wall.

Paint splatters on trim can sometimes be removed with a fingernail and some judicious scraping. If that doesn't work, or the area is too large, use a commercially available paint mistake remover, like Goof-Off®. None of these products work perfectly, but they help.

Remove the stickers from tempered-glass windows or doors carefully. Tempered glass is extremely hard, but it scratches more easily than regular glass. To clean off stickers, use water and elbow grease or a mild solvent.

That's about it. Wash the floors, vacuum the carpet, dust off the trim, and you're done. Stand back and admire your work. Have a party. Sleep for a week on the couch.

Resources

Your local home center, lumberyard, or hardware store should have almost all the tools and materials you will need to remodel your basement. If they don't have the following products, which were referenced in the text, here's where you can find them.

Aervoe Industries Inc.
1198 Mark Circle
Gardnerville, NV 89410
(800) 227-0196
www.aervoe.com
Crown Sprā-tool

Baroid Corporation
3000 N. Sam Houston
    Parkway East
Houston TX
(713) 987-4000
www.baroididp.com
bentonite
Quik-Gel (powder)
Benseal (granular)

Bonsal
P.O. Box 241148
Charlotte, NC 28224
(800) 334-0784
www.bonsal.com
Bonsal SUREWALL

ITW Brands
955 National Parkway
Schaumburg, IL 60173
(800) 982-7178
www.itwbrands.com/ez.htm
E-Z Ancor

Protective Products
    International, Inc.
1205 Karl Court Suite #116
Wauconda, IL 60084
(800) 789-6633
www.protectiveproducts.com
PROZIP
Scratch Protection
Pro Tecta Tub Kit

Sonneborn, Commercial
    Construction Products
    Division of ChemRex®
889 Valley Park Drive
Shakopee, MN 55379
(800) 433-9517
www.chemrex.com/sonneborn
Sonneborn NP-I

Tool Crib
Grand Forks, ND 58208
(800) 635-5140
www.amazon.com/toolcrib
Tools for carpentry, drywalling,
    tile setting, metalworking

The Valspar Corporation
1191 Wheeling Road
Wheeling, IL 60090
(800) 345-4530
www.goof-off.com
Goof-Off

Index